The Capability Maturity Model: Guidelines for Improving the Software Process

Carnegie Mellon University
Software Engineering Institute

Principal Contributors and Editors

Mark C. Paulk
Charles V. Weber
Bill Curtis
Mary Beth Chrissis

Other Contributors to CMM v1.0

Edward L. Averill
Judy Bamberger
Timothy C. Kasse
Mike Konrad
Jeffrey R. Perdue
Cynthia J. Wise
James V. Withey

Other Contributors to CMM v1.1

Marilyn Bush
Suzanne M. Garcia

ADDISON-WESLEY PUBLISHING COMPANY

Reading, Massachusetts · Menlo Park, California · New York
Don Mills, Ontario · Wokingham, England · Amsterdam · Bonn · Sydney
Singapore · Tokyo · Madrid · San Juan · Milan · Paris

Software Engineering Institute

The SEI Series in Software Engineering

This work was sponsored by the U.S. Department of Defense

The Capability Maturity Model for Software is a copyrighted product of CMU/SEI. Portions of *The Capability Maturity Model for Software, Version 1.1* (SEI-93-TR-24) and *Key Practices of the Capability Maturity Model for Software, Version 1.1* (SEI-93-TR-25) are used in this book with the permission of CMU/SEI.

Many of the designations used by manufacturers and sellers to distinguish their products are claimed as trademarks. Where those designations appear in this book, and Addison-Wesley was aware of a trademark claim, the designations have been printed in caps or italic caps.

Library of Congress Cataloging-in-Publication Data

The Capability maturity model : guidelines for improving the software process /
   Carnegie Mellon University / Software Engineering Institute
        p.   cm. – (SEI series in software engineering)
   Includes bibliographical references and index.
   ISBN 0-201-54664-7
   1. Computer software–Development.   I. Carnegie Mellon University
II. Series.
QA76.76.D47C37   1995
005. 1'068'5–dc20
                                  95-14497
                                  CIP

1 2 3 4 5 6 7 8 9 10–MA–9998979695

This work was sponsored by the U.S. Department of Defense.

Contents

List of Figures

List of Tables

Foreword

This book is what we were striving for eight years ago when we constructed our first version of the SEI process maturity questionnaire. When asked for a taxonomy of the maturity levels, we could describe the general criteria, but not the complete framework. In essence, my position was, "I can't tell you precisely, but I know it when I see it." The reason the Capability Maturity Model is so powerful is that it provides the detail necessary to understand the contents of each maturity level and as such permits you to examine your practices and see how they compare. You can then identify any gaps and establish improvement priorities to address your particular needs.

Perhaps the greatest contribution of this book was in the way it was produced. Many software professionals from all over the United States participated in proposing topics, reviewing drafts, critiquing changes, and testing the result. The CMM represents the combined judgment of literally hundreds of experienced engineers from all walks of government and industry. As they worked on the drafts, the key question was, "How would this work for me?" If they didn't know that a practice made sense, it wasn't included. Knowing the CMM would be used to evaluate their work, these working engineers had a vested interest in making it something they could live with. In every sense, the CMM represents the best thinking in the field today.

This raises the question of stability. Is the CMM going to change and how soon? The CMM must change. Software technology continues to evolve, and we can expect the software process to evolve at an equivalent rate. The CMM practices must therefore change to reflect new experiences and technologies. As more organizations advance to Levels 4 and 5, we can expect them to contribute many added practices and changes. Beyond being a useful guide for process improvement, the CMM thus provides a foundation for growth. It is an explicit framework software engineers can use, debate, and augment. The CMM documents must be reasonably stable, but they also must change.

Producing a document like this also entails a risk. Some individuals will always seek fixed formulas or checklists for evaluating organizations. When organizations follow this checklist strategy, they often produce piles of documents and mountains of paper to "prove" that their process is at some prescribed level. Unfortunately, this approch invariably overlooks the critical point: what the people actually do. The software process concerns people and their work and thus must be pragmatic and adjustable, or it will not be used. That is why the CMM and this book are guidelines, not rules. Their objective is to set goals for each maturity level and key process area, and to provide examples for each practice. No organization, however, should attempt to do everything in this book. Doing so would solve some problems several ways and miss others completely. That could get very expensive.

The danger of misuse will always be present, however, since some people will want rules and explicit guidelines. The best we can do is to caution readers to use judgement and to recognize that this book is a compilation of the best current thinking in the field. The CMM is comprehensive and thorough, but it is not engraved in stone. Examine the CMM with an open mind, but don't be constrained by it. Use what fits your needs, but pay most attention to the goals. Treat the detailed practices as examples, and use what applies. If you come up with better ideas, use them. Write those ideas and publish them so we can all take advantage of them.

Watts S. Humphrey
March 14, 1994
Sarasota, Florida

Preface

The Capability Maturity Model for Software is one of the best known products of the Software Engineering Institute. Thousands of copies of the two technical reports that comprise the CMM [Paulk93a, Paulk93b] have been distributed around the world. The CMM and related process products are having a significant impact on the software community, as evidenced by the current international standards effort on software process described in Appendix G.

This book integrates and elaborates the description of the CMM and how to interpret its practices. It contains the text of the key practices from [Paulk93b] verbatim, except for a few minor grammatical corrections listed in Appendix H.

The authors have added the following material:

▫ A case study of IBM Houston's Space Shuttle project, which is frequently referred to as being at Level 5 (Chapter 6)
▫ Mapping between the key practices and the goals of the key process areas (Appendix E)
▫ A comparison of ISO 9001 and the CMM (Appendix F)
▫ An overview of ISO's SPICE project, which is developing international standards for software process improvement and capability determination (Appendix G)

The book is divided into two main parts. The first part consists of the chapters describing the evolution of the CMM, the concepts of software process maturity, the structure of the model, how to interpret and use the CMM, and the case study of IBM Houston. The second part consists of the key practices of the CMM, which describe the software management engineering practices of a maturing software process. Also included are a number of appendices that provide useful reference material.

This book is targeted at anyone involved in improving the software process, including members of appraisal teams, members of software engineering process groups, software managers, and software practitioners. It complements Humphrey's *Managing the Software Process* [Humphrey89] by formalizing the maturity framework described in that book.

This book does not describe all of the work being done by the SEI's Software Process Program. In particular, the SEI's work on software process definition, measurement, and organizational change may be of value to individuals working to improve the software process. For furthur information regarding the SEI, the CMM, or its associated products, contact:

SEI Customer Relations
Software Engineering Institute
Carnegie Mellon University
Pittsburgh, PA 15213-3890
Tel: (412)268-5800
Fax: (412)268-5758
Internet: customer-relations@sei.cmu.edu

The CMM is a living document, shaped by the needs of the software community. The SEI solicits feedback from our customers. Instructions for requesting changes to the CMM and a form for doing so are contained in Appendix I.

Acknowledgments

The Capability Maturity Model for Software (CMM) was produced for the Software Engineering Institute (SEI) by a dedicated group of people who spent many hours discussing the model and its features and then documenting it in the two versions of the CMM. The principal contributors and editors of this book worked on the CMM throughout its development, but many others have contributed to its evolution.

First and foremost, the CMM is based on the vision of Watts Humphrey.

The team that initially produced the CMM for the SEI consisted of Mark Paulk, Bill Curtis, Mary Beth Chrissis, Ed Averill, Judy Bamberger, Tim Kasse, Mike Konrad, Jeff Perdue, Charlie Weber, Cindi Wise, and Jim Withey. Several drafts were necessary to produce CMM v1.0. Jim Withey, Mark Paulk, Cindi Wise, and Watts Humphrey produced early drafts. Mark Paulk then took over the model and remained book boss until the end [Paulk91]. Charlie Weber led in the development of the key practices report [Weber91]. Version 1.0 of the CMM was released in August 1991.

The team that revised the CMM to create Version 1.1 consisted of Mark Paulk (CMM project leader), Charlie Weber, Bill Curtis, Mary Beth Chrissis, Suzie Garcia, and Marilyn Bush.

At various stages, several other people contributed to the concepts expressed in the CMM. They included Joe Besselman, Anita Carleton, Marty Carlson, Susan Dart, Betty Deimel, Lionel Deimel, Peter Feiler, Mark Ginsberg,

Jim Hart, Ron Higuera, Purvis Jackson, Richard Kauffold, David Kitson, Peter Malpass, Mark Manduke, Steve Masters, Mary Merrill, Judah Mogilensky, Warren Moseley, Julia Mullaney, Jim Over, George Pandelios, Bob Park, Dick Phillips, Ginny Reddish, Mike Rissman, Jim Rozum, Jan Siegel, and Christer von Schantz.

We appreciate the administrative help from Todd Bowman, Dorothy Josephson, Debbie Punjack, Carolyn Tady, Marcia Theoret, Andy Tsounos and David White; and the editorial assistance from Suzanne Couturiaux, Bill Pollak, and Renne Dutkowski from the American Institutes for Research provided suggestions for the document design.

Special thanks go to the members of the CMM Correspondence Group for their time and effort in reviewing drafts of the CMM and providing insightful comments and recommendations, and to the members of the CMM Advisory Board for their guidance. The current members of the CMM Advisory Board are Kelley Butler, Conrad Czaplicki, Raymond Dion, Judah Mogilensky, Sue Stetak, John Vu, Charlie Weber, and Brenda Zettervall. Former members who worked with us on developing and revising the CMM include Constance Ahara, Harry Carl, Jim Hess, Martin Owens, Jerry Pixton, and Ron Willis.

PART ONE

The Capability Maturity Model for Software: Background, Concepts, Structure, and Usage

1

Introducing Software Process Maturity

Customer satisfaction has become the motto of many organizations attempting to survive and thrive in today's increasingly competitive world. At the same time that organizations are focusing on customer satisfaction, there is a growing perception that software quality is the weak link in developing high-quality products. The software crisis that has persisted over the last two or three decades has become even more critical as software pervades our day-to-day lives.

The term "software crisis" may be unfair. Software is pervasive because of its power, and software technology is advancing at a breath-taking pace. Despite these advances, it seems that the complexity of the problems being addressed by software is growing more rapidly than our ability to develop and maintain the software. The ability to develop and deliver reliable, usable software within budget and schedule commitments continues to elude most software organizations.

The search for solutions to these challenges has continued for many years. After two decades of unfulfilled promises about productivity and quality gains from applying new software methodologies and technologies, organizations are now realizing that their fundamental problem is the inability to manage the software process. In many organizations, projects are often excessively late and over budget, and the benefits of better methods and tools cannot be realized in the maelstrom of an undisciplined, chaotic project.

Examples of software catastrophes abound. An unpublished review of 17 major Department of Defense (DoD) software contracts found that the average 28-month schedule was missed by 20 months. One 4-year project was not delivered for 7 years; no project was on time. Deployment of the B1 bomber was delayed by a software problem, and the $58 billion A12 aircraft program was canceled partly for the same reason.

One recent Government Accounting Office (GAO) report [GAO-93-13] on the major software challenges states, "We have repeatedly reported on cost rising by millions of dollars, schedule delays of not months but years, and multi-billion-dollar systems that don't perform as envisioned." After summarizing more than 20 GAO case studies involving software or software-related problems in the military, this report concludes, "The understanding of software as a product and of software development as a process is not keeping pace with the growing complexity and software dependence of existing and emerging mission-critical systems."

While the military has its own unique problems, industry has its share of problems as well. Managers in industry have said, "I'd rather have it wrong than have it late. We can always fix it later." The consequences of this attitude on customer satisfaction seem clear. For many organizations, whether military or commercial, the message is that large software projects mean potential trouble.

One task force that investigated the "software crisis" [DoD87] wrote that "few fields have so large a gap between best current practice and average current practice," and went on to conclude that "today's major problems with military software development are not technical problems, but management problems."

The mission of the Software Engineering Institute (SEI) is to provide leadership in advancing the state of the practice of software engineering to improve the quality of systems that depend on software. The mission of the SEI's Software Process Program is to provide leadership in assisting software organizations to develop and continuously improve their capability to identify, adopt, and use sound management and technical practices. These practices comprise disciplined, well-defined, and effectively measured software engineering processes for the purpose of delivering quality software that meets cost and schedule commitments.

The Capability Maturity Model for Software (CMM) developed by the SEI is a framework that describes the key elements of an effective software process. The CMM describes an evolutionary improvement path for software organizations from an ad hoc, immature process to a mature, disciplined one. This path is encompassed by five levels of maturity. The characteristics and structure of these levels are described in Chapters 2 and 3, respectively.

The CMM covers practices for planning, engineering, and managing software development and maintenance. When followed, these practices improve the ability of organizations to meet goals for cost, schedule, functionality, and product quality.

The CMM guides software organizations that want to gain control of their processes for developing and maintaining software and to evolve toward a culture of software engineering and management excellence. Its purpose is to guide these organizations in selecting process improvement strategies by determining their current process maturity and identifying the few issues most critical to improving their software process and software quality. By focusing on a limited set of activities and working aggressively to achieve them, an organization can steadily improve its organization-wide software process to enable continuous and lasting gains in software process capability.

1.1 The Evolution of the CMM

In November 1986, the SEI, with assistance from the MITRE Corporation, began developing a process maturity framework that would help organizations improve their software process. This effort was initiated in response to a request to provide the federal government with a method for assessing the capability of its software contractors. In September 1987, the SEI released a brief description of the software process maturity framework [Humphrey 87a], which was later expanded in Humphrey's book, *Managing the Software Process* [Humphrey89a]. Two methods, software process assessment[1] and software capability evaluation,[2] and a maturity questionnaire [Humphrey87b] were developed to appraise software process maturity.

After four years of experience with the software process maturity framework and the 1987 maturity questionnaire, the SEI evolved the maturity framework into the Capability Maturity Model for Software [Paulk91, Weber91]. The CMM

- is based on actual practices,
- reflects the best of the state of the practice,
- reflects the needs of individuals performing software process improvement and software process appraisals,

---

[1] A software process assessment is an appraisal by a trained team of software professionals to determine the state of an organization's current software process, to determine the high-priority software process-related issues facing an organization, and to obtain the organizational support for software process improvement. An assessment is a critical step in an internal process improvement program.

[2] A software capability evaluation is an appraisal by a trained team of professionals to identify contractors qualified to perform the software work or to monitor the state of the software process used on an existing software effort.

- is documented, and
- is publicly available.

The CMM is based on knowledge acquired from software process assessments and extensive feedback from both industry and government. The initial release of the CMM was reviewed and used by the software community during 1991 and 1992. Additional knowledge and insight into software process maturity were gained by:

- studying nonsoftware organizations,
- performing and observing software process assessments and software capability evaluations,
- soliciting and analyzing change requests to the model,
- participating in meetings and workshops with industry and government representatives, and
- soliciting feedback from industry and government reviewers.

Based on this additional knowledge, the Capability Maturity Model and its practices were revised, creating the current version [Paulk93a, Paulk93b]. The CMM will continue to evolve with the software field as we develop a true engineering discipline and continue to learn about effective software process management.

During the next few years, the CMM will undergo extensive testing through use in software process appraisals and process improvement programs. It is a living document that will be continually improved, although it is anticipated that the current version of the CMM will remain the baseline until at least 1997. This provides an appropriate and realistic balance between the needs for stability and for continued improvement.

The factors that will influence the continuing evolution of the CMM include international standards activities, as well as user feedback. The SEI is working with the International Organization for Standardization (ISO) in its efforts to build international standards for software process assessment, improvement, and capability evaluation. This effort will integrate concepts from many different process improvement methods. The development of the ISO standards (and the contributions of other methods) will influence CMM v2, even as the SEI's process work is influencing the activities of the ISO. ISO's SPICE (Software Process Improvement and Capability Determination) project is described in Appendix G. The planned 1996 revision of ISO 9001 will also influence CMM revision.

1.2 Immature Versus Mature Software Organizations

To understand which improvements are most critical to an organization, one must first understand the differences between immature and mature software organizations. In an immature software organization, software processes are generally improvised by practitioners and their managers during the course of the project. Even if a software process has been specified, it is not rigorously followed or enforced. The immature software organization is reactionary, and its managers are usually focused on solving immediate crises (better known as fire fighting). These organizations routinely exceed schedules and budgets because they are not based on realistic estimates. When hard deadlines are imposed, they may compromise product functionality and quality to meet the schedule.

In an immature organization, there is no objective basis for judging product quality or for solving product or process problems. There is little understanding of how the steps of the software process affect quality, and product quality is difficult to predict. Moreover, activities intended to enhance quality, such as reviews and testing, are often curtailed or eliminated when projects fall behind schedule. The customer has little insight into the product until delivery.

A mature software organization, in contrast, possesses an organization-wide ability for managing software development and maintenance processes. It accurately communicates the software process to both existing staff and new employees, and carries out work activities according to the planned process. The processes mandated are documented, usable, and consistent with the way the work actually gets done. The process definitions are updated when necessary, and improvements are developed through controlled pilot-tests and/or cost benefit analyses. There is broad-scale, active involvement across the organization in improvement activities. Roles and responsibilities within the process are clear throughout the project and across the organization.

In a mature organization, managers monitor the quality of the software products and the process that produces them. There is an objective, quantitative basis for judging product quality and analyzing problems with the product and process. Schedules and budgets are based on historical performance and are realistic; the expected results for cost, schedule, functionality, and quality of the product are usually achieved. In general, the mature organization follows a disciplined process consistently because all of the participants understand the value of doing so, and the necessary infrastructure exists to support the process.

To use one of Humphrey's metaphors, an organization with an immature software process resembles a Little League baseball team. When the ball is hit, some players run toward the ball, while others stand around and watch, perhaps not even thinking about the game. In contrast, a mature organization is like a professional baseball team. When the ball is hit, every player reacts in a disciplined manner. Depending on the situation, the pitcher may cover home plate, infielders may set up for a double play, and outfielders prepare to back up their teammates. Although we may not normally think of it in process terms, the same kind of discipline and preparation that separates a Little League team from the professionals also separates immature and mature software organizations.

1.3 Fundamental Concepts Underlying Process Maturity

Before you can fully understand software process maturity, you must first understand some of the basic concepts that are used to describe mature organizations. The CMM focuses on the capability of software organizations to produce high-quality products consistently and predictably. Software process capability is the inherent ability of a software process to produce planned results.

What is process? A *process* is a sequence of steps performed for a given purpose. More simply stated, process is what you do. The process integrates people, tools, and procedures together, as illustrated in Fig. 1.1. Process is what people do, using procedures, methods, tools, and equipment, to transform raw material (inputs) into a product (output) that is of value to customers.

A process description is not a process. Only when activities are "performed" or methods are "used" is it accurate to speak of a process. Standards and procedures that are not used are merely shelfware; in such a case, the process is ad hoc, since the putative process description is not followed. Process and process description are frequently, if perhaps imprecisely, used interchangeably.

A *software process* can be defined as a set of activities, methods, practices, and transformations that people employ to develop and maintain software and the associated products (e.g., project plans, design documents, code, test cases, and user manuals). As an organization matures, the software process becomes better defined and more consistently implemented throughout the organization. The CMM focuses on process as a way to empower the people doing the work.

The underlying premise of software process management is that the quality of a software product is largely determined by the quality of the process used to develop and maintain it. An effective software process ties together people, tools, and methods into an integrated whole.

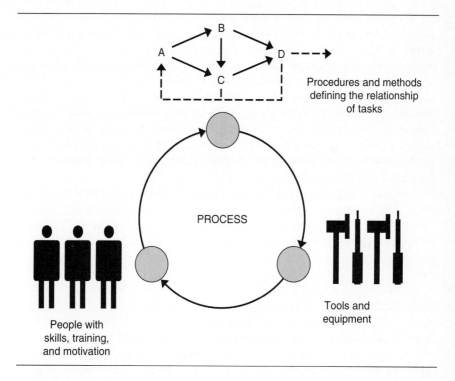

FIGURE 1.1
Process: holding the pieces together

Software process capability describes the range of expected results that can be achieved by following a software process. The software process capability of an organization provides one means of predicting the most likely outcomes to be expected from the next software project the organization undertakes.

Software process performance represents the actual results achieved by following a software process. Thus software process performance focuses on the results achieved, while software process capability focuses on results expected.

Software process maturity is the extent to which a specific process is explicitly defined, managed, measured, controlled, and effective. Maturity implies a potential for growth in capability and indicates both the richness of an organization's software process and the consistency with which it is applied in projects throughout the organization.

Software process maturity implies that software process capability must be grown. Improvement requires strong management support and a consistent long-term focus. As a software organization matures, it needs an infrastructure and culture to support its methods, practices, and procedures so that they endure after those who originally defined them have gone.

Organizational culture can be summed up as "that's the way we do things around here." It is seen in people's expectations for how they are to work together. One of the determinants of organizational culture is its infrastructure. *Infrastructure* is the underlying framework of an organization or system, including organizational structures, policies, standards, training, facilities, and tools, that supports its ongoing performance.

Institutionalization is the building of infrastructure and culture to support the methods, practices, and procedures so that they are the ongoing way of doing business. The result of institutionalization is the deployment of software processes that are effective, usable, and consistently applied across the organization.

1.4 Total Quality Management and the CMM

Although software engineers and managers often know their problems in great detail, they may disagree on which improvements are most important. Without an organized strategy for improvement, it is difficult to achieve consensus between management and the professional staff on what improvement activities to undertake first. To achieve lasting results from process improvement efforts, it is necessary to design an evolutionary path that increases an organization's software process maturity in stages. The CMM orders these stages so that improvements at each stage provide a foundation on which to build improvements undertaken at the next stage. Thus an improvement strategy drawn from a software process maturity framework provides a roadmap for continuous process improvement. It identifies deficiencies in the organization and guides advancement; it is not intended to provide a quick fix for projects in trouble.

The staged structure of the CMM is based on principles of product quality that have existed for the last 60 years. In the 1930s, Walter Shewart promulgated the principles of statistical quality control. His principles were further developed and successfully demonstrated in the work of W. Edwards Deming [Deming86] and Joseph Juran [Juran88, Juran89]. These principles have been adapted by the SEI into a maturity framework that establishes a project management and engineering foundation for quantitative control of the software process, which is the basis for continuous process improvement.

   The maturity framework into which these quality principles have been adapted was first inspired by Philip Crosby in his book *Quality Is Free* [Crosby79]. Crosby's quality management maturity grid describes five evolutionary stages in adopting quality practices. This maturity framework was adapted to the software process by Ron Radice and his colleagues, working under the direction of Watts Humphrey at IBM [Radice85]. Humphrey brought this maturity framework to the Software Engineering Institute in 1986, refined the concept of maturity levels, and developed the foundation for its current use throughout the software industry.

   The CMM is therefore an application of the process management concepts of Total Quality Management (TQM) to software, as illustrated in Fig. 1.2. TQM can be defined as the application of quantitative methods and human resources to improve the materials and services provided as inputs to an organization and to improve all of the processes within the organization. The goal of TQM is to meet the needs of the customer, now and in the future.

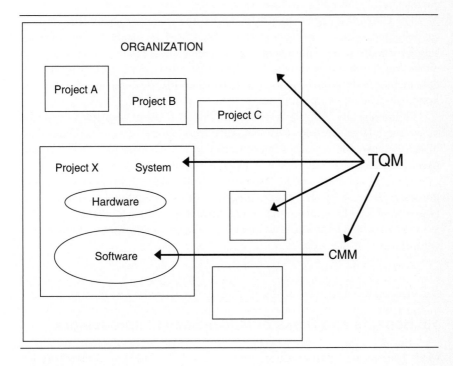

FIGURE 1.2
Applying TQM to software

When doing software process improvement, it is important to remember that the improvement effort operates inside the larger context of a business. The improvement effort should be aligned to the business needs of the organization and with any TQM efforts that may exist within the organization. This alignment will have a critical effect on the success of the software process improvement effort.

1.5 Customer Satisfaction

The goal of customer satisfaction in TQM is also the goal of the CMM. One of the drivers behind the SEI's software process work was the need of the DoD to identify qualified software contractors. The software capability evaluation method, where an acquisition agency uses the CMM to appraise the strength, weaknesses, and risks of selecting a particular software contractor and/or for monitoring a software contract, results from this customer need.

The CMM does not explicitly state that the customer should be satisfied (or delighted) with the software product. The CMM does state that the software supplier should work with the customer to understand the customer's requirements and should build software products that satisfy the customer's needs as documented in the requirements allocated to the software component of the total system or product being supplied.

Philosophically, some may argue that "delighting the customer" should be more proactively addressed. Customer satisfaction should be a critical component of any organization's process improvement or quality management efforts and should be attacked as appropriate in the organization's business environment.

There is another side to the coin as well. The CMM focuses on the processes of the software supplier, but the customer–supplier relationship is a two-way street. In a contractual context, the external customer is part of the system that produces products and shares the responsibility for providing a sane environment for the supplier.

1.6 Benefits and Risks of Model-Based Improvement

Many benefits accrue from using a model such as the CMM as a framework for improvement. The CMM helps to forge a shared vision of what software process improvement means for the organization. It establishes a common language for talking about the software process, and it defines a set of priorities for attacking software problems.

The CMM supports measurement of the software process by providing a framework for performing reliable and consistent appraisals. Although human judgment cannot be removed from these process appraisals, the CMM provides a basis for objectivity. This measurement framework also supports industry-wide comparisons through state-of-the-practice reports [Humphrey89b, Humphrey89c, Kitson92] and case studies of software process improvement [Humphrey91b, Lipke92, Dion93, Wohlwend93].

Perhaps most importantly, the CMM builds on a set of processes and practices that have been developed in collaboration with a broad selection of practitioners. Hundreds of software professionals reviewed the CMM during its development. Thousands of their comments and change requests on the various drafts of the CMM were reviewed and resolved by the CMM development and revision teams, and a CMM Advisory Board was established to help the SEI understand and resolve issues raised by the community. More than 300 people participated in the last CMM workshop before release of the current version of the CMM. While there was not unanimous agreement on the sometimes directly conflicting recommendations, it is fair to say that the CMM represents a broad-based consensus of good software engineering and management practices.

Basing improvement efforts on a model is not without its risks, however. In the words of George Box, "All models are wrong; some models are useful." Models are simplifications of the real world they represent, and the CMM is not an exhaustive description of the software process. It is not comprehensive; it only touches on other, nonprocess factors, such as people and technology, that affect the success of software projects.

The CMM is not a silver bullet and does not address all of the issues that are important for successful projects. For example, the CMM does not currently address expertise in particular application domains, advocate specific software technologies, or suggest how to select, hire, motivate, and retain competent people. Although these issues are crucial to a project's success, they are not part of the CMM.

The CMM represents a "common sense engineering" approach to software process improvement. The maturity levels, key process areas, common features, and key practices have been extensively discussed and reviewed within the software community. While the CMM is not perfect, it does represent a broad consensus of the software community and is a useful tool for guiding software process improvement efforts.

The CMM provides a conceptual structure for improving the management and development of software products in a disciplined and consistent way. It does not guarantee that software products will be successfully built or that all problems in software engineering will be adequately resolved. However, current reports from CMM-based improvement programs indicate that it can improve the likelihood that a software organization will achieve its cost, quality, and productivity goals.

The CMM identifies practices for a mature software process and provides examples of the state-of-the-practice (and in some cases, the state-of-the-art), but it is not meant to be either exhaustive or dictatorial. The CMM identifies the characteristics of an effective software process, but the mature organization addresses all issues essential to a successful project, including people and technology, as well as process.

The CMM is a tool to help software organizations improve their software processes. It can also help acquisition organizations select and manage software contractors. CMM is only a tool, however, and it must be used intelligently to help organizations address their specific business needs. The purpose of the CMM is to describe good management and engineering practices as structured by the maturity framework.

Sound judgment is necessary to use the CMM correctly and with insight. Intelligence, experience, and knowledge must shape an appropriate interpretation of the CMM in a specific environment. That interpretation should be based on the business needs and objectives of the organization and the projects. A rote, checklist-oriented application of the CMM has the potential to harm an organization rather than help it.

Achieving higher levels of software process maturity is incremental and requires a long-term commitment to continuous process improvement. Software organizations may take ten years or more to build the foundation for, and a culture oriented toward, continuous process improvement. Although a decade-long process improvement program is foreign to most software companies, this sustained effort is required to produce mature software organizations.

2

The Software Process Maturity Framework

Continuous process improvement is based on many small, evolutionary steps rather than revolutionary innovations. The CMM provides a framework for organizing these evolutionary steps into five maturity levels that lay successive foundations for continuous process improvement. These five maturity levels define an ordinal scale for measuring the maturity of an organization's software process and for evaluating its software process capability. They also help an organization prioritize its improvement efforts.

A *maturity level* is a well-defined evolutionary plateau toward achieving a mature software process. Each maturity level comprises a set of process goals that, when satisfied, stabilize an important component of the software process. Achieving each level of the maturity framework establishes a different component in the software process, resulting in an increase in the process capability of the organization.

Organizing the CMM into the five levels shown in Fig. 2.1 prioritizes improvement actions for increasing software process maturity. The labeled arrows indicate the type of process capability being institutionalized by the organization at each level of the maturity framework.

The five levels can be briefly described as:

1. Initial   The software process is characterized as ad hoc, and occasionally even chaotic. Few processes are defined, and success depends on individual effort and heroics.

2. Repeatable   Basic project management processes are established to track cost, schedule, and functionality. The necessary

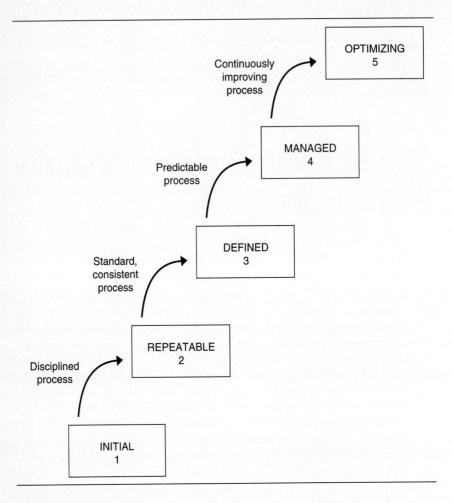

FIGURE 2.1
The five levels of software process maturity

	process discipline is in place to repeat earlier successes on projects with similar applications.
3. Defined	The software process for both management and engineering activities is documented, standardized, and integrated into a standard software process for the organization. All projects use an approved, tailored version of the organization's standard software process for developing and maintaining software.

4. Managed   Detailed measures of the software process and product quality
                   are collected. Both the software process and products are
                   quantitatively understood and controlled.

5. Optimizing   Continuous process improvement is enabled by quantitative
                   feedback from the process and from piloting innovative ideas
                   and technologies.

These five levels reflect the fact that the CMM is a model for improving the capability of software organizations. The priorities in the CMM, as expressed by these levels, are not directed at individual projects. A troubled project might well prioritize its problems differently from the taxonomy given by the CMM. Its solutions might be of limited value to the rest of the organization, because other projects might have different problems or be unable to take advantage of its solutions because they lack the necessary foundation to implement the solutions. The CMM focuses on processes that are of value across the organization.

2.1 Behavioral Characterization of the Maturity Levels

Maturity Levels 2 through 5 can be characterized through the activities performed by the organization to establish or improve the software process, by activities performed on each project, and by the resulting process capability across projects.

2.1.1 Level 1: The Initial Level

At the Initial Level, the organization typically does not provide a stable environment for developing and maintaining software. Overcommitment is a characteristic of Level 1 organizations, and such organizations frequently have difficulty making commitments that the staff can meet with an orderly engineering process, resulting in a series of crises. During a crisis, projects typically abandon planned procedures and revert to coding and testing. Success depends on having an exceptional manager and a seasoned and effective software team. Occasionally, capable and forceful software managers can withstand the pressures to take shortcuts in the software process; but when they leave the project, their stabilizing influence leaves with them. Even a strong engineering process cannot overcome the instability created by the absence of sound management practices.

In spite of this ad hoc, even chaotic, process, Level 1 organizations frequently develop products that work, even though they may exceed the budget and schedule. Success in Level 1 organizations depends on the competence and heroics of the people in the organization[1] and cannot be repeated unless the same competent individuals are assigned to the next project. Thus, at Level 1, capability is a characteristic of the individuals, not of the organization.

2.1.2 Level 2: The Repeatable Level

At the Repeatable Level, policies for managing a software project and procedures to implement those policies are established. Planning and managing new projects is based on experience with similar projects. Process capability is enhanced by establishing basic process management discipline on a project by project basis. Projects implement effective processes that are defined, documented, practiced, trained, measured, enforced, and improvable.

Projects in Level 2 organizations have installed basic software management controls. Realistic project commitments are made, based on the results observed on previous projects and on the requirements of the current project. The software managers for a project track software costs, schedules, and functionality; problems in meeting commitments are identified as they arise. Software requirements and the work products developed to satisfy them are baselined, and their integrity is controlled. Software project standards are defined, and the organization ensures they are faithfully followed. The software project works with its subcontractors, if any, to establish an effective customer–supplier relationship.

Processes may differ between projects in a Level 2 organization. The organizational requirement for achieving Level 2 is that there be organization-level policies that guide the projects in establishing the appropriate management processes.

The software process capability of Level 2 organizations can be summarized as disciplined because planning and tracking of the software project is stable and earlier successes can be repeated. The project's process is under the effective control of a project management system, following realistic plans based on the performance of previous projects.

2.1.3 Level 3: The Defined Level

At the Defined Level, a standard process (or processes) for developing and maintaining software is documented and used across the organization. Referred to throughout the CMM as the *organization's standard software process*, this standard process includes both software engineering and management processes and integrates them into a coherent whole. Processes established at Level 3 are used (and

---

[1] Selecting, hiring, developing, and retaining competent people are significant issues for organizations at all levels of maturity, but they are largely outside the scope of CMM.

changed, as appropriate) to help the software managers and technical staff perform more effectively. The organization exploits effective software engineering practices when standardizing its software processes. A group within the organization is assigned responsibility for software process activities (e.g., a software engineering process group or SEPG [Fowler90]). An organization-wide training program is implemented to ensure that the staff and managers have the knowledge and skills required to fulfill their assigned roles.

Projects tailor the organization's standard software process to develop their own defined software process, which accounts for the unique characteristics of the project. This tailored process is referred to in the CMM as the *project's defined software process*. It is the process used in performing the project's activities. A defined software process contains a coherent, integrated set of well-defined software engineering and management processes.   A well-defined process can be characterized as including readiness criteria, inputs, standards and procedures for performing the work, verification mechanisms (such as peer reviews), outputs, and completion criteria. Because the software process is well defined, management has good insight into technical progress on the project.

The software process capability of Level 3 organizations can be summarized as standard and consistent because both software engineering and management activities are stable and repeatable. Within established product lines, cost, schedule, and functionality are under control, and software quality is tracked. This process capability is based on a common, organization-wide understanding of the activities, roles, and responsibilities in a defined software process.

2.1.4 Level 4: The Managed Level

At the Managed Level, the organization sets quantitative quality goals for both software products and processes. Productivity and quality are measured for important software process activities across all projects as part of an organizational measurement program. An organization-wide software process database is used to collect and analyze the data available from the projects' defined software processes. Software processes are instrumented with well-defined and consistent measurements. These measurements establish the quantitative foundation for evaluating the projects' software processes and products.

Projects achieve control over their products and processes by narrowing the variation in their process performance to fall within acceptable quantitative boundaries. Meaningful variations in process performance can be distinguished from random variation (noise), particularly within established product lines. The risks involved in moving up the learning curve of a new application domain are known and carefully managed.

The software process capability of Level 4 organizations can be summarized as being quantifiable and predictable because the process is measured and operates within quantitative limits. This level of process capability allows an organization to predict trends in process and product quality within the quantitative bounds of these limits. Because the process is both stable and measured, when some exceptional circumstance occurs, the "special cause" of the variation can be identified and addressed. When the pre-defined limits are exceeded, actions are taken to understand and correct the situation. Software products are of predictably high quality.

2.1.5 Level 5: The Optimizing Level

At the Optimizing Level, the entire organization is focused on continuous process improvement. The organization has the means to identify weaknesses and strengthen the process proactively, with the goal of preventing the occurrence of defects. Data on the effectiveness of the software process are used to perform cost/benefit analyses of new technologies and proposed changes to the organization's software process. Innovations that exploit the best software engineering practices are identified and transferred throughout the organization.

Software teams in Level 5 organizations analyze defects to determine their causes. They evaluate software processes to prevent known types of defects from recurring and disseminate lessons learned throughout the organization.

Chronic waste, in the form of rework, can be found in any system simply due to random variation. Organized efforts to remove waste result in changing the system, that is, in improving the process by changing "common causes" of inefficiency to prevent the waste from occurring. While this is true of all the maturity levels, it is the focus of Level 5.

The software process capability of Level 5 organizations can be characterized as continuously improving because Level 5 organizations are continuously striving to improve the range of their process capability, thereby improving the process performance of their projects. Improvements occur both by incremental advancements in the existing process and by innovations using new technologies and methods. Technology and process improvements are planned and managed as ordinary business activities.

2.2 Skipping Maturity Levels

The CMM identifies the levels through which an organization should evolve to establish a culture of software engineering excellence. Because each maturity level in the CMM forms a necessary foundation on which to build the next level, trying to skip levels is almost always counterproductive.

Organizations can institute specific process improvements at any time they choose, even before they are prepared to advance to the level at which the specific practice is recommended. However, organizations should understand that the stability of these improvements is at greater risk since the foundation for their successful institutionalization has not been completed. Processes without the proper foundation may fail at the very point they are needed most—under stress.

For instance, a well-defined software process that is characteristic of a Level 3 organization can be placed at great risk if Level 2 management practices are deficient. For example, management may make a poorly planned schedule commitment or fail to control changes to the baselined requirements. Similarly, many organizations collect the detailed data characteristic of Level 4, only to find that the data are uninterpretable because of inconsistency in the software development processes and measurement definitions.

At the same time, it must be recognized that process improvement efforts should focus on the needs of the organization in the context of its business environment and that higher-level practices may address the current needs of an organization or project. For example, organizations seeking to move from Level 1 to Level 2 are frequently told to establish a software engineering process group, which is an attribute of Level 3 organizations. While an SEPG is not a necessary characteristic of a Level 2 organization, it can be a useful part of the prescription for achieving Level 2.

This is sometimes characterized as establishing a Level 1 SEPG to boot-strap the Level 1 organization up to Level 2. Level 1 software process improvement activities may depend primarily on the insight and competence of the SEPG staff until an infrastructure to support more disciplined and wide-spread improvement is in place.

Another example is the process of building software. Certainly we would expect Level 1 organizations to perform requirements analysis, design, code, and test. These activities are not described in the CMM, however, until Level 3, where they are described as coherent, well-integrated engineering processes.

Similarly, processes change in moving from Level 1 to Level 2. Process improvement occurs as an organization moves up the maturity levels. Mastery of managing continual process change is characteristic, however, of Level 5 organizations.

Such variations in implementing software process improvement are artifacts of the way key process areas are defined. A key process area describes a fully implemented and institutionalized process—one that has been mastered by an organization. Almost any process described in the CMM could be implemented, although perhaps in an incomplete or ad hoc fashion, by a Level 1 organization.

Simply because a Level 1 organization may perform a process in an ad hoc manner should not detract from the fact that it is performed. The reliability and consistency of this process can and should be subsequently improved. An organizational capability can sprout from the seed of an ad hoc process.

2.3 Visibility into the Software Process

Each level of the CMM increases visibility into the software process for both managers and the engineering staff. Software engineers have detailed insight into the state of a project because they have first-hand information on project status and performance. However, on large projects, their insight usually is drawn only from their personal experience in their area of responsibility. Those outside the project without first-hand exposure, such as senior managers, lack visibility into the project's processes and therefore rely on periodic reviews for the information they require to monitor progress. Figure 2.2, created by Jeff Perdue, illustrates the level of visibility into project status and performance afforded to management at each level of process maturity. Each succeeding maturity level incrementally provides better visibility into the software process.

At Level 1, the software process is an amorphous entity—a black box—and visibility into the project's processes is limited. Since the staging of activities is poorly defined, managers have an extremely difficult time establishing the status of the project's progress and activities.[2] Requirements flow into the software process in an uncontrolled manner, and a product results. Software development is frequently viewed as black magic, especially by managers who are unfamiliar with software. The customer can assess whether the product meets requirements only when it is delivered.

At Level 2, the customer requirements and work products are controlled, and basic project management practices have been established. These management controls allow visibility into the project on defined occasions. The process of building the software can be viewed as a succession of black boxes that allows management visibility at transition points (project milestones) as activity flows between boxes. Even though management may not know the details of what is happening in the box, the products of the process and checkpoints for confirming that the process is working are identified and known. Management reacts to problems as they occur. The customer can review the product at defined checkpoints during the software process.

At Level 3, the internal structure of the boxes, that is, the tasks in the project's defined software process, is visible. The internal structure represents the way the organization's standard software process has been applied to

---

[2] This leads to the somewhat facetious Ninety-Ninety Rule: 90% of the project is complete 90% of the time.

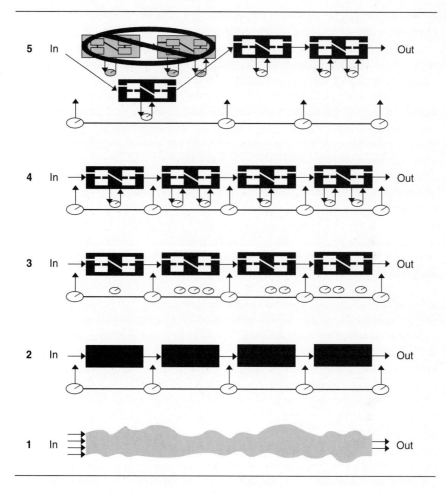

FIGURE 2.2
Visibility into the software process at each maturity level

specific projects. Both managers and engineers understand their roles and responsibilities within the process and how their activities interact at the appropriate level of detail. Management prepares proactively for risks that may arise. The customer can obtain accurate and rapid status updates because defined processes afford great visibility into project activities.

At Level 4, the defined software processes are instrumented and controlled quantitatively. Managers are able to measure progress and problems. They have an objective, quantitative basis for making decisions. Their ability to predict outcomes grows steadily more precise as the variability in the process grows smaller. The customer can establish a quantitative understanding of process capability and risk before the project begins.

At Level 5, new and improved ways of building the software are continually tried, in a controlled manner, to improve productivity and quality. Disciplined change is a way of life as inefficient or defect-prone activities are identified and replaced or revised. Insight extends beyond existing processes and into the effects of potential changes to processes. Managers are able to estimate and then quantitatively track the impact and effectiveness of change. The customer and the software organization continue to work together to establish a strong customer-supplier relationship.

Across all five levels, process capability interacts with people, technology, and measurement as an organization matures, as illustrated in Table 2.1.

2.4 Prediction of Performance

The maturity of an organization's software process helps to predict a project's ability to meet its goals. Projects in Level 1 organizations experience wide variations in achieving cost, schedule, functionality, and quality targets. Figure 2.3 illustrates the kinds of improvements expected in predictability, control, and effectiveness in the form of a probability density for the likely performance of a

TABLE 2.1
Implications of advancing through CMM levels.

	Level 1	Level 2	Level 3	Level 4	Level 5
P R O C E	Few stable processes exist or are used.	Documented and stable estimating, planning, and commitment processes are at the project level.	Integrated management and engineering processes are used across the organization.	Processes are quantitatively understood and stabilized.	Processes are continuously and systematically improved.
S S	"Just do it"	Problems are recognized and corrected as they occur.	Problems are anticipated and prevented, or their impacts are minimized.	Sources of individual problems are understood and eliminated.	Common sources of problems are understood and eliminated.

TABLE 2.1 (continued)

	Level 1	Level 2	Level 3	Level 4	Level 5
P E O P L E	Success depends on individual heroics.	Success depends on individuals; management system supports.	Project groups work together, perhaps as an integrated product team.	Strong sense of teamwork exists within each project.	Strong sense of teamwork exists across the organization.
	"Fire fighting" is a way of life.	Commitments are understood and managed	Training is planned and provided according to roles.		Everyone is involved in process improvement.
	Relationships between disciplines are uncoordinated, perhaps even adversarial.	People are trained.			
T E C H N O L O G Y	Introduction of new technology is risky.	Technology supports established, stable activities.	New technologies are evaluated on a qualitative basis.	New technologies are evaluated on a quantitative basis.	New technologies are proactively pursued and deployed.
M E A S U R E M E N T	Data collection and analysis is ad hoc.	Planning and management data used by individual projects.	Data are collected and used in all defined processes.	Data definition and collection are standardized across the organization.	Data are used to evaluate and select process improvements.
			Data are systematically shared across projects.	Data are used to understand the process quantitatively and stabilize it.	

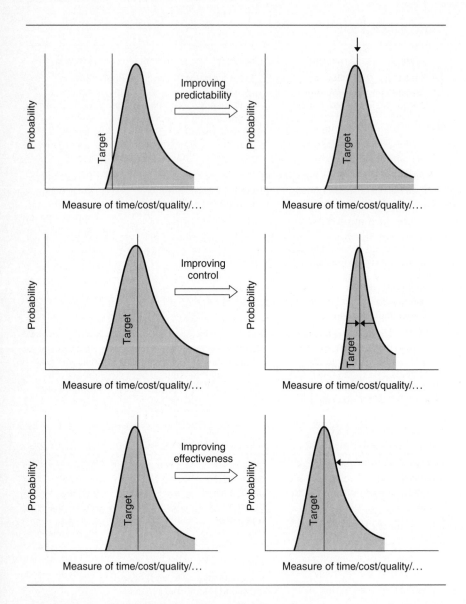

FIGURE 2.3
Improving control, predictability, and effectiveness

particular project with respect to targets, which may be schedules, cost, quality, and so on.

The first improvement expected as an organization matures is in predictability. As maturity increases, the difference between targeted results and actual results decreases across projects. For instance, Level 1 organizations often miss their originally scheduled delivery dates by a wide margin, whereas higher maturity level organizations should be able to meet targeted dates with increased accuracy.

The second improvement is in control. As maturity increases, the variability of actual results around targeted results decreases. For instance, in Level 1 organizations delivery dates for projects of similar size are unpredictable and vary widely. Similar projects in a higher maturity level organization, however, will be delivered within a smaller range.

The third improvement is in effectiveness. Targeted results improve as the maturity of the organization increases. That is, as a software organization matures, costs decrease, development time becomes shorter, and productivity and quality increase. In a Level 1 organization, development time can be quite long because of the amount of rework necessary to correct mistakes [Cooper93]. In contrast, higher maturity level organizations have increased process effectiveness and reduced costly rework, resulting in shortened development time.

As illustrated in Fig. 2.4, all three improvements are expected as the organization's software process matures. These expectations are based on the quantitative results process improvement has achieved in other industries, and they are consistent with the initial case study results reported from software organizations [Dion93, Humphrey91b, Lipke92, Wohlwend93].

Note the interaction between predictability and effectiveness as an organization moves from Level 1 to Level 2. Because of the improvement in estimating, plans become more realistic, leading to longer target schedules. At the same time, because of improvements in performing the process, cycle times shorten, leading to shorter actual schedules. In this graphic, we have chosen to emphasize the more realistic schedule by indicating that "Target N" is now "Target N+a." Schedules may be shorter at Level 2 than at Level 1, but the exact relationship will depend on the baseline effectiveness and predictability of the organization's processes when it began its software process improvement program.

The improvements in predicting a project's results represented in Fig. 2.4 assume that the software project's outcomes become more predictable as noise, often in the form of rework, is removed from the software process. Unprecedented systems complicate the picture, since new technologies and applications lower the process capability by increasing variability. Even in the case of unprecedented systems, the management and engineering practices characteristic of more mature organizations help identify and address problems earlier in the development cycle than they would have been detected in less mature organizations. In some cases, a mature process means that "failed" projects are identified early in the software life cycle, and investment in a lost cause is minimized.

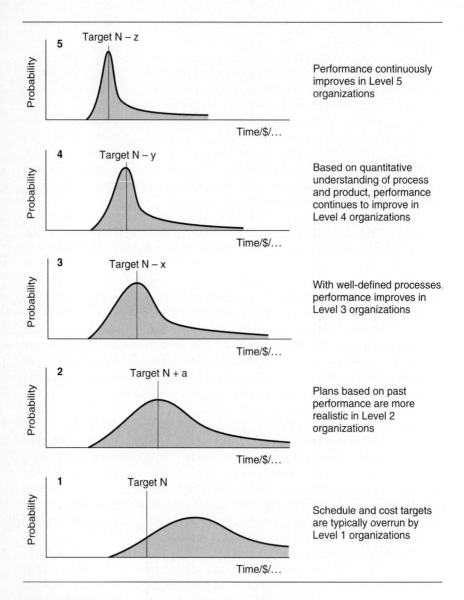

FIGURE 2.4
Process capability as indicated by maturity level

3

The Structure of the Capability Maturity Model

The CMM is a framework representing a path of improvements recommended for software organizations that want to increase their software process capability. The CMM is a descriptive model in the sense that it describes essential (or key) attributes that would be expected to characterize an organization at a particular maturity level. It is a normative model in the sense that the detailed practices characterize the normal types of behavior that would be expected in an organization doing large-scale projects in a government contracting context.

The CMM is fairly abstract so that it will not unduly constrain how the software process is implemented by an organization. The CMM describes what we would normally expect in a software process, regardless of how the process is implemented.

This operational elaboration of the CMM is designed to support the many ways it will be used, including the following five:

- Assessment teams will use the CMM to identify strengths and weaknesses in the organization.

- Evaluation teams will use the CMM to identify the risks of selecting among different contractors for awarding business and to monitor contracts.

- Appraisal method developers will use the CMM to develop other CMM-based appraisal methods that meet specific needs (e.g., the interim profile method [Whitney94]).

- Upper management will use the CMM to understand the activities necessary to launch a software process improvement program in their organization.
- Technical staff and process improvement groups, such as an SEPG, will use the CMM as a guide to help them define and improve the software process in their organization.

Because of the diverse uses of the CMM, it must be decomposed in sufficient detail that actual process recommendations can be derived from the structure of the maturity levels. This decomposition also identifies the key processes and their structure that characterize software process maturity and software process capability.

3.1 Internal Structure of the Maturity Levels

Each maturity level has been decomposed into constituent parts. With the exception of Level 1, the decomposition of each maturity level ranges from abstract summaries of each level down to their operational definition in key practices, as shown in Fig. 3.1. Each maturity level is composed of several key process areas, and each key process area is organized into five sections called common features. The common features contain the key practices that, when collectively addressed, accomplish the goals of the key process area.

3.2 Maturity Levels

A maturity level is a well-defined evolutionary plateau toward achieving a mature software process. The five maturity levels provide the top-level structure of the CMM.

Each maturity level indicates a level of process capability. Since software process capability describes the range of expected results that can be achieved by following a software process, the software process capability of an organization provides one means of predicting the most likely outcomes from the next software project the organization undertakes. For instance, at Level 2, the process capability of an organization has been elevated from ad hoc to disciplined by establishing sound project management controls.

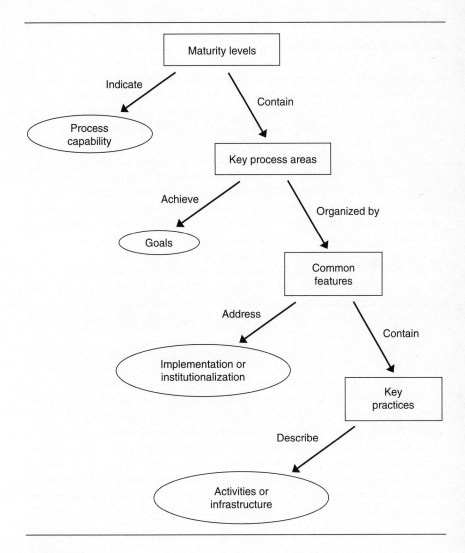

FIGURE 3.1
The CMM structure

3.3 Key Process Areas

Except for Level 1, each maturity level is decomposed into several key process areas that indicate where an organization should focus to improve its software process. Key process areas identify the issues that must be addressed to achieve a maturity level. If an organization is at Level 3, it has addressed all of the key process areas at Levels 2 and 3.[1]

Each *key process area* identifies a cluster of related activities that, when performed collectively, achieve a set of goals considered important for enhancing process capability. The key process areas have been defined to reside at a single maturity level as shown in Fig. 3.2. The path to achieving the goals of a key process area may differ across projects based on differences in application domains or environments. Nevertheless, all the goals of a key process area must be achieved for the organization to satisfy that key process area.

The adjective "key" implies that some process areas (and processes) are not key to achieving a maturity level. The CMM does not describe all the process areas that are involved with developing and maintaining software. Only those process areas identified as key determinants of process capability have been described in the CMM.

The key process areas may be considered the requirements for achieving a maturity level. To achieve a maturity level, the key process areas for that level (and the lower levels) must be satisfied and the processes must be institutionalized.

The *goals* of each key process area summarize its key practices and can be used in determining whether an organization or project has effectively implemented the key process area. The goals signify the scope, boundaries, and intent of each key process area. In adapting the key practices of a key process area to a specific project or organization situation, the goals can be used to determine whether the adaptation is a reasonable rendering of the practices. Similarly, when evaluating alternative ways to implement a key process area, the goals can be used to determine whether the alternatives satisfy the intent of the key process area.

3.3.1 Key Process Areas at Level 2

The key process areas at Level 2 focus on the software project's concerns related to establishing basic project management controls.

- The purpose of Requirements Management is to establish a common understanding between the customer and the software project of the customer's

---

[1] There is one exception. The Software Subcontract Management key process area may be "not applicable" if the organization does not do any subcontracting.

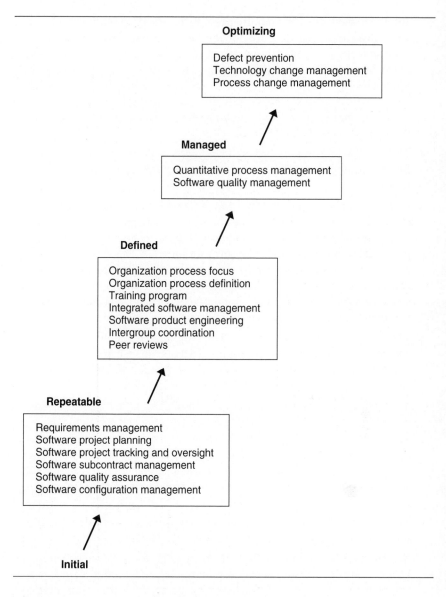

Optimizing

Defect prevention
Technology change management
Process change management

Managed

Quantitative process management
Software quality management

Defined

Organization process focus
Organization process definition
Training program
Integrated software management
Software product engineering
Intergroup coordination
Peer reviews

Repeatable

Requirements management
Software project planning
Software project tracking and oversight
Software subcontract management
Software quality assurance
Software configuration management

Initial

FIGURE 3.2
The key process areas by maturity level

requirements to be addressed by the software project. This agreement with the customer is the basis for planning and managing the software project.

An understanding of the requirements is necessary to build software that will satisfy the customer. Reviewing the requirements allocated to software and interacting with the customer (whether external or internal) is part of establishing that understanding. Since the customer's requirements will frequently evolve and change, documenting and controlling the customer requirements is a prerequisite to using them as the basis for estimating, planning, performing, and tracking the software project's activities throughout the software life cycle.

- The purpose of Software Project Planning is to establish reasonable plans for performing the software engineering and for managing the software project.

Reasonable plans are based on developing realistic estimates for the work to be performed and establishing the necessary commitments to perform that work. They begin with a statement of the work and the constraints and goals that define and bound the software project. The software planning process includes steps to estimate the size of the software work products and the resources needed, to produce a schedule, to identify and assess software risks, and to negotiate commitments. The plan is documented and maintained as a necessary tool for managing the software project.

- The purpose of Software Project Tracking and Oversight is to establish adequate visibility into actual progress so that management can take effective actions when the software project's performance deviates significantly from the software plans.

Management of the software project should be based on the software development plan. Management involves tracking and reviewing the software accomplishments and results against the plan and taking corrective action as necessary based on actual accomplishments and results. These actions may include revising the software development plan to reflect the actual accomplishments, replanning the remaining work, and/or taking actions to improve the performance.

- The purpose of Software Subcontract Management is to select qualified software subcontractors and manage them effectively.

Subcontractor selection is based on ability to perform the work, but many factors contribute to the decision to subcontract a portion of the prime contractor's work. Subcontractors may be selected based on strategic business alliances, as well as process capability and technical considerations. The work to be done by the subcontractor and the plans for the work are documented, and the prime contractor monitors performance against these plans.

- The purpose of Software Quality Assurance is to provide management with appropriate visibility into the process being used by the software project and of the products being built.

  This visibility is achieved by reviewing and auditing the software products and activities to verify that they comply with the applicable standards and procedures. Compliance issues are first addressed within the software project and resolved there if possible. For issues not resolved within the software project, the software quality assurance group escalates the issue as appropriate for resolution.

- The purpose of Software Configuration Management is to establish and maintain the integrity of the products of the software project throughout the project's software life cycle.

  Integrity of work products is achieved by identifying the configuration of the software (i.e., selected software work products and their descriptions) at given points in time, systematically controlling changes to the configuration, and maintaining the integrity and traceability of the configuration throughout the software life cycle. Software baselines are maintained in a software baseline library as they are developed. Changes to baselines and the release of software products built from the software baseline library are systematically controlled via the change control and configuration auditing functions of Software Configuration Management.

3.3.2 Key Process Areas at Level 3

The key process areas at Level 3 address both project and organizational issues, as the organization establishes an infrastructure that institutionalizes effective software engineering and management processes across all projects.

- The purpose of Organization Process Focus is to establish the organizational responsibility for software process activities that improve the organization's overall software process capability.

  Sustained process improvement involves developing and maintaining an understanding of the organization's and projects' software processes and coordinating the activities to assess, develop, maintain, and improve these processes. The word "coordinating" is deliberately chosen to emphasize that the people implementing the process must be intimately involved with its definition and improvement, although the organization provides the long-term commitments and resources to coordinate the development and maintenance of the software processes across current and future software projects.

- The purpose of Organization Process Definition is to develop and maintain a usable set of software process assets that improve process performance across the projects and provide a basis for defining meaningful data for quantitative process management. These assets provide a stable foundation that can be institutionalized via mechanisms such as training.

  Process definition involves developing and maintaining the organization's standard software process, along with related process assets, such as descriptions of software life cycles, process tailoring guidelines and criteria, the organization's software process database, and a library of software process-related documentation. These assets may be collected in many ways; for example, the descriptions of the software life cycles may be an integral part of the organization's standard software process. The taxonomy provided in this key process area outlines the aspects of process definition that need to be addressed.

- The purpose of Training Program is to develop the skills and knowledge of individuals so they can perform their roles effectively and efficiently. Training is an organizational responsibility, but the software projects are responsible for identifying their needed skills and providing the necessary training when the project's needs are unique.

  A training program begins by identifying training needs of the organization, projects, and individuals, then developing or procuring training to address the identified needs. These needs may be specific to the project or individual at a particular time, but required training can be identified based on the roles and responsibilities specified in the organization's standard software process. Some skills are effectively and efficiently imparted through informal vehicles, for example, mentoring. Other skills need more formal training vehicles, such as, classroom training.

- The purpose of Integrated Software Management is to integrate the software engineering and management activities into a coherent, defined software process that is tailored from the organization's standard software process and related process assets. This tailoring is based on the business environment and technical needs of the project.

  This key process area is the evolution of Software Project Planning and Software Project Tracking and Oversight at Level 2 to take advantage of the organizational infrastructure established at Level 3. Satisfying Integrated Software Management means that a software project is planned and managed according to a well-defined process based on organizational software process assets.

- The purpose of Software Product Engineering is to perform consistently a well-defined engineering process that integrates all the software engineering activities to produce correct, consistent software products effectively and efficiently. Software Product Engineering describes the technical activities of the project, for example, requirements analysis, design, code, and test.

These engineering processes involve documenting the software work products and maintaining traceability and consistency between them. This is necessary to ensure a controlled transition between the stages of the software life cycle and to provide high-quality software products to the customer.

- The purpose of Intergroup Coordination is to establish a means for the software engineering group to participate actively with the other engineering groups so the project is better able to satisfy the customer's needs effectively and efficiently.

The software engineering group must work proactively with other project engineering groups to address system-level requirements, objectives, and issues. Ideally, this would be some form of integrated product team or concurrent engineering. In any case, the technical working interfaces and interactions between groups need to be planned and managed to ensure the quality and integrity of the entire system. All engineering groups should be aware of the status and plans of all the groups, and system and intergroup issues should receive appropriate attention.

- The purpose of Peer Reviews is to remove defects from the software work products early and efficiently.

An important corollary effect is to develop a better understanding of the software work products and of the defects that can be prevented. The peer review is an important and effective engineering method implementable via inspections, structured walkthroughs, or a number of other collegial review methods.

3.3.3 Key Process Areas at Level 4

The key process areas at Level 4 focus on establishing a quantitative understanding of both the software process and the software products being built.

- The purpose of Quantitative Process Management is to control the process performance of the software project quantitatively.

Software process performance represents the actual results achieved from following a software process. There will be random variation (noise) in any process. With a stable process, performance is normally within known bounds (i.e., quantitative process capability). When performance falls outside those bounds, the need is to identify the "special cause" of the variation and, where appropriate, correct the circumstances that drove the transient variation to occur. The result of satisfying this key process area is a process that remains stable and quantitatively predictable.

- The purpose of Software Quality Management is to develop a quantitative understanding of the quality of the project's software products and achieve specific quality goals.

  Quantitative goals are established for software products based on the needs of the organization, the customer, and the end users. So that these goals may be achieved, the organization establishes strategies and plans, and the project specifically adjusts its defined software process to accomplish the quality goals. Software Quality Management is product focused, while Quantitative Process Management is process focused.

3.3.4 Key Process Areas at Level 5

The key process areas at Level 5 cover the issues that both the organization and the projects must address to implement continuous and measurable software process improvement.

- The purpose of Defect Prevention is to identify the causes of defects and prevent them from recurring.

  The software project analyzes defects, identifies their causes, and takes action to prevent them from recurring. Often this involves changing the project's defined software process. The causal analysis may also result in changing elements of the organization's standard software process to control common causes of variation. Defect Prevention is a mechanism for incrementally improving the software process in an evolutionary way.

- The purpose of Technology Change Management is to identify beneficial new technologies (i.e., tools, methods, and processes) and transfer them into the organization in an orderly manner.

  A focus on technology transition implies identifying, selecting, and evaluating new technologies, and incorporating effective technologies into the organization. The objective is to improve software quality, increase productivity, and decrease the cycle time for product development. The result of this focus is performing innovation efficiently in an ever-changing world. Technology Change Management deals with improving the software process in a revolutionary way.

- The purpose of Process Change Management is to improve continually the software processes used in the organization with the intent of improving software quality, increasing productivity, and decreasing the cycle time for product development.

Continuous process improvement involves defining process improvement goals and, with senior management sponsorship, proactively and systematically identifying, evaluating, and implementing improvements to the organization's standard software process and the projects' defined software processes. Process Change Management focuses on appropriately deploying both incremental, evolutionary changes and innovative, revolutionary changes.

3.4 Key Practices

Each key process area is described in terms of key practices. The *key practices* describe the activities and infrastructure that contribute most to the effective implementation and institutionalization of the key process area. The specific practices to be executed in each key process area will evolve as the organization achieves higher levels of process maturity. For instance, many of the project estimating capabilities described in the Software Project Planning key process area at Level 2 must evolve to handle the additional project data available at Level 3, as described in Integrated Software Management.

The key practices describe "what" is to be done, but they should not be interpreted as mandating "how" the process should be implemented. Alternative practices may accomplish the goals of the key process area. The key practices should be interpreted rationally to judge whether the goals of the key process area are effectively, although perhaps differently, achieved. The key practices of the CMM are in Chapters 7–10 of this book.

Each key practice consists of a single sentence, often followed by a more detailed description, which may include examples and elaboration. These key practices describe the infrastructure and activities that contribute most to the effective implementation and institutionalization of a key process area. More detailed subpractices are frequently provided under the key practice as guidance in interpreting an adequate implementation of the key practice. Examples, definitions, and cross-references to other practices are also provided as appropriate.

3.5 Common Features

For convenience, the practices that describe the key process areas are organized by common features. Common features are attributes that indicate whether the implementation and institutionalization of a key process area is effective, repeatable, and lasting. There are five common features:

Commitment to Perform — Commitment to Perform describes the actions the organization must take to ensure that the process is established and will endure. Commitment to Perform typically involves establishing organizational policies and leadership.

Ability to Perform — Ability to Perform describes the preconditions that must exist in the project or organization to implement the software process competently. Ability to Perform typically involves resources, organizational structures, and training.

Activities Performed — Activities Performed describes the activities, roles, and procedures necessary to implement a key process area. Activities Performed typically involves establishing plans and procedures, performing the work, tracking it, and taking corrective actions as necessary.

Measurement and Analysis — Measurement and Analysis describes the basic measurement practices that are necessary to determine status related to the process. These measurements are used to control and improve the process. Measurement and Analysis typically includes examples of the measurements that could be taken.

Verifying Implementation — Verifying Implementation describes the steps to ensure that the activities are performed in compliance with the process that has been established. Verifying Implementation typically encompasses reviews and audits by management and software quality assurance.

The practices in the common feature Activities Performed describe what must be implemented to establish a process capability. The other practices, taken as a whole, form the basis by which an organization can institutionalize the practices described in the Activities Performed common feature.

4

Interpreting the CMM

A reasonable interpretation of the CMM practices must be made in any context in which the CMM is applied. The CMM was written to address the process for large, complex software efforts. Informed professional judgment is especially important when the business environment differs significantly from this context. Early efforts in tailoring the CMM to different environments, however, indicate that over 90% of the key practices are applicable as written, although they must be interpreted in the context of a specific implementation.

The CMM is a commonsense application of process management and quality improvement concepts to software development and maintenance. It is not a model based on universal physical laws, such as would be seen in physics or chemistry. It represents a broad-based consensus by the software community of good engineering and management practices, but the CMM is not "engraved on stone tablets bestowed from on high."

4.1 Interpreting the Key Practices

The intention in setting down the key practices is not to require or espouse a specific model of the software life cycle, a specific organizational structure, a specific separation of responsibilities, or a specific management and technical approach to development. The intent, rather, is to provide a description of the essential elements of an effective software process.

The key practices are intended to communicate principles that apply to a wide variety of projects and organizations, that are valid across a range of typical software applications, and that will remain valid over time. Therefore the approach is to describe the principles and leave their implementation to each organization, according to its culture and the expertise of its managers and technical staff.

Although the key practices are meant to be independent of any particular implementation, specific terms and examples are consistently used in stating the key practices to improve clarity. This section describes the conventions used in the CMM for roles, responsibilities, relationships, artifacts, and activities. Organizations using the key practices should be aware of these conventions and map them appropriately to their own organization, project, and business environment.

The glossary in Appendix C contains definitions of terms, including those described in this chapter and others.

4.2 The Key Process Area Template

When reading the practices, understanding the wording consistently used throughout the CMM is helpful. A template was generally used to express the key process areas with a consistent structure and phrasing. This key process area template, with the "standard" wording used in the various key process areas, follows.

In some practices, however, the template is not followed. For example, in Verifying Implementation for SQA, the SQA group does not audit itself. The exceptions are described in Section 4.3 in the discussion of the various wording templates.

Also note:

- Goals and common features are delimited by headers, for example, **Goals** and **Commitment to Perform**.

- Key practices are labeled with a noun representing their common feature and a number, for example, Commitment 1 and Ability 2.

- Key practices are in bold type, for example, **A group that is responsible for <X> exists.**

- Subpractices are frequently preceded by a preamble; for example, the subpractices for those key practices that include the phrase "according to a documented procedure" are preceded by the preamble "This procedure typically specifies that:"

- Practices may be followed by boxed text, which contains elaboration, cross-references, or examples.

<Key Process Area X>

a key process area for Level n: <Level name>

The purpose of <Key Process Area X> is <statement>.
<Key Process Area X> involves <summary>.
<Additional elaboration on Key Process Area X as appropriate.>

Goals

Goal 1   **<Process summary statement as goal.>**

Goal 2   **<Process summary statement as goal...>**

Commitment to Perform

Commitment 1   **The project follows a written organizational policy for <X>.**

                                 or

                 The organization follows a written policy for <X>.

                 This policy typically specifies that:

                 1. <Subpractices for Commitment 1...>

Ability to Perform

Ability 1   **A group that is responsible for <X> exists.**

                 1. <Subpractices for Ability 1...>

Ability 2   **Adequate resources and funding are provided for <X>.**

                 1. <Subpractices for Ability 2...>
                 2. Tools to support the activities for <X> are made available.

> Examples of \<X\> tools include:
>
> \<examples of tools\>

Ability 3   **\<Roles\> are trained \<to perform their X activities\>.**

or

\<Roles\> receive required training \<to perform their X activities\>.

> Examples of training include:
>
> \<examples of training\>

Ability 4   **\<Roles\> receive orientation in \<X\>.**

> Examples of orientation include:
>
> \<examples of orientation training\>

Activities Performed

Activity 1   **\<Activity performed in Key Process Area X.\>**

1. \<Subpractice for Activity 1, possibly affecting different groups.\>

> Examples of affected groups include:
>
> \<list of affected groups\>

2. \<Additional subpractices for Activity 1...\>
3. \<Software work products, as appropriate\> are placed under configuration management.

> Refer to the Software Configuration Management key process area.

Activity 2   **<Activity performed in Key Process Area X> according to a documented procedure.**

This procedure typically specifies that:

1. <Subpractices for Activity 2, possibly with cross reference(s) to key practice(s) in another key process area.>

> Refer to Activity N of the <Z> key process area for practices <related to Activity 2.1>.

2. <Additional subpractices for Activity 2...>
3. <Software work products> undergo peer review <according to appropriate criteria>.

> Refer to the Peer Reviews key process area.

4. <Software work products, as appropriate> are managed and controlled.

> "Managed and controlled" implies that the version of the work product in use at a given time (past or present) is known (i.e., version control), and changes are incorporated in a controlled manner (i.e., change control).
>
> If a greater degree of formality than is implied by "managed and controlled" is desired, the work product can be placed under the full discipline of configuration management, as is described in the Software Configuration Management key process area.

Measurement and Analysis

Measurement 1   **Measurements are made and used to determine the status of the activities for <X>.**

> Examples of measurements include:
>
> <measurement examples>

Verifying Implementation

Verification 1   **The activities for <X> are reviewed with senior management on a periodic basis.**

    1. <Subpractices for Verification 1...>

Verification 2   **The activities for <X> are reviewed with the project manager on both a periodic and event-driven basis.**

    1. <Subpractices for Verification 1...>

Verification 3   **The software quality assurance group reviews and/or audits the activities and work products for <X> and reports the results.**

> Refer to the Software Quality Assurance key process area.

At a minimum, these reviews and/or audits verify that:

    1. <Subpractices for Verification 3...>

4.3 Interpreting the Common Features

In this section, the structural conventions described in the key process area template are described in detail. The description addresses the definition of the structural elements within the common features, discusses their implications, and itemizes the variations in that structure.

4.3.1 Commitment to Perform

The key practices in the Commitment to Perform common feature describe the actions the organization must take to ensure that the process is established and will endure. They typically involve establishing organizational policies and leadership.

**Policy
statements**

Where policy statements are used, they generally refer to the project following a written, organizational policy for the practices of that key process area. This is to emphasize the connection between organizational commitment and the projects that are actually performing the work.

The subpractices for the policy statement generally summarize activities that are covered later in the key process area and are particularly suitable to institutionalization via a written policy.

Every key process area has a policy statement in Commitment to Perform. In some key process areas (e.g., Organization Process Focus), the focus of the activities for the key process area is the organization, not the project. In those cases, the policy statement is reworded and refers to the organization following a written policy.

The key process areas that have policy statements for the organization[1] to follow are:

Organization Process Focus

Organization Process Definition

Training Program

Quantitative Process Management

Defect Prevention

Technology Change Management

Process Change Management

Leadership

In some key process areas, Commitment to Perform contains a statement that addresses the assignment of a leadership role (e.g., project software manager) or that describes particular sponsorship activities that are necessary for the key process area to be successfully institutionalized.

The key process areas that have leadership practices are:

Software Project Planning

Software Project Tracking and Oversight

Software Subcontract Management

---

[1] Quantitative Process Management and Defect Prevention have both project and organization policy statements.

Organization Process Focus

Technology Change Management

Process Change Management

4.3.2 Ability to Perform

The key practices in the Ability to Perform common feature describe the preconditions in the project or organization necessary to implement the software process
competently. They typically involve resources, organizational structures, and
training.

Organizational
structures

Some key process areas contain a key practice that describes
a particular kind of organizational structure that supports the
key process area.

In some cases there is an underlying reason for establishing
this structure, such as the need for independence (or objectivity) that leads to an SQA group. In other cases, such as for
an SCM group or an SEPG, this is the normative behavior in
building the capability of large organizations performing
under contract. Section 4.4 on "Organizational Structure and
Roles" discusses this in more detail.

The key process areas that have practices on organizational
structure are:

Software Quality Assurance

Software Configuration Management

Organization Process Focus

Training Program

Quantitative Process Management

Defect Prevention

Technology Change Management

Resources
and funding

Every key process area contains a key practice that reflects
the need for adequate resources and funding for the activities
covered by the key process area. These resources and funding, described by the subpractices, generally fall into three
categories: access to special skills, adequate funding, and
access to tools. Tools that may be of use in performing the
activities of the key process area are listed as examples.

The word "funding" is used rather than "budget" to emphasize that what is delivered and used is more pertinent to the actual process than what was promised.

Training
The CMM's context for the term "training" is somewhat broader than might normally be considered when using the term. Training is provided to make an individual proficient with specialized instruction and practice and may include informal as well as formal vehicles for transferring skills and knowledge to the individuals in the organization.

Although classroom training is a common mechanism that many organizations use to build the skills of their employees, the CMM also accommodates other vehicles, such as facilitated video, computer-aided instruction, or formal mentoring and apprenticeship programs.

Every key process area has a training practice except for the Training Program key process area, where Ability 3 focuses on the members of the training group having the necessary skills and knowledge to perform their training activities.

Two templates to describe training are generally found throughout the CMM. At Level 2, the phrase "receive training" is used. At Levels 3 and above, the phrase "receive required training" is used. The intention in using these different templates is to recognize that training at Level 2 is not likely to have been based on roles in a well-defined process and institutionalized across the organization. At Levels 3 and above, the key practices of the Training Program key process area are expected to govern the organization's training activities.

In all the key process areas, potential training topics are expressed as example boxes, to recognize that different organizational situations are likely to drive different specific training needs.

Orientation
In some key process areas, key practices that describe orientation are found. The term "orientation" is used broadly to indicate less depth of skill or knowledge being transferred than would be expected via training. Orientation is an overview or introduction to a topic for those overseeing or interfacing with the individuals responsible for performing the

work in the topic area.

The key process areas that include orientation practices are:

Software Project Tracking and Oversight

Software Subcontract Management

Software Quality Assurance

Organization Process Focus

Training Program

Software Product Engineering

Intergroup Coordination

Quantitative Process Management

Prerequisites

Some key process areas contain key practices that express a need for prerequisites. For example, a software development plan is a prerequisite for Software Project Tracking and Oversight.

In some cases, these prerequisites are expected as outputs from the activities of another key process area. In other cases, they are items expected to be obtained from outside the realm of the software project (e.g., the system requirements allocated to software are a prerequisite for Requirements Management). Other prerequisites include the delegation of responsibility for performing a function (e.g., establishing a software configuration control board is a prerequisite for change control in Software Configuration Management).

In keeping with the CMM philosophy of highlighting "key" practices, not all prerequisite items are listed for each key process area. Only those found to be particularly critical for implementing the key process area are cited in the CMM.

The key process areas that include prerequisites are:

Requirements Management

Software Project Planning

Software Project Tracking and Oversight

Software Configuration Management

Intergroup Coordination

Quantitative Process Management

Technology Change Management

4.3.3 Activities Performed

The key practices in the Activities Performed common feature describe the activities, roles, and procedures necessary to implement a key process area. They typically involve establishing plans and procedures, performing the work, tracking it, and taking corrective actions as necessary.

Of all the common features, Activities Performed shows the greatest amount of structural variability, because the implementation activities for the key process areas vary in level of detail, organizational focus (e.g., project or organization), and need for planning and documentation.

Types of plans   Two major types of plans are described in the key practices: formal plans (e.g., software development plan, software quality assurance plan, and software configuration management plan) and informal plans (e.g., peer review plan, risk management plan, and technology management plan).

The informal plans will typically be documented as part of a formal plan (e.g., the peer review plan may be documented as part of the software development plan) or as an adjunct to a formal plan (e.g., peer review schedules). Formal plans require a high degree of management commitment, both from the standpoint of creating them and ensuring that they are followed. In contractual environments, these formal plans are usually deliverable to the customer who contracted the effort.

Informal plans   Informal plans are usually described by a single key practice. The subpractices include information about the contents of the plan as well as the procedure for developing or revising the plan.

The key process areas that include informal plans are:

Organization Process Focus

Intergroup Coordination

Peer Reviews

Defect Prevention

Technology Change Management

Formal plans

When formal plans are called out, there are usually two key practices that specifically address the planning activities: a key practice that requires that the plan be developed or revised according to a documented procedure, and one that requires that the activities of the key process area be based on the plan.

The subpractices referring to a documented procedure generally cover what the inputs to the plan need to be, as well as the expected steps for obtaining commitment and support required for the plan. These subpractices identify the typical reviewers of the plan. They also highlight what levels of approval would be expected.

The subpractices that refer to the plan being the basis for activities describe the expected contents of the plan under discussion. Depending on the type of plan and need for organizational flexibility in covering the general topics of the plan, varying levels of detail are provided to describe the plan's contents.

The key process areas that include formal plans are:

Software Project Planning

Software Subcontract Management

Software Quality Assurance

Software Configuration Management

Training Program

Integrated Software Management

Quantitative Process Management

Software Quality Management

Process Change Management

According to a documented procedure

Most key process areas contain one or more key practices that describe activities performed according to a documented procedure. A documented procedure is usually needed so that the individuals responsible for a task or activity are able to perform it in a repeatable way, so that others with general knowledge of the area will be able to learn and perform the task or activity in the same way, and so that those who depend on the consistency of the results are satisfied. This is one aspect of institutionalizing a process.

One of the common themes running throughout the CMM is the need to build organizational capability by documenting the process and then practicing it as documented. To quote the auditors, "Say what you do; do what you say."

The formality and level of detail of a documented procedure can vary significantly, from a handwritten individual desk procedure to a formal organizational standard operating procedure that is managed and controlled. The formality and level of detail depend on who will perform the task or activity (e.g., individual or team), how often it is performed, the importance and intended use of the results, and the intended recipients of the results.

Key process areas at Levels 3 and above may use the phrase "according to the project's defined software process" in place of "according to a documented procedure." A defined software process is not only documented in procedures and standards; it is also well defined, with readiness criteria, inputs, verification mechanisms, outputs, and completion criteria.

System requirements allocated to software

The system requirements allocated to software, usually referred to as the "allocated requirements" in the CMM, are the subset of the system requirements that are to be implemented in the software components of the system. The allocated requirements are a primary input to the software development plan. The software requirements analysis task elaborates and refines the allocated requirements and results in documented software requirements. The software requirements are the basis for the software design.

Customer requirements involve a complete system, not just software. In the CMM, discussion of customer requirements centers on those customer requirements to be implemented in software. System requirements typically are allocated to hardware, software, and so on by a system engineering group as part of the overall system design. The system requirements allocated to the software project include both technical requirements (functionality, performance, etc.) and non-technical requirements (delivery dates, cost, etc.).

This allocation illustrates a CMM scoping issue: the CMM is written from a software perspective. It covers the software process and addresses only those requirements allocated to software. The CMM does not cover the processes of the customer or the system engineering group. It does describe intergroup interfaces that the software engineering group should proactively address, hopefully in a spirit of teamwork and an effective customer–supplier relationship.

Customer–supplier relationship

The customer may be internal or external to the organization. An example of an internal customer is a marketing group; an example of an external customer is the DoD. The end user may also differ from the external customer. The CMM is expressed in terms that relate to a software organization's developing a critical software component for an external customer.

Where necessary, the boundaries between groups, as stated in the CMM, must be appropriately interpreted. For example, in software-only procurements, there may be no system engineering group between the customer and the software engineering group. In such a case, customer requirements, system requirements, and allocated requirements may be synonymous, and the responsibilities of the system engineering group may be divided between the customer and the software engineering group.

Tracking and taking corrective action versus managing

In Software Project Tracking and Oversight at Level 2, many of the key practices use the phrase, "… is tracked … corrective actions are taken as appropriate." In Integrated Software Management at Level 3, many of the similar key practices use the phrase, "is managed."

This difference in wording reflects the project's possible lack of a completely defined software process at Level 2. Management actions at Level 2 are likely to be reactions to actual problems.

At Level 3, the project has a completely defined software process, and the relationships between the various software work products, tasks, and activities are well defined. Management is better able to anticipate problems and proactively prevent them from occurring. When interventions are required, the effect on the entire software process is understood, and these interventions can be more effectively defined and applied.

Reviewed versus undergoes peer reviews

The CMM includes both reviews and peer reviews. In a review, a software work product, or set of work products, is presented to managers, the customer, end users, or other interested individuals for their comment or approval. Reviews typically occur at the end of a task.

In a peer review, a software work product, or set of work products, is presented to the producer's colleagues to identify defects. Managers, the customer, and end users are typically not present in a peer review. Peer reviews are an integral, in-process part of a task. They are performed so that defects can be removed early, leading to higher productivity and high-quality products. Some software work products will be reviewed; some will undergo peer review; and some will undergo both peer reviews and reviews.

Placed under configuration management versus managed and controlled

Some software work products (for example, the software design and the code) should have baselines established at predetermined points. These baselines are formally reviewed and agreed on and serve as the basis for further development. A rigorous change control process is applied to baselined items. These baselines provide control and stability when interacting with the customer. This is sometimes referred to as baseline configuration management. The phrase "placed under configuration management" is used for such software work products.

When control of the configuration is exercised by the developers, it is usually referred to as developmental configuration management. Some items under developmental configuration management may be placed under baseline configuration management at predetermined points in their development. The phrase "placed under configuration management" in the CMM means baseline configuration management. Developmental configuration management is not required by the CMM, although it is a desirable engineering practice.

Some software work products, such as estimates or the software development plan, that may not have to be under configuration management, still need to be "managed and controlled." This phrase is used to characterize the process of identifying and defining software work products that are not part of a baseline and are therefore not placed under configuration management but that must be controlled for the project to proceed in a disciplined manner. "Managed and controlled" implies that the version of the work product in use at a given time (past or present) is known (i.e., version control), and that changes are incorporated in a controlled manner (i.e., change control).

For example, planning data should be "managed and controlled." It may not need to be placed under formal configuration management in the sense of baselining and applying rigorous change control.

4.3.4 Measurement and Analysis

The key practices in the Measurement and Analysis common feature describe basic measurement practices that are necessary to determine status related to the process. Measurements included in this common feature are used to control and improve the process.

Some Measurement and Analysis practices go beyond status:

- the quality of the training program (Training Program),
- the effectiveness of management (Integrated Software Management), and
- the functionality and quality of software products (Software Product Engineering).

Examples of suggested measurements are expressed as supplementary information, because the variability in project environments may lead to different measurement needs and approaches. There are currently no universally accepted measures of software process or quality.

4.3.5 Verifying Implementation

The key practices in the Verifying Implementation common feature describe the steps to ensure that the activities are performed in compliance with the process that has been established. They generally include key practices that relate to oversight by senior management and project management, as well as specific verification activities that the software quality assurance group or others are expected to perform to verify that the process is being performed properly.

Senior management oversight on a periodic basis

Most key process areas contain a key practice on senior management oversight of the process. The primary purpose of periodic reviews by senior management is to provide awareness of, and insight into, software process activities at an appropriate level of abstraction and in a timely manner. The time between reviews should meet the needs of the organization and may be lengthy, as long as adequate mechanisms for exception reporting are available.

The scope and content of senior management reviews will greatly depend on which senior manager is involved in the review. Reviews by the senior manager responsible for all software activities of an organization are expected to occur on a different schedule, and address different topics, than those performed by the senior executive of the entire organization. Senior management reviews would also be expected to cover different topics, or similar topics at a higher level of abstraction, than would project management oversight reviews.

The key process areas that do not include a senior management oversight practice are:

Organization Process Definition

Peer Reviews

Project management oversight on both a periodic and event-driven basis

The template "both on a periodic and event-driven basis" is used in the key practices to emphasize that projects have needs for different types of review at different stages and depending on the project characteristics. Project management should maintain an ongoing awareness of the status of the software effort and be informed when significant events on the software project occur. This awareness comes from project management participation in formal reviews, such as critical design reviews, as well as reviews that encompass process issues such as status of process improvement planning and resolution of process noncompliance issues.

At the project level, project management oversight is expected to be at a more detailed level than that of senior management, reflecting project management's more active involvement in the operational aspects of a project.

The key process areas that do not include a project management oversight practice are:

Organization Process Focus

Organization Process Definition

Training Program

Peer Reviews

Technology Change Management

Process Change Management

Software quality assurance activities

The particular activities that are considered appropriate for review and/or audit by the software quality assurance (SQA) group are described as a key practice. In particular cases, where the SQA group would not be expected to have authority, SQA verification activities are not described.

Because it would be a conflict of interest for SQA to audit itself, independent experts review its activities. There is no SQA practice for Organization Process Focus because of its tight coupling with Organization Process Definition; separate SQA practices for these two key process areas were felt to be redundant. Training Program activities are audited, but not necessarily by the **software** quality assurance group. This is because the training group will likely cover all of the organization's training needs, not just software.

The key process areas that do not include an SQA practice are:

Software Quality Assurance

Organization Process Focus

Training Program

There are two other minor variations of the template for Verifying Implementation. Software Configuration Management includes a practice on configuration audits, and Training Program includes a practice on independent evaluation of training.

4.4 Organizational Structure and Roles

Although the CMM attempts to remain independent of specific organizational structures and models, it is necessary to express the practices in the CMM consistently using terminology related to organizational structure and roles that may differ from those followed by any specific organization. The following sections describe the various concepts related to organizations, projects, and roles that are necessary for interpreting the key practices of the CMM.

4.4.1 Organizational Roles

A role is a unit of defined responsibilities that may be assumed by one or more individuals. The following descriptions of roles are frequently used in the key practices:

Manager	A manager provides technical and administrative direction and control to individuals performing tasks or activities within the manager's area of responsibility. The traditional functions of a manager include planning, organizing, directing, and controlling work within an area of responsibility.
Senior manager	A senior manager fulfills a management role at a high enough level in an organization such that the primary focus is on the long-term vitality of the organization, rather than short-term project and contractual concerns and pressures. In general, a senior manager for engineering would have responsibility for multiple projects. A senior manager also provides and protects resources for long-term improvement of the software process (e.g., a software engineering process group).
	Senior management, as used in the CMM, can denote any manager who satisfies the above description, up to and including the head of the organization. As used in the key practices, the term "senior management" should be interpreted in the context of the key process area and the projects and organization under consideration.
Project manager	A project manager has total business responsibility for an entire project. The project manager directs, controls, administers, and regulates a project to build a software or hard-

ware/software system. The project manager is ultimately responsible to the customer.

In a project-oriented organizational structure, most of the people working on a project would report to the project manager, although some disciplines might have a matrix reporting relationship. In a matrix organizational structure, it may be only the business staff who report to the project manager. The engineering groups would then have an indirect reporting relationship to the project manager.

Project software manager

A project software manager has total responsibility for all the software activities for a project. The project software manager controls all the software resources for a project and is the individual whom the project manager deals with in terms of software commitments.

The software engineering group on a project would report to the project software manager, although some activities such as tools development might have a matrix reporting relationship.

In a large project, the project software manager is likely to be a second-, third-, or fourth-line manager. In a small project, the project software manager might be the first-line software manager.

First-line software manager

A first-line software manager fulfills the role with direct management responsibility (including providing technical direction and administering the personnel and salary functions) for the staffing and activities of a single organizational unit (e.g., a department or project team) of software engineers and other related staff.

Software task leader

A software task leader fulfills the role of leader of a technical team for a specific task and has technical responsibility and provides technical direction to the staff working on the task.

The software task leader usually reports to the same first-line software manager as do the other people working on the task.

Staff, software engineering staff, individuals

Several terms are used in the CMM to denote the individuals who perform the various technical roles described in various key practices of the CMM. The staff are the individuals, including task leaders, who are responsible for accomplishing an assigned function, such as software development or software configuration management, but who are not managers.

The software engineering staff are the software technical people (e.g., analysts, programmers, and engineers), including software task leaders, who perform the software development and maintenance activities for the project, but who are not managers.

The term "individuals" as used in the key practices is qualified and bounded by the context in which the term appears (e.g., "the individual involved in managing the software subcontract").

A similar breakout of roles can be identified for other engineering groups such as system engineering or system test.

In a particular project or organization, there need not be a one-to-one correspondence between these roles and individuals. One person could perform in multiple roles, or each role could be performed by separate individuals.

For example, on a small, software-only project, one person might have as many as six management roles: the system engineering first-line manager, the project system engineering manager, the software first-line manager, the project software manager, the project manager, and the software configuration management manager.

On a slightly larger project, one person might act as the system engineering first-line manager, the project system engineering manager, and the project manager while another person might act as both the first-line software manager and the project software manager. These two managers might be in the same or a different second-line organization.

On a large project, many roles, especially those of management, would likely be filled by separate individuals.

4.4.2 Organizational Structure

The fundamental concepts of organization, project, and group must be understood to properly interpret the key practices of the CMM. The following paragraphs define the use of these concepts in the CMM:

Organization   An organization is a unit within a company or other entity within which many projects are managed as a whole.

An operational definition for "organization" is the scope of an appraisal or process improvement effort. Organizational analysis is necessary to define exactly what that scope will be.

Examples of an organization include

- a company,
- a division of a corporation,
- a government agency, and
- a branch of service.

All projects within an organization share a common top-level manager and common policies.

Project

A project is an undertaking requiring concerted effort that is focused on developing and/or maintaining a specific product.

The product may include hardware, software, and other components. The product may be delivered on a single occasion, or several deliveries with varying functionality may be spread over time, or the same product may be delivered to many customers (as is the case for commercial software products). Typically, a project has its own funding, cost accounting, and delivery schedule.

Group

A group is the collection of departments, managers, and individuals who have responsibility for a set of tasks or activities.

Examples of a group could include:

- a single individual assigned part time, to
- several part-time individuals assigned from different departments, to
- several individuals dedicated full time, to
- one or more departments dedicated full-time.

Groups commonly referred to in the CMM are described next.

Software engineering group

The software engineering group is the collection of individuals (both managers and technical staff) who have responsibility for performing the software development and maintenance activities (i.e., requirements analysis, design, code, and test) for a project.

Groups performing software-related work, such as the software quality assurance group, the software configuration management group, and the software engineering process group, are not included in the software engineering group. These groups are considered to be one of the "other software-related groups."

Software-related groups

A software-related group is the collection of individuals (both managers and technical staff) representing a software engineering discipline that supports, but is not directly responsible for, performing software development and/or maintenance.

Examples of software-related disciplines include software quality assurance, software configuration management and process engineering.

When encountered in the key practices, the term "software-related group" should be interpreted in the context of the key process area and the organization. Only those software-related groups that are involved or affected should be included. For example, the software engineering process group is not involved with managing customer requirements as described in Requirements Management.

Software engineering process group

The software engineering process group is the group of specialists who facilitate the definition, maintenance, and improvement of the software process used by the organization. In the key practices, this group is generically referred to as "the group responsible for the organization's software process activities."

System engineering group

The system engineering group is the collection of individuals (both managers and technical staff) who have responsibility for specifying the system requirements; allocating the system requirements to the hardware, software, and other components; specifying the interfaces between the hardware, software, and other components; and monitoring the design and development of these components to ensure conformance with their specifications.

System test group

The system test group is the collection of individuals (both managers and technical staff) who have responsibility for planning and performing the independent system testing of the software to determine whether the software product satisfies its requirements.

Software quality assurance group	The software quality assurance group is the collection of individuals (both managers and technical staff) who plan and implement the project's quality assurance activities to ensure the software process steps and standards are followed. Organizational issues concerning software quality assurance are discussed in Section 4.4.3.
Software configuration management group	The software configuration management group is the collection of individuals (both managers and technical staff) who have responsibility for planning, coordinating, and implementing the formal configuration management activities for the software project.
Training group	The training group is the collection of individuals (both managers and staff) who are responsible for coordinating and arranging the training activities for an organization. This group typically prepares and conducts most of the training courses and coordinates use of other training vehicles.

4.4.3 Independence and Organizational Structure

The organization must take care that the key practices that call for independence are appropriately interpreted and followed. This is particularly true for small projects and small organizations. The key practices call for independence when technical or organizational biases may affect the quality or risks associated with the project. For example, the following two subpractices deal with independence:

- The SQA group has a reporting channel to senior management that is independent of the project manager, the project's software engineering group, and the other software-related groups (Commitment 1.2 in Software Quality Assurance).

- The (system and acceptance) test cases and test procedures are planned and prepared by a test group that is independent of the software developers (Activity 7.3 in Software Product Engineering).

The need for independence of the system and acceptance testing is based on technical considerations. Such independence ensures that the testers are not inappropriately influenced by the design and implementation decisions made by the software developers or maintainers.

The independence of the SQA group is necessary so its members can perform their jobs without being influenced by project schedule and cost pressures. Ensuring effective operational independence without the organizational independence is difficult. For example, an employee reporting to the project manager may be reluctant to stop a test activity even though serious noncompliance issues exist.

Organizations must determine the organizational structure that will support activities that require independence, such as SQA, in the context of their strategic business goals and business environment.

Independence should:

- provide the individuals performing the SQA role with the organizational freedom to be the "eyes and ears" of senior management on the project,

- protect the individuals performing the SQA role from adverse personnel actions when there is a need to escalate deviations outside the project, and

- provide senior management with confidence that objective information on the process and products of the project is being reported.

Since the key practices allow interpretation of the independence criteria, professional judgment must be exercised by the organization in determining whether the goals of the key process area are achieved. The related goal in the Software Quality Assurance key process area states that adherence is objectively verified. "Objectively" was deliberately used in the goals to support flexibility; "independence" was used in the practices to reinforce the expectation that the normal behavior is to establish an independent SQA group. Alternative implementations should be able to demonstrate how objectivity is achieved and noncompliance issues are resolved.

4.5 Understanding Software Process Definition

Software process definition is fundamental for achieving higher levels of maturity. This section discusses aspects of software process definition that are helpful in using the key practices related to process definition, beginning with Organization Process Definition at Level 3.

The key practices in Organization Process Definition are presented using terms that reflect an approach to process definition that supports both stability and flexibility. This approach is depicted in Fig. 4.1, and its key elements are described in the following paragraphs.

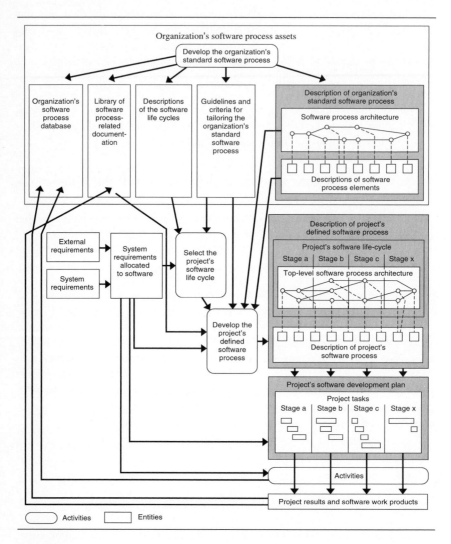

FIGURE 4.1
Conceptal software process framework used in the CMM

4.5.1 Process Definition Concepts

A fundamental concept that supports the approach taken by the SEI in its process definition work is that processes can be developed and maintained in a way similar to the way products are developed and maintained. There must be:

- requirements that define what process is to be described,
- an architecture and design that provide information on how the process will be defined,
- implementation of the process design in a project or organizational situation,
- validation of the process description via measurement, and
- deployment of the process into widespread operation within the organization or project for which the process is intended.

Using the analogy of product development, a framework for software process development and maintenance has evolved that translates these concepts into ones that are more specific to the process development discipline (similar to the specificity of terminology used for developing real-time embedded systems versus management information systems). The key elements of this framework, which are referred to as the organization's software process assets, are illustrated in Fig. 4.1 and described briefly below.[2]

4.5.2 Concepts Related to the Organization's Software Process Assets

Software process assets are a collection of entities maintained by an organization, for use by projects in developing, tailoring, maintaining, and implementing their software processes. Any entity that the organization considers useful in performing the activities of process definition and maintenance could be included as a process asset.

Organization's software process assets

The organization establishes and maintains a set of software process assets as shown in Fig. 4.1. These software process assets include:

- the organization's standard software process (including the software process architecture and software process elements),
- the descriptions of software life cycles approved for use,
- the guidelines and criteria for tailoring the organization's standard software process,

---

[2] For further reading on the concepts of process definition that are being developed within the process engineering community, refer to [Feiler92] and [Armitage93].

- the organization's software process database, and
- the library of software process-related documentation.

The software process assets are available for use by the projects in developing, maintaining, and implementing their defined software process.

An organization may bundle the software process assets in many ways, depending on its approach to establishing its standard software process. For example, the description of the software life cycle may be an integral part of the organization's standard software process. Another example is that parts of the library of software process-related documentation may be stored in the organization's software process database.

Organization's standard software process

An organization's standard software process is the operational definition of the basic process that guides the establishment of a common software process across the software projects in the organization. It describes the fundamental *software process elements* that each software project is expected to incorporate into its defined software process. It also describes the relationships (e.g., ordering and interfaces) between these software process elements.[3] It establishes a consistent way of performing the software activities across the organization and is essential for long-term stability and improvement.

The organization's standard software process forms the basis for the projects' defined software processes. It provides continuity in the organization's process activities and is the reference for the measurements and long-term improvement of the software processes used in the organization.

The organization's standard software process is not meant to imply that an organization will have one monolithic process for all software projects in all application domains. For example, if the organizational assets support both waterfall

---

[3] The relationship between software process elements is sometimes referred to as a "software process architecture."

and evolutionary life cycles, then at least two different software processes may be supported.

Software process architecture

The software process architecture is a high-level (i.e., summary) description of the organization's standard software process. It describes the ordering, interfaces, interdependencies, and other relationships between the software process elements of the organization's standard software process. It also describes the interfaces, dependencies, and other relationships to other external processes (e.g., system engineering, hardware engineering, and contract management).

Software process element

A software process element is a constituent element of a software process description. Each process element covers a well-defined, bounded, closely related set of activities (e.g., software estimating element, software design element, coding element, and peer review element). The descriptions of the process elements may be templates to be filled in, fragments to be completed, abstractions to be refined, or complete descriptions to be modified or used unmodified.

Description of software life cycles approved for use

A software life cycle is the period of time that begins when a software product is conceived and ends when the software is no longer available for use. The software life cycle typically includes a concept stage, requirements stage, design stage, implementation stage, test stage, installation and checkout stage, operation and maintenance stage, and sometimes, retirement stage [IEEE-STD-610].

Because an organization may be producing software for a variety of contractual and/or commercial customers and users, one software life cycle may not be appropriate for all situations. Therefore the organization may identify more than one software life cycle for use by the projects. These software life cycles are typically obtained from software engineering literature and may be modified for the organization. They are available to be used, in combination with the organization's standard software process, in developing a project's defined software process.

The key practices are not meant to limit the choice of a software life cycle. People who have extensively used one particular software life cycle may perceive elements of that life cycle in the organization and structure of the key practices. However, there is no intent either to encourage or preclude the use of any particular software life cycle.

Guidelines and criteria for tailoring

The organization's standard software process is described at a general level that may not be directly usable by a project. Guidelines are established to guide the software projects in (1) selecting a software life cycle from those approved for use and (2) tailoring and elaborating the organization's standard software process and the selected software life cycle to fit the specific characteristics of the project.

These guidelines and criteria help ensure that there is a common basis across all software projects for planning, implementing, measuring, analyzing, and improving the projects' defined software processes and the organization's standard software process. They describe what can and cannot be tailored and identify process elements that should be considered for tailoring.

Organization's software process database

The purpose of the organization's software process database is to collect and make available data on the software processes and resulting software work products, particularly as they relate to the organization's standard software process. The database contains or references both the actual measurement data and the related information needed to understand the measurement data and assess it for reasonableness and applicability.

Examples of process and work product data include estimates of software size, effort, and cost; actual data on software size, effort, and cost; productivity data; peer review coverage and efficiency; and number and severity of defects found in the software code.

Library of software process-related documentation

A library of software process-related documentation is established to (1) store process documents that are potentially useful to other current and future projects, particularly as they relate to the organization's standard software process, and (2) make them available for sharing across the organization. This library contains example documents and document fragments that are expected to be of use to future projects when they are tailoring the organization's standard software process. The examples may cover artifacts such as a project's defined software process, standards, procedures, software development plans, measurement plans, and process training materials. This library is an important resource that can help to reduce the amount of effort required to start a new project, by providing examples of successful projects as a starting point.

4.5.3 Concepts Related to the Project's Defined Software Process

At the organizational level, the organization's standard software process needs to be described, managed, controlled, and improved in a formal manner. At the project level, the emphasis is on the usability of the project's defined software process and the value it adds to the project.

Description of project's defined software process

The description of the project's defined software process is the operational definition of the software process used by the project. The project's defined software process is well characterized and understood and is described in terms of software standards, procedures, tools, and methods. It is developed by tailoring the organization's standard software process to fit the specific characteristics of the project.

This tailoring includes selecting a software life cycle from those approved by the organization and modifying the organization's standard software process to fit the specific characteristics of the project.

The project's defined software process provides the basis for planning, performing, and improving the activities of the managers and technical staff performing the project's tasks and activities. It is possible for a project to have more than one defined software process (e.g., for the operational software and for the test support software).

The more generic term "defined process" can be used to characterize all well-defined processes at both the organization and project levels that share these attributes.

Stages

A stage is a partition of the software effort that is of a manageable size and that represents a meaningful and measurable set of related tasks that are performed by the project. A stage is usually considered a subdivision of a software life cycle and is often completed with a formal review (or other well-defined criteria) prior to the onset of the following stage.

The term "stage" is used to refer to a defined partition of the software project's effort, but the term should not be tied to any specific software life cycle. As used in the key practices, "stage" can mean rigidly sequential stages or overlapping and iterative stages.

Tasks

The work to be performed is broken down into tasks. A task is a well-defined unit of work in the software process that provides management with a visible checkpoint into the status of the project. Tasks have readiness criteria (preconditions) and completion criteria (postconditions).

Within the context of process definition, a task is a well-defined component of a defined process. All tasks can be considered activities, but not all activities are well enough defined to be considered tasks (although an activity may include a task). For this reason, use of "task" in the Level 2 key practices is avoided and the less rigorous term "activity" is used.

Activities

An activity is any step taken or function performed, both mental and physical, toward achieving some objective. Activities include all the work the managers and technical staff do to perform the work of the project and organization.

Software work products (project results)

The results of activities and tasks primarily consist of software work products. A software work product is any artifact created as part of defining, maintaining, or using a software process. They can include process descriptions, plans, procedures, computer programs, and associated documentation, which may or may not be intended for delivery to a customer or end user. Work products become an input to the next step in the process or provide archival information on the software project for use in future projects.

Examples of software work products include plans, estimates, data on actual effort, corrective action documentation, and requirements documents. The subset of software work products that are deliverable to the customer or end user are referred to as software products.

Software products

The software products are the complete set, or any of the individual items of the set, of computer programs, procedures, and associated documentation and data designated for delivery to a customer or end user [IEEE-STD-610].

All software products are also software work products. A software work product that will not be delivered to a customer or end user is not, however, a software product.

4.5.4 Relationship Between the Project's Defined Software Process and the Software Development Plan

The description of the project's defined software process is usually not specific enough to be performed directly. Although the description typically identifies such things as roles (i.e., who performs a task) and types of software work products needed to perform a task, it does not specify the individual who will assume the roles, the specific software work products that will be created, or the schedule for performing the tasks and activities.

The project's software development plan, as either a single document or a collection of plans that can collectively be referred to as a software development plan, provides the bridge between the project's defined software process (what will be done and how it will be done) and the specifics of how the project will be performed (e.g., which individuals will produce which software work products according to what schedule). The combination of the project's defined software process and its software development plan makes it possible to actually perform the process.

4.5.5 Documentation and the CMM

The key practices describe a number of process-related documents, each one covering specific areas of content. The key practices do not require a one-to-one relationship between the documents named within them and the actual work products of an organization or project. Nor is there an intended one-to-one relationship to documents specified by the customer or to standards such as DOD-STD-2167A or IEEE software standards. The key practices require only that the applicable contents of these documents be part of the organization's or project's written work products.

In terms of document structure, the contents of a document referred to in the key practices could be part of a larger document or separated into several individual documents. For example, a project might have a software development plan that includes the essentials of the software risk management plan.

Another project, however, could develop three documents—a software development plan, a software management plan, and a project work breakdown structure—to satisfy the key practices for a software project's software risk management, software quality assurance, and software development plans.

4.6 The Evolution of Processes

Relationships link the key process areas, as illustrated in Fig. 4.2. The Management process category contains the project management activities as they evolve from planning and tracking at Level 2, to managing according to a defined software process at Level 3, to quantitative management at Level 4, to management in a constantly changing environment at Level 5.

The Organizational process category contains the cross-project responsibilities as the organization matures, beginning with a focus on process issues at Level 3, continuing to a quantitative understanding of the process at Level 4, and culminating with the management of change in an environment of continuous process improvement at Level 5.

The Engineering process category contains the technical activities, such as requirements analysis, design, code, and test, that are performed at all levels but that evolve toward an engineering discipline at Level 3, quantitative product control at Level 4, and continuous measured improvement at Level 5.

One of the more controversial decisions in developing the CMM was defining key process areas to reside at a single maturity level. The primary reason for this decision was to simplify the presentation of how to achieve the next maturity level. Separating out the issues specific to achieving a maturity level clarified the understanding of what was needed to achieve a maturity level.

Key process areas are not processes, as this controversy highlights. A process changes over time and hopefully matures. A process is dynamic. A key process area describes essential attributes (i.e., key practices) of a process when that process is fully realized. A key process area is static; it describes a process at a high level of abstraction and does not tell how the process is performed.

Processes evolve through the maturity levels; key process areas reside at a single maturity level. The CMM allows for this evolution by describing processes in general terms, and the practices in a key process area should be appropriately interpreted as a process evolves. Where critical distinctions need to be made at higher maturity levels, the key process areas at higher levels are applied, as illustrated in Fig. 4.3 for software project management.

Software project management evolves as the organization matures. At Level 1, software project management is only as good as the software project manager. At Level 2, documented and realistic plans are the basis for

Process categories	Management	Organizational	Engineering
Levels	Software project planning, management, etc.	Cross-project processes, training, infrastructure, etc.	Requirements analysis, design, code, test, etc.
Optimizing	Technology change management		
	Process change management		Defect prevention
Managed	Quantitative process management		Software quality management
Defined	Integrated software management Intergroup coordination	Organization process focus Organization process definition Training program	Software product engineering Peer reviews
Repeatable	Requirements management Software project planning Software project tracking and oversight Software subcontract management Software quality assurance Software configuration management		
Initial	Ad hoc processes		

FIGURE 4.2
The key process areas assigned to process categories

managing the software project. At Level 3, software project management is based on a defined software process derived from organizational assets. At Level 4, quantitative and statistical techniques are used to manage process

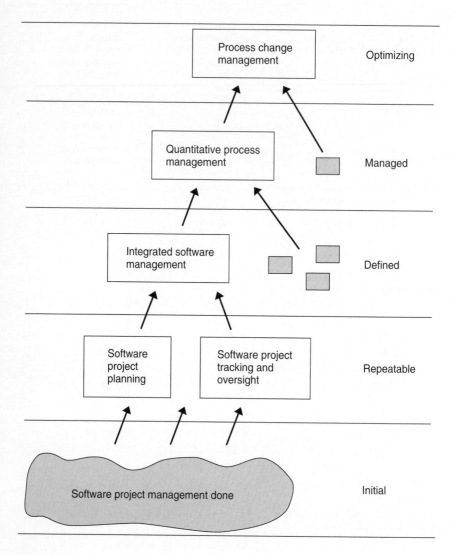

FIGURE 4.3
The evolution of software project management

performance and product quality. At Level 5, management operates in an environment of continuous improvement. Similar examples may be derived from Table 2.1.

4.7 Applying Professional Judgment

Professional judgment is necessary for interpreting the key practices and how they contribute to the goals of a key process area. In general, the key process areas describe a fundamental set of behaviors that all software organizations should exhibit, regardless of their size or their products. The key practices in the CMM, however, must be interpreted in light of a project's or organization's business environment and specific circumstances. This interpretation should be based on an informed knowledge of both the CMM and the organization and its projects.

To provide a complete set of valid principles that apply to a wide range of situations, the key practices are intentionally stated to allow for flexibility. Throughout the key practices, nonspecific phrases like "affected groups," "as appropriate," and "as necessary" are used. These phrases may have different meanings for two different organizations, for two projects in a single organization, or for one project at different points in its life cycle. Each project or organization should identify an appropriate meaning for such phrases in its processes.

Interpreting the practices requires the organization or project to consider the overall context in which they are used. The goals of the key process areas provide a structure for making this interpretation. Professional judgment is used to determine whether a specific interpretation or implementation satisfies the goals of a key process area.

If an organization's implementation of a key process area satisfies the goals but differs significantly from the key practices, the rationale for the interpretation should be documented. A documented rationale will help appraisal teams understand why certain practices are implemented the way they are.

Applying professional judgment leads to the issue of the "goodness" of the software process. The CMM does not place "goodness" requirements on the software process, although it does establish minimal criteria for a "mature" software process. The objective of process management is to establish processes that are used and can act as a foundation for systematic improvement based on the organization's business needs.

What are the criteria for a "mature" software process? A software process that is mature with respect to the CMM is effective in building organizational capability and satisfies the requirements of a defined process. Specifically, it is

- defined
- documented,
- trained,

- practiced,
- supported,
- maintained,
- controlled,
- verified,
- validated,
- measured, and
- able to improve.

An example of interpretation: If an organization established a software process for estimating that consisted of rolling the dice, would that constitute a mature process? It could certainly be documented and consistently followed. Some might even argue that it would be as realistic as many current estimating techniques. "Rolling the dice" would not be judged an adequate estimating process by most software professionals. It is not sufficient with respect to the CMM because it responds only to the laws of probability and therefore cannot be improved.

Could a documented procedure that states, "Go ask George" be sufficient? This could be an effective method for estimating. As long as George is around, it could even be consistent and repeatable. However, for this to be acceptable, George must define and document the procedure he uses. He also should collect measures and use them to improve his process. There are also several other factors that must be considered. Is everyone in the organization using George to generate estimates? Is the organization small enough for everyone to use George? Does the organization verify that George follows his process? If yes is the answer to all of these questions, this might be considered a mature process. However, we do not recommend that you define a process in this manner since on the surface it appears (and usually is) a person-centered process that cannot be repeated without George.

"Go ask George" may be an accurate reflection of the current estimating procedure, but it highlights a risk. It may be the first step in an improvement program. The organization may even decide that this is an acceptable risk if more pressing problems need to be addressed immediately. Such a procedure requires further investigation.

In contrast, a size estimating approach based on a Delphi technique[4] would be judged a reasonable and effective process, even though the Delphi method

---

[4] In a Delphi technique, experts in a subject review the issues under consideration and come to consensus on the recommendations related to the issue in a highly structured way. The Delphi technique is discussed in Section 22.2 "Expert Judgment" of [Boehm81].

is a person-centered process. An organizational capability can be based on a structured technique such as the Delphi method.

The CMM is expressed in terms of the highly structured environment of a large, complex software project. A process that is adequate for a small project will frequently be ineffective for a large project, and the corresponding large project process will frequently be inefficient in the small project environment. The CMM is not a checklist that can be used the same way in all environments, although the detailed practices in the CMM provide guidance in making judgments.

Both maturity and effectiveness should be interpreted in the context of the business environment and the specific circumstances of the project and the organization. Process maturity can be judged in comparison to a model such as the CMM. Process effectiveness can be determined only with regard to the organization's business objectives.

5

Using the CMM

The CMM establishes a set of publicly available criteria describing the characteristics of mature software organizations. These criteria can be used by organizations to improve their processes for developing and maintaining software or by government or commercial organizations to evaluate the risks of contracting a software project to another particular organization.

The improvement approach developed by the SEI is referred to as the IDEAL approach and is illustrated in Fig. 5.1. IDEAL is an acronym that encompasses the five stages of the software process improvement cycle:

- Initiating
- Diagnosing
- Evaluating
- Acting
- Leveraging

The IDEAL approach is an overall framework that describes the necessary phases, activities, and resources needed for a successful process improvement effort. The CMM can be used as the basis for diagnosing an organization's software processes, establishing priorities, and acting on them. This chapter provides an overview of a CMM-based method for diagnosing the maturity of an organization's execution of the software process and discusses some of the issues to be aware of when acting to improve the software process.

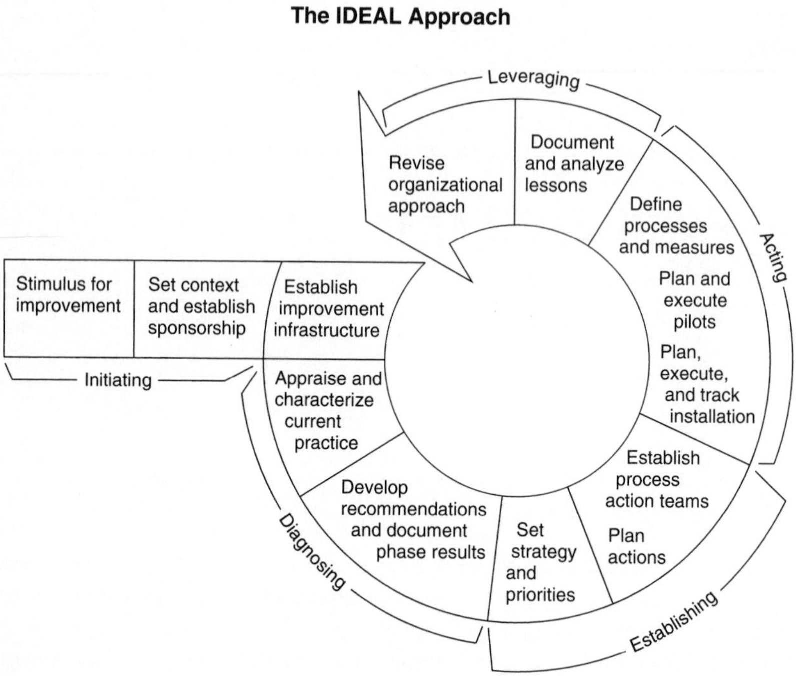

The IDEAL Approach

FIGURE 5.1
The IDEAL approach to software process improvement

There are two general classes of appraisal: software process assessment and software capability evaluation.

- *Software process assessments* are used to determine the state of an organization's current software process, to determine the high-priority software process-related issues facing an organization, and to obtain the organizational support for software process improvement.

- *Software capability evaluations* are used to identify contractors who are qualified to perform the software work or to monitor the state of the software process used on an existing software effort.

An appraisal method based on the CMM provides a structured basis for the investigation and permits the rapid and reasonably consistent development of findings that identify the organization's key strengths and weaknesses. This overview of the CMM-based appraisal method is high-level, however, and is not sufficient by itself for readers to conduct either an assessment or evaluation. Anyone wishing to apply the CMM through these methods should request further information from the SEI on assessment and evaluation training.

The significant difference between assessments and evaluations comes from the way the results are used. For an assessment, the results form the basis for an action plan for organizational self-improvement. For an evaluation, they guide the development of a risk profile. In source selection, this risk profile augments the traditional criteria used to select the most responsive and capable vendors. In contract monitoring, the risk profile may also be used to motivate the contractor's process improvement efforts.

5.1 A CMM-Based Appraisal Method

The CMM establishes a common frame of reference for performing software process appraisals. Although assessments and evaluations differ in purpose, both use the CMM as a foundation for appraising software process maturity. Figure 5.2 provides a summary description of the common steps in assessments and evaluations.

The first step in an appraisal method is to select a team. This team should be trained in the fundamental concepts of the CMM as well as the specifics of the assessment or evaluation method. The members of the team should be professionals knowledgeable in software engineering and management.

The second step is to have representatives from the site to be appraised complete the software process maturity questionnaire and other diagnostic instruments. Once this activity is completed, the appraisal team performs a response analysis (step 3), which tallies the responses to the questions and identifies those areas where further exploration is warranted. The areas to be investigated correspond to the CMM key process areas.

The team is now ready to visit the site being appraised (step 4). Beginning with the results of the response analysis, the team conducts interviews and reviews documentation to gain an understanding of the software process followed by the site. The key process areas and key practices in the CMM guide the team members in questioning, listening, reviewing, and synthesizing the information received from the interviews and documents. The team applies professional judgment in deciding whether the site's implementation of the key process areas satisfies the relevant key process area goals.[1] When there are

[1] These judgments may have to take place without complete information when company proprietary or security issues are involved.

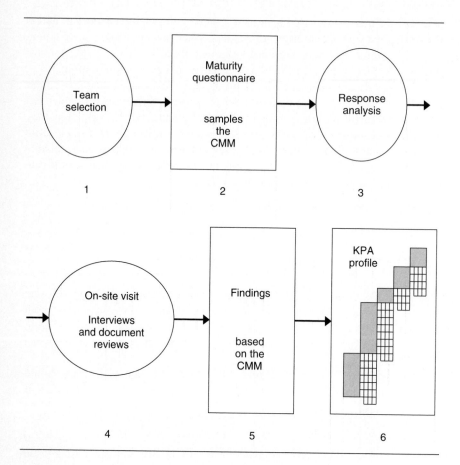

FIGURE 5.2
A software process appraisal method based on the CMM

clear differences between the key practices in the CMM and the site's practices, the team documents its rationale for judging that key process area.

At the end of the on-site period, the team produces a list of findings (step 5) that identifies the strengths and weaknesses of the organization's software process. In a software process assessment, the findings become the basis for recommendations for process improvement; in a software capability evaluation, the findings become part of the risk analysis performed by the acquisition agency.

Finally, the team prepares a key process area profile (step 6) that shows the areas where the organization has, and has not, satisfied the goals of the key process areas. A key process area can be satisfied and still have associated findings, provided the findings do not identify major problems that inhibit achieving any goals of the key process areas.

In summary, the CMM-based appraisal method:

- uses the software process maturity questionnaire as a springboard for the on-site visit,
- uses the CMM as a map that guides the on-site investigation,
- develops findings that identify software process strengths and weaknesses in terms of the key process areas in the CMM,
- derives a profile based on an analysis of the satisfaction of the goals within the key process area, and
- presents the appraisal results, to the appropriate audience, in terms of findings and a key process area profile.

5.2 Software Process Assessments and Software Capability Evaluations

In spite of these similarities, the results of an appraisal may differ, even on successive applications of the same method. This is most obviously a concern when the appraisals are a software process assessment versus a software capability evaluation.

One reason for differences is that the scope of the appraisal may vary. First, the organization being investigated must be determined. For a large company, several different definitions for "organization" are possible. The scope may be based on common senior management, common geographical location, designation as a profit-and-loss center, common application domain, or other considerations. The term "organization" is operationally defined as part of the appraisal process.

Second, even in what appears to be the same organization, the sample of projects selected may affect the scope. A division within a company may be appraised, with the team arriving at findings based on a division-wide scope. Later, a product line in that division may be appraised, with that team arriving at its findings based on a much narrower scope. This may be a project sampling issue or a subtle difference in defining what the organization is. Comparison between the results without understanding the context is problematic.

Software process assessments and software capability evaluations differ in motivation, objective, outcome, and ownership of the results. These factors lead to substantive differences in the dynamics of interviews, the scope of inquiry, the information gathered, and the formulation of the outcome. The assessment and evaluation methods are quite different when the detailed procedures employed are examined. Assessment training does not prepare a team to perform evaluations, or vice versa.

Software process assessments are performed in an open, collaborative environment. Their success depends on a commitment from both management and the professional staff to improve the organization. The objective is to surface problems and help managers and engineers improve their organization. While the maturity questionnaire is valuable in focusing the assessment team on maturity level issues, the emphasis is on structured and unstructured interviews as tools for understanding the organization's software process. Aside from identifying the software process issues facing the organization, the buy-in to improvement, the organization-wide focus on process, and the motivation and enthusiasm in executing an action plan are the most valuable outcomes of an assessment.

Software capability evaluations, on the other hand, are performed in a more audit-oriented environment. The objective is tied to monetary considerations, since the team's recommendations will help select contractors or set award fees. The emphasis is on a documented audit trail that reveals the software process actually implemented by the organization.

This does not mean, however, that the results of software process assessments and software capability evaluations should not be comparable. Since both methods are CMM-based, the points of comparison and difference should be evident and explainable.

5.3 Software Process Improvement

For software engineering process groups or others trying to improve their software process, the CMM has specific value in the areas of action planning, implementing action plans, and defining processes. During action planning, the members of the software engineering process group, equipped with knowledge of their software process issues and business environment, can compare their current practices against the goals and key practices of the CMM. The key practices should be examined in relation to corporate goals, management priorities, the level of performance of the practice, the value of implementing each practice to the organization, and the ability of the organization to implement a practice in light of its culture.

The software engineering process group must next determine which process improvements are needed, how to effect the change, and obtain the necessary buy-in. The CMM aids this activity by providing a starting point for discussion about process improvement and by helping to surface disparate assumptions about commonly accepted software engineering practices. In implementing the action plan, the CMM can be used by the process group to construct parts of the operational action plan and to define the software process.

One of the prerequisites to establishing a software process improvement program is to obtain the necessary management sponsorship. Executives frequently ask what is the data on the effect of software process improvement— what is the return on investment? Their concern is appropriate. Software process improvement should be done to help the business —not for its own sake.

Unfortunately, no formal validation study has been done on the impact of moving up the maturity levels. The success of CMM-based improvement efforts is based on three factors:

- the plausibility of the maturity levels and key process areas in terms of common sense
- general data from TQM efforts
- the limited number of case studies that have been published

The best known data comes from:

- Hughes, Ground Systems Group, Software Engineering Division [Humphrey91b]
- Tinker Air Force Base, Aircraft Software Division, Oklahoma City Air Logistics Center [Lipke92]
- Schlumberger Laboratory for Computer Science [Wohlwend93]
- Raytheon, Equipment Division, Software Systems Laboratory [Dion93]

Hughes reported moving from Level 2 in 1987 to Level 3 in 1991. They spent $445K over two years and achieved a $2M annual reduction in cost overruns, for a return on investment (ROI) of 4.5 to 1.

Tinker started their improvement effort in 1990 and won the Air Force Logistics Command and Air Force Quality Improvement Prototype award in 1991. They invested $462K and received a $2.9M return, for an ROI of 6.35 to 1.

Schlumberger started their improvement effort in 1990. They reported improving from 0.22/KSLOC for 400K programs to 0.13/KSLOC for 700K programs, and customer-reported defects from 25% to 10%. Productivity increased more than two times. They went from 51% of projects on schedule in 1990 to 94% on schedule in 1992, and from 50% schedule slip in 1990 to 1% schedule slip in 1992.

Raytheon moved from Level 1 in 1988 to Level 3 in 1991. Spending $1M annually, they reported being awarded two contracts based on process. Their

payments. Rework costs decreased \$15.8M, from 41% to 11%. Productivity increased 2.3 times in 4.5 years. Project costs decreased 30%, integration time decreased 80%, retesting time decreased 50%, and projects were typically 4–6% under budget.

In addition to quantified data, all of these organizations reported significant intangible benefits. Some of these benefits included:

- improved employee morale
- improved quality of work life
- fewer overtime hours
- more stable work environment
- lower turnover of staff
- improved communication
- improved quality as reported by customers

Increased customer satisfaction and competitive advantage, as reported by these companies, are where "the rubber meets the road" for executives contemplating investing in software process improvement. It must be remembered, however, that case studies are not rigorous proof. A pilot study on validation was begun in 1993 by the SEI, but it will be some time before a rigorous analysis of the effect of software process improvement is available.

This is only a sampling of software process improvement efforts. The typical return on investment, based on data from organizations that have done software process improvement for more than 3 years, is about 7:1, with an average gain in productivity of 37% per year, an average 18% increase each year in the proportion of defects found in pre-test, an average 19% reduction in time to market, and an average 45% reduction in field error reports per year. This is comparable to published TQM reports.

Numbers such as these should not be used to establish arbitrary goals for an improvement effort. There are many factors that influence the impact of an improvement initiative, including the active sponsorship of senior management, an understanding of where the organization is starting from, and a clear vision of where the organization is going and how it is to get there on the part of all involved—senior management, project managers, software managers, SEPG staff, the technical staff, and other participants. These numbers come from successful programs. Many improvement efforts fail because of mergers, reorganizations, loss of sponsorship, and so forth. Successful improvement efforts depend on sustained effort, which can be at risk in a tumultuous business environment.

5.4 Using the CMM in Context

The CMM was deliberately created to focus on the software process. There is a larger business context, where one might see TQM applied. If there is a TQM initiative in an organization, the software process improvement effort should be aligned with it. Even if not, the software process improvement initiative should be aligned with the business goals of the organization. Without this alignment, long-term improvement will usually not be sustained.

The real world contains many possible ways of defining and implementing processes that contribute to building high quality products which satisfy the customer. Since the CMM describes what a process should address rather than how it should be implemented, there are many "implementation details" to be worked out when doing software process improvement. Figure 5.3 illustrates the middle ground held by the CMM: below the larger business concerns, focused on software issues, yet not mandating the specific implementation of the process.

Since the CMM is focused on software issues, there are a number of other issues that should be considered as part of an overall improvement program, but which are only touched on in the CMM. These include topics such as strategic business planning, establishing product lines, adopting effective technologies, and managing the human resource.

If an organization is building a product that no one wants to buy, then no matter how efficient its processes are, it will go out of business. The CMM does not address what kind of business the organization should be in, although from a TQM perspective, it is essential to identify your customers and build products that address their needs.

It is senior management's responsibility to establish a strategic business plan. It is the responsibility of the different organizational units, including the software organization, to align their efforts with the business goals of the organization.

Besselman, in work unpublished at this time, has done research indicating that higher maturity organizations are either developing commercial products or have their government procurements structured around product lines. Such organizations derive significant life cycle benefits beyond those of simply developing a software product one time; they reuse software, processes, and the expertise of their people in a disciplined way to gain significant competitive advantage.

Technology is another leverage point in gaining competitive advantage. The CMM neither requires nor precludes specific software technologies, such

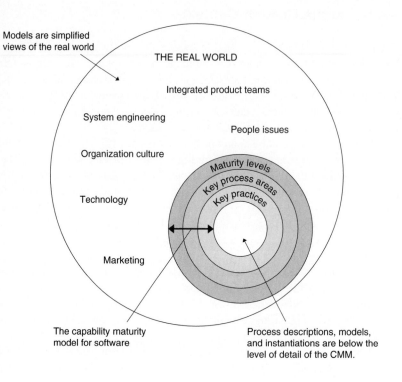

Models are simplified views of the real world

THE REAL WORLD

Integrated product teams

System engineering

People issues

Organization culture

Maturity levels

Key process areas

Key practices

Technology

Marketing

The capability maturity model for software

Process descriptions, models, and instantiations are below the level of detail of the CMM.

FIGURE 5.3
"M" is for model

as prototyping, object oriented design, or reusing software requirements, design, code, or other elements. This is not intended to imply that technology is not an important factor in developing an effective and efficient software process. The provision of tools to support the process are called out in the resource practices under Ability to Perform.

There is no general consensus within the software community, however, on what the appropriate tools and methodologies are to support all application domains and all software engineering environments. Object oriented approaches and reuse are among the most popular and powerful software methods used today, yet they are not universally used, and their appropriateness is questioned in some environments.

The CMM emphasizes the process of making an informed, reasoned decision about what the appropriate technologies are for a given need. The CMM does not specify what those decisions should be. The organization and/or project is in the best position to make technology decisions that address their needs. If an informed decision is made, it would be presumptuous for anyone outside the organization (or contractual relationship) to declare the technology chosen inappropriate.

Last, but not least, is the power conveyed by having competent people working for the organization. The CMM focuses on process management rather than people issues, but this does not imply that the human resource is unimportant. The success of any human-intensive effort, such as software engineering, will always depend on the competence of the people doing the work. To quote Watts Humphrey [Humphrey89a, page 20]:

> In the software process, people are the most important ingredient. It
> is essential to recognize their desire to do good work. The need is
> thus to focus on repairing the process and not the people. If manage-
> ment feels that the people are the problem, process improvement
> will appear threatening, the people will worry about their jobs, and
> this worry will likely cause resistance to change.

The CMM directly addresses the people dimension only in training. Other issues, such as selecting, hiring, and retaining competent people, are outside the scope of the CMM. They are not, however, outside the scope of management responsibility or outside the scope of organizational needs. An effective process can empower people to work more effectively.

The CMM focuses on a high leverage point—the software process—that can have a dramatic effect on the effectiveness of people in doing their work and the adoption of effective technologies, all of which will help the organization attain its business objectives.

6

A High-Maturity Example: Space Shuttle Onboard Software

6.1 Introduction

Prior to every launch of a space shuttle, managers of the Space Shuttle Onboard Software (hereafter called Onboard Shuttle) project at IBM–Houston[1] sign a Certificate of Flight Readiness, wherein they attest that there are no known faults in the shuttle's flight software that would endanger the shuttle or its crew. For over a

---

[1] In this chapter we will be describing work originally performed by IBM Federal Systems Company in Houston, Texas. In the spring of 1994 this organization was sold to Loral Corporation and has merged into Loral's Space Information Systems Division. The first three authors of this book visited this project for three days in September, 1993, and this chapter was developed from their findings. We are indebted to Ted Keller who arranged this visit and provided opportunities to view the process at work first hand. We are also grateful to Julie Barnard, Shirley Demerson, Barry Eiland, Maureen Judd, Karen Kelley, Barbara Kolkhorst, Tony Macina, Anne Martt, Jim Orr, Tom Peterson, and Patti Thornton for their briefings and insights. The figures presented in this chapter are used with permission of the Onboard Shuttle project. For additional information on this project we recommend an excellent article in the *IBM Systems Journal* [Billings94].

decade the Onboard Shuttle project team has striven to ensure there were no faults in the Space Shuttle Orbiter Primary Avionics Software System (flight software) when new releases are delivered to NASA's Johnson Space Center.

To satisfy NASA's requirement for software that meets the highest safety and reliability standards, the Onboard Shuttle project evolved a software process that yields a highly predictable quality result. The team believed that, given a defined process that produces products at a known level of quality, the best way to ensure that the next product will exhibit the same quality is to execute the process faithfully to a process standard. After two decades of work, the shuttle's flight software is being developed using a process that exhibits some of the same characteristics exhibited by manufacturing processes under statistical quality control. As a result, the flight software produced by this process is predictably near zero-defects, giving Onboard Shuttle managers confidence they have met the requirements for signing the Certificate of Flight Readiness.

The last known safety-related fault that flew onboard during a shuttle mission was detected in October 1986, and only one software failure (a benign annunciation fault in 1989) has occurred during flight since 1985. Figure 6.1 displays the failure history since 1988 of Onboard Shuttle software after its delivery to NASA. These data include failures occurring during NASA's testing, during use on flight simulators, during flight, or during any use by other

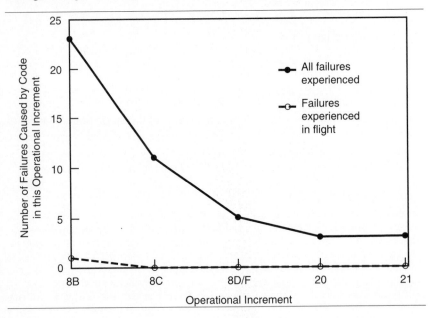

FIGURE 6.1
Failure history for delivered operational increments of Onboard shuttle software since 1988.

contractors. Any behavior of the software that deviates from the requirements in any way, however benign, constitutes a failure. Contrast this level of commitment with the cavalier attitude expressed toward users in most warranties offered by vendors of personal computer software.

By continually improving software processes, the Onboard Shuttle project achieved two orders of magnitude reduction in the defects it delivered per thousand lines of code and a 300% improvement in productivity since it started improvements in the mid-1970s. NASA recently awarded the 10-year follow-on contract to the Onboard Shuttle project without competitive bidding. This sole-source award was justified by arguing that the current contractor possessed unique skills and was the only entity known to be able to perform the process that was producing the results NASA required.

The results of a software capability evaluation performed in 1989 were reported as follows; "The NASA Headquarters SRM&QA Survey team has determined that the Flight Software Project is at Level 5." The Onboard Shuttle project has twice been named IBM Best Software Lab and is the only contractor to have received NASA's Excellence Award twice. To understand how an organization behaves at higher maturity levels, this chapter describes the Onboard Shuttle project as it has evolved over the past two decades.

6.2 Background

6.2.1 The Product

The shuttle's flight software (Primary Avionics Software System) is responsible for the guidance, navigation, and flight control functions performed during all phases of shuttle flight (Fig. 6.2). In addition, the software supports all interface functions between the shuttle and ground operations, monitors and manages all onboard systems, performs fault detection and annunciation, and performs shuttle checkout and safing procedures. The flight software consists of approximately 420,000 lines of code that run on the shuttle's onboard computers. Although the operating system component is written in assembler, the rest of the flight software is written in HAL/S.

During critical phases of shuttle flight (e.g., ascent, reentry) the flight software runs redundantly on four of the five onboard computers, creating extraordinary real-time synchronization requirements. A backup flight system developed independently by another contractor is available should the primary flight software experience a serious failure. Because of the reliability built into the primary system, this backup system has never been used during flight.

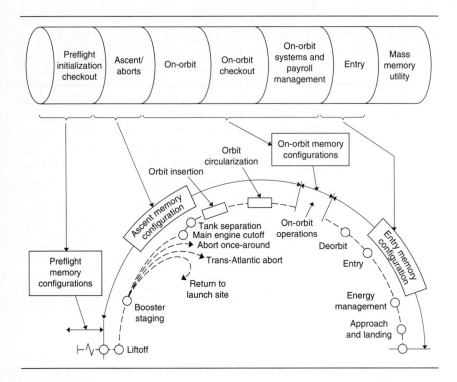

FIGURE 6.2
Functional structure of Onboard Shuttle Flight Software.

The Onboard Shuttle project also develops and maintains 1.7 million lines of Flight Software Application Tools that support configuration management, software builds, test and simulation, automatic verification, and software reconfiguration. These tools run on an IBM S/370 equivalent computer and are required for developing, testing, integrating, and managing the flight software.

6.2.2 The Life Cycle

The Onboard Shuttle project consists of an evolutionary series of releases, called operational increments, each of which adds incremental functionality to the flight software. The flight software for each of the first six shuttle missions consisted of the software from the previous flight plus added functions. As the frequency of flights increased, it became necessary to decouple the software development process from shuttle operations. Thus in 1986 the development of new functionality was separated from the reconfiguration of software to support each launch. New functionality is added through the process of developing new operational increments. A separate organization is responsible for shuttle operations (not the Onboard Shuttle project) and for reconfiguring the currently released operational increment to the unique mission profile for each launch.

Through the end of 1993, 17 operational increments had been delivered to NASA. While each operational increment is developed in a manner resembling a waterfall process, the overall model for the project is evolutionary and iterative. Each operational increment is developed through three phases:

1. Customer requirements definition
2. Software design, development, and integration
3. Independent verification

Each operational increment takes about two years to develop, and their development is overlapped so that one is released about every 12 months. These phases are followed by ongoing operational support of the released flight software. Prior to each shuttle launch another contractor reconfigures the generic flight software to support the specific mission requirements of the upcoming flight. Onboard Shuttle staff test and certify the correctness of the reconfigured software to be loaded into the shuttle before signing the Certificate of Flight Readiness.

6.2.3 Project Characteristics

The Onboard Shuttle project employs approximately 270 people. Because of extreme reliability and safety requirements, 26% of these staff are involved in flight software verification, but only 18% are involved in developing it (Fig. 6.3). The verification team is independent of the development team, with its own management reporting chain. Many of the staff are young and extremely diverse. New hires are initially assigned to the Onboard Shuttle project in order to acquire rigorous development habits they can carry to other projects. Generally staff stay with the Onboard Shuttle project for five to seven years before transferring to another project.

The environment surrounding the Onboard Shuttle project is one of constantly changing requirements. NASA occasionally changes requirements late in an operational increment because of functional priorities for an upcoming flight. Flight dates also change. To respond effectively in this environment without sacrificing product quality, the Onboard Shuttle project found that it had to have a formally defined process to ensure that crucial steps were not missed while trying to satisfy the customer. The team found that most automated project management tools were not sufficient for such a dynamic environment and that many management functions were more effectively performed manually.

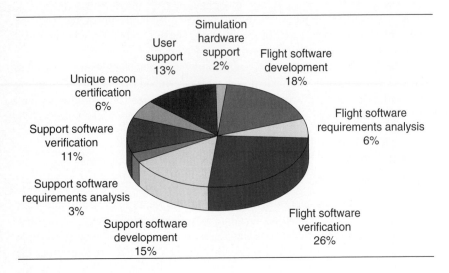

FIGURE 6.3
Allocation of Onboard Shuttle staff by function.

6.3 Approaches to Process Improvement

6.3.1 Improvement History

To satisfy NASA's requirements for near zero-defect software, the Onboard Shuttle project made continuous improvements to its software process beginning in the 1970s (Fig. 6.4). These changes, sometimes coupled with technology improvements, were considered to be the most effective means to ensure that the product met NASA's expectations for failure-free performance. Several of the most important changes are described in the following sections.

The Onboard Shuttle project identified four primary hurdles that inhibit the production of high-quality software. The first inhibitor was poor project management, especially the inability to manage within constraints set by cost, schedule, functionality, and quality. The second was driving projects from schedule, not quality requirements. The third inhibitor was failure to control the contents of requirements and software product baselines. The fourth was failure to track errors and to make process changes that eliminate their causes.

The continuing process improvement program that the Onboard Shuttle project implemented over the last two decades has been designed to systematically overcome and eliminate these inhibitors. In some cases process changes took up to two years to demonstrate results. However, the aggregate of the

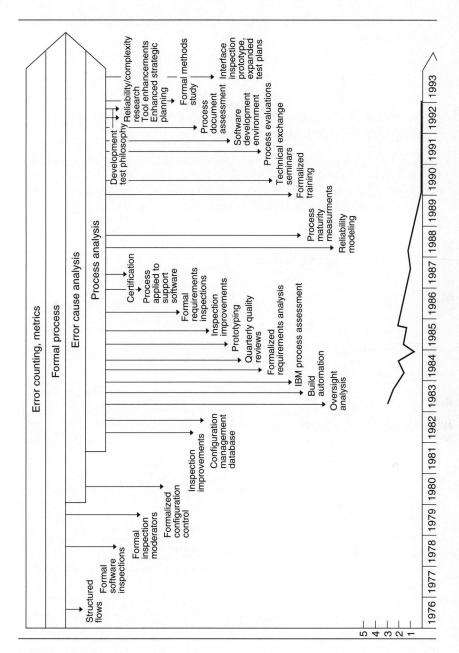

FIGURE 6.4
Chronology of process improvements implemented by the Onboard Shuttle
project.

changes being made in different areas over time combine to demonstrate steady and continuous improvement in project results. The project reported a 300% improvement in productivity and two orders of magnitude reduction in defect rates.

6.3.2 Project Management Planning and Tracking and Intergroup Coordination

The Onboard Shuttle project inherited strong project management skills from IBM Federal Systems Company that had been developed on other NASA programs dating from the 1960s. The Onboard Shuttle project is managed through a series of control boards that parallel similar boards established by NASA (Fig. 6.5). This

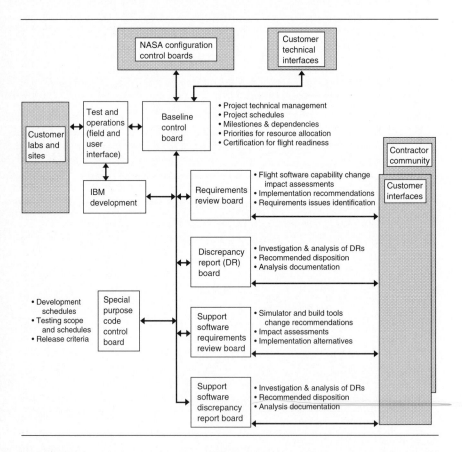

FIGURE 6.5
Control board structure for managing the Onboard Shuttle project.

parallel structure among project and customer boards establishes a single point of contact for each of the functions crucial to the customer. The top-level boards in this structure are the Onboard Shuttle project's Baseline Control Board and NASA's Configuration Control Board.

Each of the Onboard Shuttle project's control boards provides a point of coordination on a crucial issue across the entire project. Each board has a chair and representatives from each relevant functional area in the Onboard Shuttle project. Through this cross-functional structure, Onboard Shuttle teams are better able to understand the interdependencies of their decisions across the project. The boards provide a common and supportive forum for raising concerns that affect other groups.

These boards counteract the natural tendency to build functional fiefdoms in which managers might try to protect their own operations at the expense of the overall project. The chairs of these boards report to a staff manager who is independent of the operational managers. Thus the Onboard Shuttle project has both a vertical and horizontal management structure, each with different roles and areas of authority. Senior project managers believe this structure is necessary on any project involving three or more functional managers (i.e., any project of over approximately 60 people).

The members of the project's Baseline Control Board consist of second-line managers, board chairmen from other boards, and specific project coordinators. With responsibility for commitments for software content, schedules, and resources, this board has the authority to set project priorities, resolve intra-project technical issues, coordinate integrated project positions, and oversee software processes.

When the baseline for an operational increment is approved, the lead software coordinators draft a build plan consisting of contents and dates for various builds. These are coordinated with line managers and negotiated with the customer if necessary. The Baseline Control Board resolves any conflicts and baselines the plan. Dates are baselined only after each affected organization has made its input on the proposed date.

The Baseline Control Board meets weekly to review project status and areas of concern. Contents of software builds whose constituents come from different groups are altered only with board approval, as are changes in build dates. The board has responsibility to ensure that quality is never sacrificed to schedule pressures. The Baseline Control Board chair is responsible for monitoring resource utilization throughout the project and for determining the effort and schedule impacts of requirements changes.

The Onboard Shuttle project maintains a buffer of uncommitted project effort in order to absorb changes requiring additional effort without renegotiating delivery milestones. When it appears this buffer will be exhausted, the Baseline Control Board is responsible for negotiating trade-offs with NASA and revising project plans. Since the Onboard Shuttle project is a level-of-effort contract (fixed cost), trade-offs are made in either the scheduled milestones or the delivered functionality. Over time the project and NASA have learned to balance workloads across operational increments more effectively to avoid overcommitting against the contracted level of effort.

The Discrepancy Report Review Board handles problems reported against flight software. These reports could come from members of the Onboard Shuttle project, other contractors, or NASA. The board determines the Onboard Shuttle project's position on a problem and its resolution and develops a position on when and how the problem should be fixed (e.g., the next flight, the next operational increment, etc.). The board submits its recommendation to NASA's Configuration Control Board and gives NASA a single point of contact with the Onboard Shuttle project for resolving potential software problems.

The Requirements Review Board is responsible for ensuring a proper balance between the content of the operational baseline and the availability of the resources required to build and verify it. This board reviews the proposed content for each operational increment and ensures that adequate resources are available for implementing it on the schedule proposed. Throughout each operational increment this board monitors baseline content, proposed baseline changes, and resource utilization to ensure that the Onboard Shuttle project does not become overcommitted. This board reviews each proposed change to the software and determines the risks associated with making the change in the context of both resource availability and other proposed changes.

Other boards have been developed as the need arose. For instance, there is a board for controlling software patches. Further, a similar set of boards has been constructed for the support software. Boards are created when there is a fundamental issue that must be carefully managed and coordinated across the different groups composing the project.

The role of project managers has evolved dramatically as these control boards assumed their responsibilities. Management is now less concerned with progress tracking (the boards now do this) and more concerned with resourcing and people management. For instance, they continually ensure that appropriately trained staff are available as backup for every critical position on the project.

Traditional management responsibilities have been delegated to the control boards. Managers feel comfortable delegating these responsibilities because of the power of the measurement system. Measures present them with continuous information on project status and allow them to take management action on an exception basis. Because of their confidence in the measurement and the control board systems, managers have empowered lower levels of the organization to manage the ordinary processes performed on the project. Project management is freed to focus on longer-term strategic and operational issues.

Managers for the Onboard Shuttle project are developed from within the project's existing staff. Traditional management styles are inconsistent with the level of empowerment given to the project's technical staff. For instance, in low-maturity organizations process improvement is driven from the top down, whereas in the Onboard Shuttle project, process improvement is driven from the bottom up, since the process has been internalized and the staff is empowered to improve it. Even people who have managed elsewhere are not allowed to move immediately into management responsibilities after joining the project. They must first work on the project for several years to understand the process and proper role for managers within a participatory environment.

6.3.3 Configuration Control

Configuration control and measurement were established at the beginning of the Onboard Shuttle project. Configuration control was made rigorous and formal in 1980. Nevertheless, much of the tracking was still done manually. In 1982 a configuration management database was established, designed around good software management practices. One year later software builds were automated using the configuration management database to define the proper inputs and outputs vis-a-vis the requirements. Where feasible, the automation of configuration control and error checking improved productivity by freeing staff from performing these tasks.

It is notable that the Onboard Shuttle project originally implemented configuration management without an automated library. Rather, the configuration data were maintained on paper. Nevertheless, the objective of controlling the configuration of work products was accomplished. In time, a productivity boost from technology was added when appropriate tools became available. However, accomplishing the goals of configuration management was the primary focus rather than waiting for automated tools.

The configuration control procedures track several process-related attributes to each individual line. For instance, for each line of code in the flight software it is possible to determine in which release the line of code was created and its change history in all subsequent releases. Thus it is possible to identify during which operational increment a recently discovered fault was actually injected. Approximately 80% of the failures detected by NASA are in lines of code that have been in the system for over 10 years. The improved development and verification methods have been extremely effective in removing faults in the functions added during subsequent operational increments.

6.3.4 Requirements Management

In 1979 the requirements analysis group and the performance verification group were combined into a single function. Thus those who analyze the requirements also verify the performance of the implemented system. In 1984 the requirements analysis process was formally defined and required. The analysis focused on determining whether the requirements were implementable, allowing requirements problems and issues to be addressed with the customer long before they were implemented.

In 1986 formal inspections were implemented on requirements. Moderators did not sign off on inspections until either all issues were closed or a resolution was sufficiently clear to indicate that the risk entailed in the issue had been mitigated. Data on problems and issues began to be tracked internally within the Onboard Shuttle project. Within a year after installation of requirements inspections, the number of problems and issues being raised had declined by 75%, in part because the customer became more aware of requirements issues. Requirements inspections were now performed prior to approving the baseline for the operational increment.

In the mid-1980s a shift occurred in the attitude of requirements analysts toward the requirements. Previously requirements had been treated as a NASA product to be understood and analyzed for correctness. After the requirements inspection process was introduced, requirements analysts accepted requirements quality as their own responsibility. Accepting the ownership of requirements quality was part of a larger culture change. Within this culture, a change request is considered a requirements problem and it is analyzed to determine how the requirements writing process could be improved to reduce changes in the future.

A study in the mid-1980s indicated that 20% of errors were caused by a misinterpretation of the requirements. As a result, requirements analysts began to ensure that the requirements were documented in a manner that made the intended behavior of the system unambiguous. Requirements problems or ambiguities that used to be accepted are now written up in discrepancy reports to ensure that they are eliminated early as a source of faults. Methods such as facilitating joint meetings are used to ensure an accurate communication of intent between customers and developers. They also serve as liaisons between customers and developers throughout the project.

In 1990 scenario-based inspections were instituted to help the development and verification organizations better understand the requirements and the capability they were expected to create. A year later the requirements process was formally documented by a team that took responsibility for owning the requirements processes. A summary of the requirements management process is presented in Fig. 6.6. A requirements postmortem was added to determine strengths and weaknesses of the process so that process changes could be implemented in the next operational increment. Changed requirements processes were baselined at the initiation of the most recently released operational increment.

The most recent improvements to the requirements management process include studying the potential benefits of adopting formal methods for stating

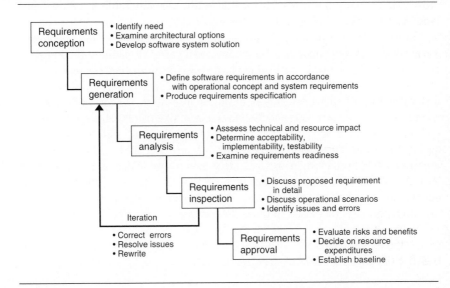

FIGURE 6.6
The requirements management process for the Onboard Shuttle project.

requirements and inspecting interfaces to address interface issues during requirements analysis. The project continues to pursue a more consistent methodology for documenting requirements. Requirements writing methods have
been investigated as a way to reduce unnecessary differences in styles of
documenting requirements across different writers.

6.3.5 Peer Reviews and Inspections

Flight software was developed using structured flows from the inception of the
Onboard Shuttle project. Structured programming was enforced, and only well-
defined constructs were allowed. However, structured programming was not
sufficient for eliminating defects from the product. In 1978 formal software
inspections were required for both the design and the code. In 1979 all inspections
were required to have moderators trained in how to conduct Fagan-style inspections
[Fagan76].

In the early 1980s a chief moderator was appointed, and teams of moderators and lead software personnel began to analyze inspection weaknesses that
allowed software defects to escape detection in the inspection process. This
was an early example of software process analysis. Although the inspection

process is formally defined with explicit roles, it is tailorable to address the unique attributes of different functional areas.

Inspections have proven to be one of the most powerful techniques deployed for improving product quality. The focus on early error detection shifted project costs from the testing and verification phases into the design and implementation phases, where the costs of fixing defects were lower. The project has established that if the cost of fixing a defect is $1 during an inspection, the cost of the fix will rise to $13 during system test and $92 if it must be fixed after delivery. As can be seen in Fig. 6.7, the percent of total injected faults detected prior to verification testing has grown steadily from below 50% to just over 80%. This percentage improvement is even more impressive, since the number of defects being injected into the software per thousand lines of code has been dropping steadily across operational increments. Thus it is clear that the Onboard Shuttle project has been installing processes that result in fewer defects than were detected earlier.

6.3.6 Software Product Engineering

6.3.6.1 Prototyping

In 1985 the Onboard Shuttle project began jointly exploring with NASA the use of prototyping proposed changes to critical software before making a hard commitment to a new set of requirements. Each prototype was an exploratory version

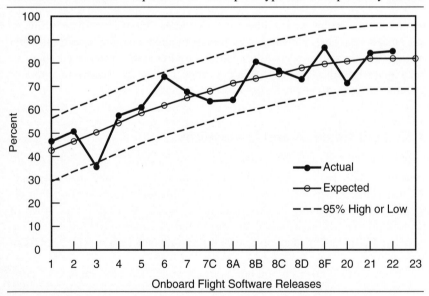

FIGURE 6.7
Percentage of total injected faults defected prior to verification testing.

of an operational increment that had been developed using an expedited version of the standard development process. The prototype allowed the project and customer to identify requirements mistakes before committing to the formal requirements for an operational increment and to identify some design and coding mistakes to be avoided during the full-up implementation. The project reported substantial quality improvements from finding requirements, design, and coding faults in prototypes rather than in product code.

The prototype was never taken as a starting point for the product, only as a basis for clarifying requirements. When the requirements had been determined, the prototype was put aside. The deliverable flight software was then developed from the revised requirements using the project's standard, defined development process.

6.3.6.2 Independent Verification

Much of the cost of the flight software was in verifying the existence of quality in order to certify the readiness of shuttle software. In the 1970s verification of flight software was assigned to an organization that was managerially independent of the software development team. That is, although they were part of the Onboard Shuttle project, their management chain reported directly into the overall project manager and was lateral to, and independent of, the development staff.

The verification process was designed to achieve the seemingly contradictory goals of providing verifiers with insight into the software and requirements while ensuring they conduct testing as if they were receiving untested software. For instance, in the 1980s verification personnel were included in design and code inspections, but to protect their independence they did not attend reviews of items related to development testing such as unit and functional test plans. Including verification testers in design and code reviews dramatically increased the early detection of defects, since testers found as many as 20% of review problems. Products produced by verification testers such as test plans, test documents, and test cases were kept under configuration control.

In 1981 verification techniques were documented, and a year later storage of error data in the configuration management system was implemented. Prologues (comments) were stored in code modules that described change authorization, the lines changed, and so on. Later, similar prologues were also stored with test cases and became important data in identifying process causes of defects. Verification staff began attending design and code inspections when it was learned that over 50% of all defects were found through static analysis and code inspections. In 1984 an automated test case status system was developed to aid tracking progress, and an automated test case library was developed a year later. At the same time inspections of verification test procedures were begun. In 1986 a test coverage analysis tool was adopted into the verification process.

During the late 1980s broader communication was established among the verification staff through electronic forums for exchanging tips, solutions, and the like. Also meetings were held to ensure that all interfaces between functional areas were covered and coordinated. More emphasis was also placed on earlier definition of the verification test plan and its completion by project milestones.

In 1991 a verification process ownership team was formed. The Tools Control Board provided greater visibility and access to test and analysis tools developed by members of the verification staff. A year later, functional test teams were developed to ensure that new staff members learned verification techniques applicable to their particular area from experienced members of the staff. Through this mechanism, backup skills were developed for important areas, and the workload could be better balanced. To expand knowledge and available test cases for less active areas of the flight software that may be candidates for future changes, testing beyond that required for the current operational increment is being explored.

The structured approach taken to the verification process contributed strongly to finding essentially all defects prior to release to the customer. Fig. 6.8 displays the dramatic decline in the number of defects per thousand lines of code being detected during verification testing. These data must be interpreted in the context of the decreasing number of defects escaping detection during development and the sharp decline in defects released to NASA. The defined verification process included the development and inspection of a verification test plan, the formal control of test cases, and the documenting and customer review of test case results and issue closures.

6.3.7 Software Quality Management and Defect Prevention

For the Onboard Shuttle project a software failure is any performance of the software that deviates from the stated requirement, regardless of how insignificant. However, if a problem occurs that can be traced to an incorrect requirement rather than a fault in the software, then it is counted as a requirements fault, not a software fault. This strict separation between requirements faults and the generic flight software software faults is crucial, since project data can be used only to determine the fidelity with which the requirements have been implemented into a software product. These data are not relevant to the quality of the requirements or the process by which requirements were developed, since these processes are outside the scope of the Onboard Shuttle project. Nevertheless, the Onboard Shuttle project has taken steps to improve the requirements development process.

From time to time the Discrepancy Report Board conducted in-depth analyses of faults that were of particular concern to NASA. In 1983 formal oversight analysis was established. Faults were now analyzed for their causes and the reasons that any subsequent inspection, test, or verification activities

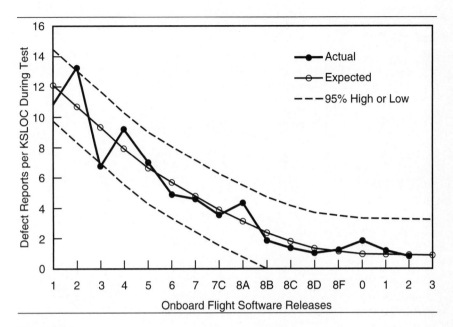

FIGURE 6.8
Faults detected per thousand lines of code during the verification testing of
Onboard Shuttle software.

failed to detect faults. This practice has evolved into the four stage defect
prevention process presented in Fig. 6.9.

In the first stage, faults are analyzed for their technical cause and corrections are made to eliminate them. In the second stage, the process cause of the
fault is identified, and the process is changed to eliminate the possibility of the
underlying error occurring in the future. In the third stage, any inspections,
test, or verification procedures from which the fault escaped undetected are
improved to detect similar faults in the future. In the final stage, if similar
functions were used elsewhere in the flight software, those areas of the product
are reinspected to determine whether a similar fault may have escaped detection
elsewhere in the system. The results of these analyses are recorded, and trends
in the data are investigated.

Part of the root cause analysis of software faults involves getting a detailed
scenario of how the software was used from the person who experienced the
failure. Lessons learned from these scenarios are fed back into the development
process. Identifying usage scenarios has been especially effective in improving
the ability of the verification process to detect faults that would occur under
low-probability conditions. The power of usage scenarios has been so great
that they are now generated as part of the requirements analysis and inspection
process.

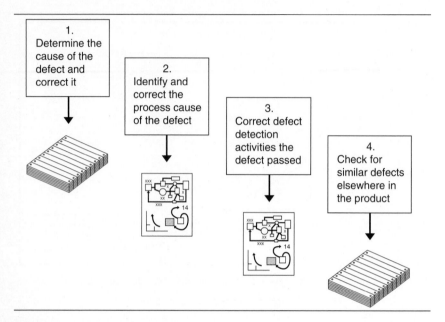

FIGURE 6.9
The Onboard Shuttle software defect prevention process.

Because of the time required, this level of defect analysis and prevention is difficult to apply when the product is riddled with faults. Further, the data would be extremely difficult to analyze in an environment where processes are performed inconsistently. However, as the process matures and faults are captured much nearer the point they are injected, there are fewer faults and more time available to analyze them.

The power of these quality management activities is presented in Fig. 6.10. The Onboard Shuttle project begins tracking the number of faults detected during all of its various inspection and test activities beginning approximately 400 days prior to delivery of each operational increment. The result of almost two decades of process improvement is that the process performs within known quantitative boundaries. Thus the project team expects to find a certain number of faults during each inspection or test phase. When they do not detect the number of faults they would expect to find based on historical trends, the Onboard Shuttle staff have reason to suspect the possibility of a problem in either the product or the process.

It is evident in Fig. 6.10 that the Onboard Shuttle project was operating near the upper boundaries of its defect detection experience beginning around the 210th day prior to the release of Operational Increment 22. After analyzing their process, project staff found that they had not updated their defect detection

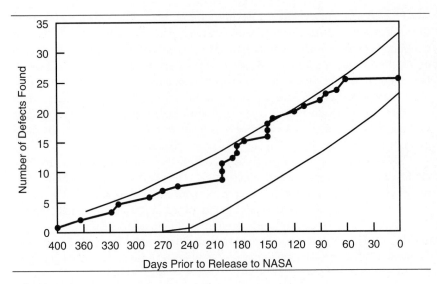

FIGURE 6.10
Fault detection experience for Operational Increment 22.

confidence intervals to accommodate an accelerated defect detection capability
that resulted from improvements made to the testing process. These testing
improvements were made as a result of lessons learned on previous operational
increments.

In 1984 managers at all levels were trained in the quality management
principles and techniques developed by Deming, Juran, and Crosby. A quality
coordinator was established, and resources were committed to improve both
process and product quality. Site executives now decide what quality goals and
measures should be established throughout the project and reported by responsible managers and executives each quarter. These quality goals are periodically updated to reflect lessons learned on recently released operational
increments. Goals are also updated to challenge the project to improve its
process capability and performance.

Quality measures are developed by each group or department for measuring
the processes for which they are responsible. Definitions of measures are
developed bottom up rather than top down to ensure their fidelity to the process
they measure and their acceptance by the team responsible for performing the
process. Measurement definitions have been found to have a settling-in time
of about six months. During this time experience is gained in the use and
interpretation of the measures, and their definitions are revised to improve their
value. Over time, measures are driven to finer levels of granularity in order to
drive process improvements deeper into the process under consideration.

Process and quality data are never used to evaluate individual members of the project staff. Using the data exclusively for process analysis in a culture of continuous process improvement reduces the tendency to game the process in order to make the measures look good. Problems with individual staff members show up in other areas such as missed schedules. If an individual continually causes project coordination problems by missing schedules, then management will step in and manage a performance problem. Management will consider a number of factors such as whether the individual was given an assignment for which he or she had not been properly prepared.

NASA has become integrally involved in the Onboard Shuttle project's quality and process improvement activities. The results of these activities are reviewed with NASA at least quarterly. Review meetings occasionally run far longer than scheduled as NASA staff get involved in interpreting and using the data. NASA staff frequently ask for additional data and for new views of the existing data. The continuous improvement activities have produced an environment of trust between customer and supplier that supports a partnership in quality improvement.

The Onboard Shuttle project's NASA customer has made changes based on lessons learned in the project's continuing improvement program. They have adopted a process philosophy and have implemented control board structures with other contractors similar to those used in managing the Onboard Shuttle project.

In 1988 reliability modeling was initiated using the SMERFS model because it was conservative and worked well with the data produced on the project. Once validated, the results were shared with NASA. More recently, software metrics research has been initiated to identify software characteristics that predict software quality or faults. They have observed that the frequency of inspection problems predicts the frequency of discrepancy reports. Discrepancy reports are also predicted by the frequency of requirements changes in a particular area.

6.3.8 Process Change Management

In 1984 an IBM team led by Ron Radice performed a two week review of the Onboard Shuttle project. The procedure used in this review was the predecessor of the Software Process Assessment method that Watts Humphrey would develop at the SEI. The project scored a 3 on a 5-point scale that was similar to, but not exactly mapped to, the 1987 SEI questionnaire or the CMM. In 1988 a software process assessment team comprised of members from NASA, the Jet Propulsion Laboratory, and the SEI assessed the Onboard Shuttle project at level 5 using the pre-CMM 1987 questionnaire. As a result of this assessment, the project began to focus on formalizing process documentation and enhancing the education process.

In 1990 project staff began joint efforts with experts in both industry and academia to benchmark best practices and to adopt those that demonstrated potential for contributing to process or product quality. Other reviews against the Baldrige Award criteria raised awareness of the need to define processes for conducting process improvement.

Process ownership teams were formed in 1990 to become the technical owners of processes. Ownership teams have been formed in nine areas: requirements evaluation; design and code; inspection; development test; functional verification; guidance, navigation and control verification; system software verification; application tools; and boards. These process ownership teams are comprised of the people who perform the process and are therefore in the best position to know what improvements should be made. The teams are responsible for documenting and benchmarking the process, collecting and analyzing measures of the process, improving the process, and providing process education. Once documented, the processes are placed under configuration control, and a formal change request and approval process must be executed to change the process.

The leaders of the process ownership teams also participate on a Process Evaluation Team that includes a senior engineer as chair, a representative from quality assurance, and suppliers and customers of the process (sometimes even an external customer). The role of the Process Evaluation Team is to determine the level of various processes by establishing criteria for their maturity. While the CMM treats maturity as an organizational attribute, this form of process evaluation extends the maturity concept down into the technical processes. Table 6.1 presents the generic criteria from which explicit criteria are developed in each of the nine process areas.

TABLE 6.1
Process Evaluation Criteria

Level 1:
— Process is defined and documented.
— Quality measurements are established with realistic goals for internal processes and those used by subcontractors.
— Quality measurements are agreed to by customer.
— Process technical ownership team is established and functioning.
— Configuration control mechanism is established and functioning.
— Process weaknesses are deemed containable based on error rates and severities.
Level 2:
— Customer satisfaction measures are set with realistic goals.
— Productivity measures are established with realistic goals for both internal and subcontractor processes.

TABLE 6.1 (*continued*)
— Defect analysis and feedback mechanism is in place.
— Process improvement teams are in operation
— Progress on process actions is demonstrated.
— Quality measurement data are being collected and positive trends are established.
— Training program for new analysts/programmers is in place and operating.
— Process is effective and no significant operational or control exposures exist.
Level 3:
— Customer satisfaction measurement shows positive trend toward acceptable goal.
— Productivity measurement shows positive trend toward acceptable goal.
— Sustained positive trends are achieved on all quality measures.
— New technologies or methodologies for process use are evaluated.
— Majority of employees are involved in process improvement.
— Actions from process/defect analysis are carried through to implementation.
— Self sustaining process education program is in place.
— Recognition methods are identified and applied.
— Measurements are established for process simplification and cycle time reduction.
— Process effectiveness can be projected.
Level 4:
— Sustained positive trends are achieved on productivity measures.
— Sustained positive trends are achieved on customer satisfaction measures.
— Process simplification and cycle time reduction measurement shows positive trend toward acceptance goal.
— Plans are in place to move ahead to new technologies and methodologies.
— Benchmark data are established and used to set quality and productivity goals.
— Recognition methods are ingrained in the process.
— All employees are involved in the search for process improvement.
Level 5:
— Products are defect free (6 sigma).
— Sustained positive trends on cycle time reduction and process simplification are achieved.
— Process is an industry resource in technology and methodology.
— Process projections are validated by two years of actual performance comparisons.
— Data from industry indicate this process is best of breed.

These criteria were developed from the CMM, the Baldrige Award, and internal IBM guides. Although the process evaluation criteria are clustered into five levels like the CMM, closer examination indicates that these scales are quite different from the organization of key practices in the CMM. In fact, many of the criteria at lower levels of the Onboard Shuttle's process evaluation framework represent issues addressed at levels 4 and 5 of the CMM. The final definition of these criteria for each process area impacts the level of control expected over the process and the aggressiveness with which process innovation is pursued.

The Process Evaluation Team establishes an expected rating level for each process through negotiation with the process's technical owners. Depending on the criticality of the process to defect elimination, some processes are allowed to be self-audited. If a process fails to meet minimum standards upon evaluation, its performance could be stopped until it is improved.

Process owners target an evaluation level for each process and develop a plan to improve the process to satisfy those criteria. Recommended process changes can be piloted against the evaluation criteria to determine whether they will benefit the process prior to implementation. Process owners have complete authority over process changes provided improvement is ultimately achieved against the criteria. However, the Process Evaluation Team can also serve as a forum for developing consensus on controversial process changes. Progress on process improvements is reported to software, program, and general managers and also to the customer during periodic quality reviews.

The Process Evaluation Team provides a forum for unsolicited process improvement suggestions and for those received from outside the Onboard Shuttle project team. They also track actions taken to improve processes. This team tries to balance the empowerment of staff members to change the process, with both the need to encourage process improvement that meets organizational criteria and the need to maintain coordination among different processes.

To spread improved processes, methods, and technologies across the site, a Site Software Engineering Council was formed. This council makes policy regarding software engineering issues across the various projects executed at the Houston site and provides the interface with the other sites in Federal Systems Company on these same issues. The council is composed of technical and management representatives from all software projects; representatives from the education, quality assurance, and other support groups; and representatives from other relevant groups and boards such as the site Software Engineering Process Group, Systems Engineering Board, and Test Engineering Council.[2]

In recent years the Onboard Shuttle project has participated in several evaluative activities to identify additional opportunities for improvement. Some of these efforts involve object-oriented process modeling and enhancements to the development environment for enacting some processes. Process documentation has been used more seriously to evaluate subprocesses, resulting in the definition and implementation of these subprocesses.

---

[2] Since the sale to Loral, this function has been redefined into the charter of a Software Engineering Process Group.

6.3.9 Training and Mentoring

In 1993 four teams were formed to improve education in the Onboard Shuttle project: education process, knowledge base, curriculum, and customer interface. The curriculum team performed a training needs analysis and developed training objectives for 116 needs. This team also developed curricula for six job types. The process team developed an on-line system that provided access to all training information on the project. The goal was to allow the storage and retrieval of courses and materials developed from time to time on the project.

Originally an informal mentoring program was conducted using office-mates or peers to help new project members adjust and learn their jobs. In 1993 a formal mentoring program was established for educating new hires through a planned curriculum assisted by a trained mentor. Volunteers for mentoring assignments were solicited, and applicants were screened to ensure they had appropriate skills. Those selected underwent a training program and were provided a mentor handbook. The success of the program was monitored by evaluating the nature of problem reports and defect cause analyses, conducting education opinion surveys, evaluating the mentoring program, and tracking the progress of the spread of the educational development on the project.

The mentoring curriculum consists of a roadmap of the knowledge a mentee should acquire during the first and second months, the third and fourth months, the fifth and sixth months, and continuous education after six months on the project. The knowledge to be imparted is grouped into 6 categories: general Shuttle, general skills, processes/procedures, languages, tools, and miscellaneous. Thus the roadmap defines the primary and secondary require-ments for knowledge during each of several time periods. Onboard Shuttle managers report that while it used to take about 12 months to achieve journey-man status and 18 months to become truly proficient in performing assigned tasks on the project, the mentoring process has shortened this apprentice period and increased productivity.

The mentoring program is part of the Onboard Shuttle quality improvement process. When the root cause of a fault is identified as a lack of knowledge on the part of a programmer, the mentoring process is analyzed to determine whether it failed to provide the required knowledge in a timely manner to avoid the error. Any shortcoming identified in the mentoring process becomes the subject of process improvement. In this way the project blames knowledge shortfalls on the process and not on the person. The project philosophy is that no one should be assigned a task until they have been properly prepared to perform it. A well-run process does not leave people on their own to develop skills.

6.4 Overall Lessons

6.4.1 Management Lessons

In their lengthy effort to develop a process that produces a product of predictably high quality, the Onboard Shuttle project has learned many lessons in how to use process improvement to achieve technical and business objectives. Foremost among these lessons is that process improvement must be applied with constant attention to its impact on results. When applied inflexibly, processes become more a matter of dogma than of productivity or quality improvement.

The Onboard Shuttle project found that some of the practices adopted when the project was functioning at the equivalent of CMM levels 1, 2, or 3 could become so ingrained that they became a hindrance to continued improvement. For example, the way that the project was managed and the role of managers changed as the control and coordination board structure evolved. Some functions once performed by managers are now performed by the technical staff through their roles on project control boards.

In a high-maturity organization, the process becomes so internalized by the staff that they willingly take responsibility for managing it. The staff are often the most effective locus of process management, since they are the closest to it and are best able to interpret process data. For instance, most quality assurance issues are resolved at lower levels of the Onboard Shuttle project.

The Onboard Shuttle project presents an excellent example of what Humphrey [Humphrey89] described as decoupling the concepts of management and managers. Managers have roles with assigned responsibilities, and there are phenomena that need to be managed. The management of some of those phenomena may be assigned to managers, and the management of other phenomena may be assigned to nonmanagers. The important issue from a process perspective is that a role or roles exist somewhere in the project with responsibility for exercising management oversight and control in each area where it is needed. Decoupling the concepts of management and manager allows an organization to empower its staff to manage activities to which they are closest and frees management to become concerned with strategic longer-term issues.

Executives in the Onboard Shuttle project have found that they need not be concerned with the drive for excellence on the part of individual staff members, since a culture of excellence has been internalized. However, they do focus on ensuring that the staff does not become complacent, and they constantly focus on improving the process performance of the project. They tend not to be concerned as much with milestones but instead with error rates, since these are a primary indicator of how efficiently the process is operating.

In low-maturity organizations, processes must be brought under control before they can be improved. Getting the development process under management control sometimes leaves engineers less flexibility in implementing software processes. Engineers in mature organizations that have brought their process under control can be empowered to make improvements in it because of their process mastery. The empowerment of mature engineers to change the process is crucial, since the process must continue to respond to project conditions that are changing. An inflexible process will be quickly outdated as technology, competition, or development conditions change.

6.4.2 People Lessons

Success in immature organizations often depends on heroes who perform technical miracles under unfavorable conditions. The Onboard Shuttle project has evolved a process that is not dependent on heroes to succeed. This should never be interpreted to imply any lack of emphasis on technical excellence in the staff. In fact, the mentoring program is designed to accelerate the development of technical skills.

The Onboard Shuttle process is designed to eliminate single points of failure in the project. That is, if a fault slips through detection and is delivered to the customer, no single individual can be blamed for the problem. Each single line of code in the flight software is reviewed by at least six different people before being released to the customer. The inspection process is designed to ensure that each new or changed line of code is reviewed against a number of quality concerns by people inspecting the product with these different perspectives.

Individual programmers are reassured that the process will protect them from making mistakes that will be delivered to the customer. Thus any delivered fault is a team fault. A single programmer may have made a mistake, but numerous others failed to detect it. For this reason, the analysis of faults focuses on the process and not on individuals.

The design of the Onboard Shuttle project process has helped overcome variations in individual staff skills in two ways. The process is less affected by someone whose skills are not sufficient, because each element of the product is reviewed by so many other project members. It is extremely unlikely that the results of poor performance could escape detection and be delivered to the customer. More importantly, however, the design of the process transfers knowledge and skills across the staff much faster than a less mature process.

Thus through knowledge gained in mentoring, inspections, and other processes, the Onboard Shuttle project is increasing the average skill of each staff member at a faster rate than would be observed on less-mature projects. Further, the process detects evidence of ineffective performance much more quickly than would be true in a less-mature process, and steps can be taken to manage it much sooner.

6.4.3 Cost Lessons

The Onboard Shuttle project has developed the capability to consistently predict its costs to within 10% of actual expenditures, and they have only missed 1 deadline in 15 years. The cost of the Onboard Shuttle flight software is high because of the process required to achieve the exceptional reliability requirements for human-rated avionics software. Project managers report that they believe that the human-rated reliability and safety requirements increase the cost of the software by a factor of 3 to 4. However, they would not change the architecture of the process were they to begin building nonhuman-rated software with lower reliability require-ments. The cost of such a system would decline because the amount of verification activity would be reduced.

Since the Onboard Shuttle project is able to quantify the performance of its process so effectively, they are able to characterize the cost of different levels of reliability. Figure 6.11 presents a comparison developed by Kyle Rone of the cost of software developed through the Onboard Shuttle process as related to different levels of defect density. As the required defect density levels move below 1 defect per thousand lines of code, the costs begin to escalate rapidly. The dramatically higher costs for human-rated software derive from the greater difficulty of designing test cases for detecting faults that would occur only under low probability conditions. The scenarios underlying these test cases take extraordinary effort to develop.

6.4.4 Process Transfer Lessons

How successfully can a mature process be transferred to another organization? The most difficult things to transfer are

- the exact organization-wide software process to an organization in a dif-ferent application area,
- the lessons learned about how to best execute processes,
- the historical data, which may not apply in a new area.

However, the principles behind process maturity growth can be transferred and used as a guide for improving another organization.

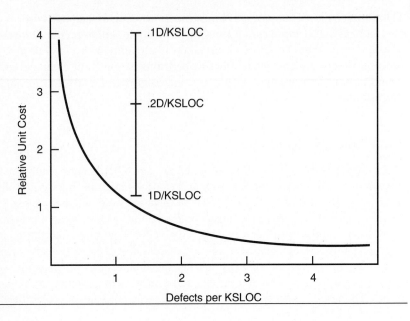

FIGURE 6.11
Relative cost of a line of code as a function of delivered defect density.

The Onboard Shuttle project has attempted to transfer its software processes and methods to other projects. Associated with the Onboard Shuttle project is a project to build support tools called the Flight Software Application Tools (FSWAT). This project began adopting some of the methods pioneered on the Onboard Shuttle project. Since its implementation of these processes is younger and less mature, FSWAT remains more influenced by variations in the skills of its technical staff than is true in the Onboard Shuttle project.

Through process improvement, the FSWAT project has continually improved its delivered software quality. For instance, transfer of the requirements analysis and code inspection processes to FSWAT in the 1980s reduced product defect rates from 0.72 defects per thousand lines of code in 1986 to 0.30 in 1993. However, the required reliability of FSWAT software is lower than that of flight software because it is not human-rated. Therefore the project costs for FSWAT are lower by a factor of 3. These costs are lower because of the reduced level of independent test and verification required. Some development processes are simpler on FSWAT. For instance, where there might be 50 items on an inspection checklist for flight software, there may be only 10 for FSWAT.

The Onboard Shuttle project has also transferred some of its process knowledge to the Space Station Freedom software project that was initiated during the 1980s (this project has since been canceled in a budget reduction effort by the U.S. Congress). Since the Space Station project was substantially different in both application and contract type from the Onboard Shuttle project, it was difficult to apply the defined software process used for flight software. The site Software Engineering Process Group has developed some sitewide software processes and has adopted some process definitions from other areas of the parent company. However, it was not possible to apply a common process to both projects. In some business circumstances it may be necessary for the organization to support two or more standard software processes from which new projects can tailor their defined software processes.

Nevertheless, the principles for developing mature processes could be transferred for application on new projects. The method for transferring these principles into practice on new projects was to transfer managers and technical staff. Thus, rather than just transfer static documents, the most effective transfer occurred with the reassignment of people possessing the dynamic knowledge about how to apply mature processes and improvement methods. One of the most important lessons from this project is that while low-maturity organizations look on talented staff as the best way to save troubled projects, mature organizations look on talented staff as the best way to transfer the culture and methods to new applications.

PART TWO

The Key Practices of the Capability Maturity Model for Software

7

The Key Process Areas for Level 2: Repeatable

Basic project management processes are established to track cost, schedule, and functionality. The necessary process discipline is in place to repeat earlier successes on projects with similar applications.

The key process areas for Level 2 are:

7.1   Requirements Management
7.2   Software Project Planning
7.3   Software Project Tracking and Oversight
7.4   Software Subcontract Management
7.5   Software Quality Assurance
7.6   Software Configuration Management

7.1 Requirements Management

a key process area for Level 2: Repeatable

The purpose of Requirements Management is to establish a common understanding between the customer and the software project of the customer's requirements that will be addressed by the software project.

Requirements Management involves establishing and maintaining an agreement with the customer on the requirements for the software project. This agreement is referred to as the "system requirements allocated to the software." The "customer" may be interpreted as the system engineering group, the marketing group, another internal organization, or an external customer. The agreement covers both the technical and nontechnical (e.g., delivery dates) requirements. The agreement forms the basis for estimating, planning, performing, and tracking the software project's activities throughout the software life cycle.

The allocation of the system requirements to software, hardware, and other system components (e.g., humans) may be performed by a group external to the software engineering group (e.g., the system engineering group), and the software engineering group may have no direct control of this allocation. Within the constraints of the project, the software engineering group takes appropriate steps to ensure that the system requirements allocated to software, which it is responsible for addressing, are documented and controlled.

To achieve this control, the software engineering group reviews the initial and revised system requirements allocated to software to resolve issues before they are incorporated into the software project. Whenever the system requirements allocated to software are changed, the affected software plans, work products, and activities are adjusted to remain consistent with the updated requirements.

Goals

Goal 1   **System requirements allocated to software are controlled to establish a baseline for software engineering and management use.**

Goal 2   **Software plans, products and activities are kept consistent with the system requirements allocated to software.**

Commitment to Perform

Commitment 1   **The project follows a written organizational policy for managing the system requirements allocated to software.**

> The system requirements allocated to the software are referred to as "allocated requirements" in these practices.
>
> The allocated requirements are the subset of the system requirements that are to be implemented in the software components of the system. The allocated requirements are a primary input to the software development plan. Software requirements analysis elaborates and refines the allocated requirements and results in software requirements which are documented.

This policy typically specifies that:

1. The allocated requirements are documented.

2. The allocated requirements are reviewed by:

   □ the software managers, and

   □ other affected groups.

> Examples of affected groups include:
>
> system test,
>
> software engineering (including all subgroups, such as software design),
>
> system engineering,
>
> software quality assurance,
>
> software configuration management, and
>
> documentation support.

3. The software plans, work products, and activities are changed to be consistent with changes to the allocated requirements.

Ability to Perform

Ability 1

For each project, responsibility is established for analyzing the system requirements and allocating them to hardware, software, and other system components.

> Analysis and allocation of the system requirements is not the responsibility of the software engineering group but is a prerequisite for their work.

This responsibility covers:

1. Managing and documenting the system requirements and their allocation throughout the project's life.
2. Effecting changes to the system requirements and their allocation.

Ability 2

The allocated requirements are documented.

The allocated requirements include:

1. The nontechnical requirements (i.e., the agreements, conditions, and/or contractual terms) that affect and determine the activities of the software project.

> Examples of agreements, conditions, and contractual terms include:
>
>   products to be delivered,
>
>   delivery dates, and
>
>   milestones.

2. The technical requirements for the software.

> Examples of technical requirements include:
>
>   end user, operator, support, or integration functions;
>
>   performance requirements;
>
>   design constraints;
>
>   programming language; and
>
>   interface requirements.

3. The acceptance criteria that will be used to validate that the software products satisfy the allocated requirements.

Ability 3

Adequate resources and funding are provided for managing the allocated requirements.

1. Individuals who have experience and expertise in the application domain and in software engineering are assigned to manage the allocated requirements.

2. Tools to support the activities for managing requirements are made available.

> Examples of support tools include:
>
> > spreadsheet programs,
> >
> > tools for configuration management,
> >
> > tools for traceability, and
> >
> > tools for text management.

Ability 4

Members of the software engineering group and other software-related groups are trained to perform their requirements management activities.

> Examples of training include:
>
> > the methods, standards, and procedures used by the project, and
> >
> > the application domain.

Activities Performed

Activity 1

The software engineering group reviews the allocated requirements before they are incorporated into the software project.

1. Incomplete and missing allocated requirements are identified.

2. The allocated requirements are reviewed to determine whether they are:

  □ feasible and appropriate to implement in software,

  □ clearly and properly stated,

  □ consistent with each other, and

  □ testable.

3. Any allocated requirements identified as having potential problems are reviewed with the group responsible for analyzing and allocating system requirements, and necessary changes are made.

4. Commitments resulting from the allocated requirements are negotiated with the affected groups.

Examples of affected groups include:

  software engineering (including all subgroups, such as software design),

  software estimating,

  system engineering,

  system test,

  software quality assurance,

  software configuration management,

  contract management, and

  documentation support.

Refer to Activity 6 of the Software Project Planning key process area for practices covering negotiating commitments.

Activity 2   **The software engineering group uses the allocated requirements as the basis for software plans, work products, and activities.**

The allocated requirements:

1. Are managed and controlled.

"Managed and controlled" implies that the version of the work product in use at a given time (past or present) is known (i.e., version control), and changes are incorporated in a controlled manner (i.e., change control).

> If a greater degree of formality than is implied by "managed and controlled" is desired, the work product can be placed under the full discipline of configuration management, as is described in the Software Configuration Management key process area.

2. Are the basis for the software development plan.

3. Are the basis for developing the software requirements.

Activity 3

Changes to the allocated requirements are reviewed and incorporated into the software project.

1. The impact to existing commitments is assessed, and changes are negotiated as appropriate.

   □ Changes to commitments made to individuals and groups external to the organization are reviewed with senior management.

> Refer to Activity 4 of the Software Project Planning key process area and Activity 3 of the Software Project Tracking and Oversight key process area for practices covering commitments made external to the organization.

   □ Changes to commitments within the organization are negotiated with the affected groups.

> Refer to Activities 5, 6, 7, and 8 of the Software Project Tracking and Oversight key process area for practices covering negotiating changes to commitments.

2. Changes that need to be made to the software plans, work products, and activities resulting from changes to the allocated requirements are:

   □ identified,

   □ evaluated,

   □ assessed for risk,

   □ documented,

□ planned,

□ communicated to the affected groups and individuals, and

□ tracked to completion.

Measurement and Analysis

Measurement 1   **Measurements are made and used to determine the status of the activities for managing the allocated requirements.**

> Examples of measurements include:
>
> status of each of the allocated requirements;
>
> change activity for the allocated requirements; and
>
> cumulative number of changes to the allocated requirements, including total number of changes proposed, open, approved, and incorporated into the system baseline.

Verifying Implementation

Verification 1   **The activities for managing the allocated requirements are reviewed with senior management on a periodic basis.**

> The primary purpose of periodic reviews by senior management is to provide awareness of and insight into software process activities at an appropriate level of abstraction and in a timely manner. The time between reviews should meet the needs of the organization and may be lengthy, as long as adequate mechanisms for exception reporting are available.

> Refer to Verification 1 of the Software Project Tracking and Oversight key process area for practices covering the typical content of senior management oversight reviews.

Verification 2   **The activities for managing the allocated requirements are reviewed with the project manager on both a periodic and event-driven basis.**

> Refer to Verification 2 of the Software Project Tracking and Oversight key process area for practices covering the typical content of project management oversight reviews.

Verification 3   **The software quality assurance group reviews and/or audits the activities and work products for managing the allocated requirements and reports the results.**

> Refer to the Software Quality Assurance key process area.

At a minimum, these reviews and/or audits verify that:

1. The allocated requirements are reviewed, and problems are resolved before the software engineering group commits to them.

2. The software plans, work products, and activities are appropriately revised when the allocated requirements change.

3. Changes to commitments resulting from changes to the allocated requirements are negotiated with the affected groups.

7.2 Software Project Planning

a key process area for Level 2: Repeatable

The purpose of Software Project Planning is to establish reasonable plans for performing the software engineering and for managing the software project.

Software Project Planning involves developing estimates for the work to be performed, establishing the necessary commitments, and defining the plan to perform the work.

The software planning begins with a statement of the work to be performed and other constraints and goals that define and bound the software project (those established by the practices of the Requirements Management key process area). The software planning process includes steps to estimate the size of the software work products and the resources needed, produce a schedule, identify and assess software risks, and negotiate commitments. Iterating through these steps may be necessary to establish the plan for the software project (i.e., the software development plan).

This plan provides the basis for performing and managing the software project's activities and addresses the commitments to the software project's customer according to the resources, constraints, and capabilities of the software project.

Goals

Goal 1   **Software estimates are documented for use in planning and tracking the software project.**

Goal 2   **Software project activities and commitments are planned and documented.**

Goal 3   **Affected groups and individuals agree to their commitments related to the software project.**

Commitment to Perform

Commitment 1   **A project software manager is designated to be responsible for negotiating commitments and developing the project's software development plan.**

Commitment 2   **The project follows a written organizational policy for planning a software project.**

This policy typically specifies that:

1. The system requirements allocated to software are used as the basis for planning the software project.

> Refer to Activity 2 of the Requirements Management key process area.

2. The software project's commitments are negotiated between:

        □ the project manager,

        □ the project software manager, and

        □ the other software managers.

3. Involvement of other engineering groups in the software activities is negotiated with these groups and is documented.

Examples of other engineering groups include:

    system engineering,

    hardware engineering, and

    system test.

---

4. Affected groups review the software project's:

        □ software size estimates,

        □ effort and cost estimates,

        □ schedules, and

        □ other commitments.

Examples of affected groups include:

    software engineering (including all subgroups, such as software design),

    software estimating,

    system engineering,

    system test,

    software quality assurance,

    software configuration management,

    contract management, and

    documentation support.

---

5. Senior management reviews all software project commitments made to individuals and groups external to the organization.

6. The project's software development plan is managed and controlled.

> The term "software development plan" is used throughout these practices to refer to the overall plan for managing the software project. The use of "development" terminology is not intended to exclude software maintenance or support projects and should be appropriately interpreted in the context of the individual project.

> "Managed and controlled" implies that the version of the work product in use at a given time (past or present) is known (i.e., version control) and changes are incorporated in a controlled manner (i.e., change control).
>
> If a greater degree of control than is implied by "managed and controlled" is desired, the work product can be placed under the full discipline of configuration management, as is described in the Software Configuration Management key process area.

Ability to Perform

Ability 1   **A documented and approved statement of work exists for the software project.**

1. The statement of work covers:
   - scope of the work,
   - technical goals and objectives,
   - identification of customers and end users,

> The end users referred to in these practices are the customer designated end users or representatives of the end users.

   - imposed standards,
   - assigned responsibilities,
   - cost and schedule constraints and goals,
   - dependencies between the software project and other organizations,

> Examples of other organizations include:
>
> > the customer,
> >
> > subcontractors, and
> >
> > joint venture partners.

- □ resource constraints and goals, and
- □ other constraints and goals for development and/or maintenance.

2. The statement of work is reviewed by:

- □ the project manager,
- □ the project software manager,
- □ the other software managers, and
- □ other affected groups.

3. The statement of work is managed and controlled.

Ability 2

Responsibilities for developing the software development plan are assigned.

1. The project software manager, directly or by delegation, coordinates the project's software planning.

2. Responsibilities for the software work products and activities are partitioned and assigned to software managers in a traceable, accountable manner.

> Examples of software work products include:
>
> > work products for delivery to the external customer or end users, as appropriate;
> >
> > work products for use by other engineering groups; and
> >
> > major work products for internal use by the software engineering group.

Ability 3

Adequate resources and funding are provided for planning the software project.

1. Where feasible, experienced individuals, who have expertise in the application domain of the software

project being planned, are available to develop the software development plan.

2. Tools to support the software project planning activities are made available.

> Examples of support tools include:
>
> > spreadsheet programs,
> >
> > estimating models, and
> >
> > project planning and scheduling programs.

Ability 4   **The software managers, software engineers, and other individuals involved in the software project planning are trained in the software estimating and planning procedures applicable to their areas of responsibility.**

Activities Performed

Activity 1   **The software engineering group participates on the project proposal team.**

1. The software engineering group is involved in:

   □ proposal preparation and submission,

   □ clarification discussions and submissions, and

   □ negotiations of changes to commitments that affect the software project.

2. The software engineering group reviews the project's proposed commitments.

> Examples of project commitments include:
>
> > the project's technical goals and objectives;
> >
> > the system and software technical solution;
> >
> > the software budget, schedule, and resources; and
> >
> > the software standards and procedures.

Activity 2   **Software project planning is initiated in the early stages of, and in parallel with, the overall project planning.**

Activity 3

The software engineering group participates with other affected groups in the overall project planning throughout the project's life.

1. The software engineering group reviews the project-level plans.

Activity 4

Software project commitments made to individuals and groups external to the organization are reviewed with senior management according to a documented procedure.

Activity 5

A software life cycle with predefined stages of manageable size is identified or defined.

> Examples of software life cycles include:
>
>   waterfall,
>
>   overlapping waterfall,
>
>   spiral,
>
>   serial build, and
>
>   single prototype/overlapping waterfall.

Activity 6

The project's software development plan is developed according to a documented procedure.

This procedure typically specifies that:

1. The software development plan is based on and conforms to:

    □ the customer's standards, as appropriate;

    □ the project's standards;

    □ the approved statement of work; and

    □ the allocated requirements.

2. Plans for software-related groups and other engineering groups involved in the activities of the software engineering group are negotiated with those groups, the support efforts are budgeted, and the agreements are documented.

Examples of software-related groups include:

software quality assurance,

software configuration management, and

documentation support.

Examples of other engineering groups include:

system engineering,

hardware engineering, and

system test.

3. Plans for involvement of the software engineering group in the activities of other software-related groups and other engineering groups are negotiated with those groups, the support efforts are budgeted, and the agreements are documented.

4. The software development plan is reviewed by:

- the project manager,
- the project software manager,
- the other software managers, and
- other affected groups.

5. The software development plan is managed and controlled.

Activity 7   **The plan for the software project is documented.**

In the key practices, this plan or collection of plans is referred to as the software development plan.

Refer to Activity 1 of the Software Project Tracking and Oversight key process area for practices concerning the project's use of the software development plan.

The software development plan covers:

1. The software project's purpose, scope, goals, and objectives.
2. Selection of a software life cycle.
3. Identification of the selected procedures, methods, and standards for developing and/or maintaining the software.

Examples of software standards and procedures include:

    software development planning,

    software configuration management,

    software quality assurance,

    software design,

    problem tracking and resolution, and

    software measurement.

---

4. Identification of software work products to be developed.
5. Size estimates of the software work products and any changes to the software work products.
6. Estimates of the software project's effort and costs.
7. Estimated use of critical computer resources.
8. The software project's schedules, including identification of milestones and reviews.
9. Identification and assessment of the project's software risks.
10. Plans for the project's software engineering facilities and support tools.

Activity 8

Software work products that are needed to establish and maintain control of the software project are identified.

Refer to Activity 4 of the Software Configuration Management key process area.

Activity 9   **Estimates for the size of the software work products (or changes to the size of software work products) are derived according to a documented procedure.**

This procedure typically specifies that:

1. Size estimates are made for all major software work products and activities.

> Examples of software size measurements include:
>
> > function points,
> >
> > feature points,
> >
> > lines of code,
> >
> > number of requirements, and
> >
> > number of pages.

> Examples of types of work products and activities for which size estimates are made include:
>
> > operational software and support software,
> >
> > deliverable and nondeliverable work products,
> >
> > software and nonsoftware work products (e.g., documents), and
> >
> > activities for developing, verifying, and validating work products.

2. Software work products are decomposed to the granularity needed to meet the estimating objectives.

3. Historical data are used where available.

4. Size estimating assumptions are documented.

5. Size estimates are documented, reviewed, and agreed to.

> Examples of groups and individuals who review and agree to size estimates include:
>
> > the project manager,
> >
> > the project software manager, and
> >
> > the other software managers.

Activity 10

Estimates for the software project's effort and costs are derived according to a documented procedure.

This procedure typically specifies that:

1. Estimates for the software project's effort and costs are related to the size estimates of the software work products (or the size of the changes).

2. Productivity data (historical and/or current) are used for the estimates when available; sources and rationale for these data are documented.

   □ The productivity and cost data are from the organization's projects when possible.

   □ The productivity and cost data take into account the effort and significant costs that go into making the software work products.

> Examples of significant costs that go into making the software work products include:
>
>   direct labor expenses,
>
>   overhead expenses,
>
>   travel expenses, and
>
>   computer use costs.

3. Effort, staffing, and cost estimates are based on past experience.

   □ Similar projects should be used when possible.

   □ Time phasing of activities is derived.

   □ Distributions of the effort, staffing, and cost estimates over the software life cycle are prepared.

4. Estimates and the assumptions made in deriving the estimates are documented, reviewed, and agreed to.

Activity 11

Estimates for the project's critical computer resources are derived according to a documented procedure.

> Critical computer resources may be in the host environment, in the integration and testing environment, in the target environment, or in any combination of these.

This procedure typically specifies that:

1. Critical computer resources for the project are identified.

> Examples of critical computer resources include:
>
>   computer memory capacity,
>
>   computer processor use, and
>
>   communications channel capacity.

2. Estimates for the critical computer resources are related to the estimates of:
   □ the size of the software work products,
   □ the operational processing load, and
   □ the communications traffic.

3. Estimates of the critical computer resources are documented, reviewed, and agreed to.

Activity 12

The project's software schedule is derived according to a documented procedure.

This procedure typically specifies that:

1. The software schedule is related to:
   □ the size estimate of the software work products (or the size of changes), and
   □ the software effort and costs.

2. The software schedule is based on past experience.
   □ Similar projects are used when possible.

3. The software schedule accommodates the imposed milestone dates, critical dependency dates, and other constraints.

4. The software schedule activities are of appropriate duration and the milestones are of appropriate time separation to support accuracy in progress measurement.

5. Assumptions made in deriving the schedule are documented.

6. The software schedule is documented, reviewed, and agreed to.

Activity 13

The software risks associated with the cost, resource, schedule, and technical aspects of the project are identified, assessed, and documented.

1. The risks are analyzed and prioritized based on their potential impact to the project.

2. Contingencies for the risks are identified.

Examples of contingencies include:

schedule buffers,

alternate staffing plans, and

alternate plans for additional computing equipment.

Activity 14

Plans for the project's software engineering facilities and support tools are prepared.

1. Estimates of capacity requirements for these facilities and support tools are based on the size estimates of the software work products and other characteristics.

Examples of software development facilities and support tools include:

software development computers and peripherals,

software test computers and peripherals,

target computer environment software, and

other support software.

---

2. Responsibilities are assigned and commitments are negotiated to procure or develop these facilities and support tools.

3. The plans are reviewed by all affected groups.

Activity 15

Software planning data are recorded.

1. Information recorded includes the estimates and the associated information needed to reconstruct the estimates and assess their reasonableness.

> **2.** The software planning data are managed and controlled.

Measurement and Analysis

Measurement 1   **Measurements are made and used to determine the status of the software planning activities.**

> Examples of measurements include:
>
> completions of milestones for the software project planning activities compared to the plan; and
>
> work completed, effort expended, and funds expended in the software project planning activities compared to the plan.

Verifying Implementation

Verification 1   **The activities for software project planning are reviewed with senior management on a periodic basis.**

> The primary purpose of periodic reviews by senior management is to provide awareness of, and insight into, software process activities at an appropriate level of abstraction and in a timely manner. The time between reviews should meet the needs of the organization and may be lengthy, as long as adequate mechanisms for exception reporting are available.

1. The technical, cost, staffing, and schedule performance is reviewed.
2. Conflicts and issues not resolvable at lower levels are addressed.
3. Software project risks are addressed.
4. Action items are assigned, reviewed, and tracked to closure.
5. A summary report from each meeting is prepared and distributed to the affected groups and individuals.

Verification 2

The activities for software project planning are reviewed with the project manager on both a periodic and event-driven basis.

1. Affected groups are represented.

2. Status and current results of the software project planning activities are reviewed against the software project's statement of work and allocated requirements.

3. Dependencies between groups are addressed.

4. Conflicts and issues not resolvable at lower levels are addressed.

5. Software project risks are reviewed.

6. Action items are assigned, reviewed, and tracked to closure.

7. A summary report from each meeting is prepared and distributed to the affected groups and individuals.

Verification 3

The software quality assurance group reviews and/or audits the activities and work products for software project planning and reports the results.

> Refer to the Software Quality Assurance key process area.

At a minimum, the reviews and/or audits verify:

1. The activities for software estimating and planning.

2. The activities for reviewing and making project commitments.

3. The activities for preparing the software development plan.

4. The standards used for preparing the software development plan.

5. The content of the software development plan.

7.3 Software Project Tracking and Oversight

a key process area for Level 2: Repeatable

The purpose of Software Project Tracking and Oversight is to provide adequate visibility into actual progress so that management can take effective actions when the software project's performance deviates significantly from the software plans.

Software Project Tracking and Oversight involves tracking and reviewing the software accomplishments and results against documented estimates, commitments, and plans, and adjusting these plans based on the actual accomplishments and results.

A documented plan for the software project (i.e., the software development plan, as described in the Software Project Planning key process area) is used as the basis for tracking the software activities, communicating status, and revising plans. Software activities are monitored by the management. Progress is primarily determined by comparing the actual software size, effort, cost, and schedule to the plan when selected software work products are completed and at selected milestones. When it is determined that the software project's plans are not being met, corrective actions are taken. These actions may include revising the software development plan to reflect the actual accomplishments and replanning the remaining work or taking actions to improve the performance.

Goals

Goal 1   **Actual results and performance are tracked against the software plans.**

Goal 2   **Corrective actions are taken and managed to closure when actual results and performance deviate significantly from the software plans.**

Goal 3   **Changes to software commitments are agreed to by the affected groups and individuals.**

Commitment to Perform

Commitment 1   **A project software manager is designated to be responsible for the project's software activities and results.**

Commitment 2   **The project follows a written organizational policy for managing the software project.**

This policy typically specifies that:

1. A documented software development plan is used and maintained as the basis for tracking the software project.

2. The project manager is kept informed of the software project's status and issues.

3. Corrective actions are taken when the software plan is not being achieved, either by adjusting performance or by adjusting the plans.

4. Changes to the software commitments are made with the involvement and agreement of the affected groups.

Examples of affected groups include:

software engineering (including all subgroups, such as software design),

software estimating,

system engineering,

system test,

software quality assurance,

software configuration management,

contract management, and

documentation support.

---

5. Senior management reviews all commitment changes and new software project commitments made to individuals and groups external to the organization.

Ability to Perform

Ability 1

A software development plan for the software project is documented and approved.

Refer to Activities 6 and 7 of the Software Project Planning key process area for practices covering the software development plan.

Ability 2   **The project software manager explicitly assigns responsibility for software work products and activities.**

The assigned responsibilities cover:

1. The software work products to be developed or services to be provided.
2. The effort and cost for these software activities.
3. The schedule for these software activities.
4. The budget for these software activities.

Ability 3   **Adequate resources and funding are provided for tracking the software project.**

1. The software managers and the software task leaders are assigned specific responsibilities for tracking the software project.
2. Tools to support software tracking are made available.

> Examples of support tools include:
>
> spreadsheet programs and
>
> project planning/scheduling programs.

Ability 4   **The software managers are trained in managing the technical and personnel aspects of the software project.**

> Examples of training include:
>
> managing technical projects;
>
> tracking and oversight of software size, effort, cost, and schedule; and
>
> managing people.

Ability 5   **First-line software managers receive orientation in the technical aspects of the software project.**

> Examples of orientation include:
>
> > the project's software engineering standards and procedures and
> >
> > the project's application domain.

Activities Performed

Activity 1

A documented software development plan is used for tracking the software activities and communicating status.

> Refer to Activity 7 of the Software Project Planning key process area for practices covering the content of the software development plan.

This software development plan is:

1. Updated as the work progresses to reflect accomplishments, particularly when milestones are completed.
2. Readily available to:

   □ the software engineering group (including all subgroups, such as software design),

   □ the software managers,

   □ the project manager,

   □ senior management, and

   □ other affected groups.

Activity 2

The project's software development plan is revised according to a documented procedure.

> Refer to Activity 6 of the Software Project Planning key process area for practices covering the activities for producing the software development plan.

This procedure typically specifies that:

1. The software development plan is revised, as appropriate, to incorporate plan refinements and incorporate

plan changes, particularly when plans change significantly.

> Interdependencies between the system requirements allo-
> cated to software, design constraints, resources, costs, and
> schedule need to be reflected in all changes to the plan.

2. The software development plan is updated to incorporate all new software project commitments and
   changes to commitments.
3. The software development plan is reviewed at each
   revision.
4. The software development plan is managed and controlled.

> "Managed and controlled" implies that the version of the
> work product in use at a given time (past or present) is
> known (i.e., version control) and changes are incorporated
> in a controlled manner (i.e., change control).
>
> If a greater degree of control than is implied by
> "managed and controlled" is desired, the work product can
> be placed under the full discipline of configuration man-
> agement, as is described in the Software Configuration
> Management key process area.

Activity 3

**Software project commitments and changes to commit-
ments made to individuals and groups external to the
organization are reviewed with senior management according to a documented procedure.**

Activity 4

**Approved changes to commitments that affect the soft-
ware project are communicated to the members of the
software engineering group and other software-related
groups.**

> Examples of other software-related groups include:
>
> software quality assurance,
>
> software configuration management, and
>
> documentation support.

Activity 5

The sizes of the software work products (or sizes of the changes to the software work products) are tracked, and corrective actions are taken as necessary.

> Refer to Activity 9 of the Software Project Planning key process area for practices covering derivation of size estimates.

1. Sizes for all major software work products (or the sizes of the changes) are tracked.

2. Actual size of code (generated, fully tested, and delivered) is compared to the estimates documented in the software development plan.

3. Actual units of delivered documentation are compared to the estimates documented in the software development plan.

4. Overall projected size of the software work products (estimates combined with actuals) is refined, monitored, and adjusted on a regular basis.

5. Changes in size estimates of the software work products that affect software commitments are negotiated with the affected groups and are documented.

Activity 6

The project's software effort and costs are tracked, and corrective actions are taken as necessary.

> Refer to Activity 10 of the Software Project Planning key process area for practices covering the derivation of cost estimates.

1. Actual expenditures of effort and costs over time and against work completed are compared to the estimates documented in the software development plan to identify potential overruns and underruns.

2. Software costs are tracked and compared to the estimates documented in the software development plan.

3. Effort and staffing are compared to the estimates documented in the software development plan.

4. Changes in staffing and other software costs that affect software commitments are negotiated with the affected groups and are documented.

Activity 7 **The project's critical computer resources are tracked, and corrective actions are taken as necessary.**

> Refer to Activity 11 of the Software Project Planning key process area for practices covering the derivation of computer resource estimates.

1. The actual and projected uses of the project's critical computer resources are tracked and compared to the estimates for each major software component as documented in the software development plan.
2. Changes in estimates of critical computer resources that affect software commitments are negotiated with the affected groups and are documented.

Activity 8 **The project's software schedule is tracked, and corrective actions are taken as necessary.**

> Refer to Activity 12 of the Software Project Planning key process area for practices covering derivation of the schedule.

1. Actual completion of software activities, milestones, and other commitments is compared against the software development plan.
2. Effects of late and early completion of software activities, milestones, and other commitments are evaluated for impacts on future activities and milestones.
3. Software schedule revisions that affect software commitments are negotiated with the affected groups and are documented.

Activity 9 **Software engineering technical activities are tracked, and corrective actions are taken as necessary.**

1. Members of the software engineering group report their technical status to their first-line manager on a regular basis.

2. Software release contents for successive builds are compared to the plans documented in the software development plan.

3. Problems identified in any of the software work products are reported and documented.

4. Problem reports are tracked to closure.

Activity 10   **The software risks associated with cost, resource, schedule, and technical aspects of the project are tracked.**

> Refer to Activity 13 of the Software Project Planning key process area for practices covering identification of risks.

1. The priorities of the risks and the contingencies for the risks are adjusted as additional information becomes available.

2. High-risk areas are reviewed with the project manager on a regular basis.

Activity 11   **Actual measurement data and replanning data for the software project are recorded.**

> Refer to Activity 15 of the Software Project Planning key process area for practices covering recording of project data.

1. Information recorded includes the estimates and associated information needed to reconstruct the estimates and verify their reasonableness.

2. The software replanning data are managed and controlled.

3. The software planning data, replanning data, and the actual measurement data are archived for use by ongoing and future projects.

Activity 12   **The software engineering group conducts periodic internal reviews to track technical progress, plans, performance, and issues against the software development plan.**

These reviews are conducted between:

1. The first-line software managers and their software task leaders.
2. The project software manager, first-line software managers, and other software managers, as appropriate.

Activity 13   **Formal reviews to address the accomplishments and results of the software project are conducted at selected project milestones according to a documented procedure.**

These reviews:

1. Are planned to occur at meaningful points in the software project's schedule, such as the beginning or completion of selected stages.
2. Are conducted with the customer, end user, and affected groups within the organization, as appropriate.

> The end users referred to in these practices are the customer designated end users or representatives of the end users.

3. Use materials that are reviewed and approved by the responsible software managers.
4. Address the commitments, plans, and status of the software activities.
5. Result in the identification and documentation of significant issues, action items, and decisions.
6. Address the software project risks.
7. Result in the refinement of the software development plan, as necessary.

Measurement and Analysis

Measurement 1   **Measurements are made and used to determine the status of the software tracking and oversight activities.**

> Examples of measurements include:
>
> effort and other resources expended in performing the tracking and oversight activities; and
>
> change activity for the software development plan, which includes changes to size estimates of the software work products, software cost estimates, critical computer resource estimates, and schedule.

Verifying Implementation

Verification 1   **The activities for software project tracking and oversight are reviewed with senior management on a periodic basis.**

> The primary purpose of periodic reviews by senior management is to provide awareness of, and insight into, software process activities at an appropriate level of abstraction and in a timely manner. The time between reviews should meet the needs of the organization and may be lengthy, as long as adequate mechanisms for exception reporting are available.

1. The technical, cost, staffing, and schedule performance is reviewed.
2. Conflicts and issues not resolvable at lower levels are addressed.
3. Software project risks are addressed.
4. Action items are assigned, reviewed, and tracked to closure.
5. A summary status report from each meeting is prepared and distributed to the affected groups.

Verification 2   **The activities for software project tracking and oversight are reviewed with the project manager on both a periodic and event-driven basis.**

1. Affected groups are represented.

2. The technical, cost, staffing, and schedule performance is reviewed against the software development plan.

3. Use of critical computer resources is reviewed; current estimates and actual use of these critical computer resources are reported against the original estimates.

4. Dependencies between groups are addressed.

5. Conflicts and issues not resolvable at lower levels are addressed.

6. Software project risks are addressed.

7. Action items are assigned, reviewed, and tracked to closure.

8. A summary report from each meeting is prepared and distributed to the affected groups.

Verification 3   **The software quality assurance group reviews and/or audits the activities and work products for software project tracking and oversight and reports the results.**

> Refer to the Software Quality Assurance key process area.

At a minimum, the reviews and/or audits verify:

1. The activities for reviewing and revising commitments.

2. The activities for revising the software development plan.

3. The content of the revised software development plan.

4. The activities for tracking the software project's cost, schedule, risks, technical and design constraints, and functionality and performance.

5. The activities for conducting the planned technical and management reviews.

7.4 Software Subcontract Management

a key process for Level 2: Repeatable

The purpose of Software Subcontract Management is to select qualified software subcontractors and manage them effectively.

Software Subcontract Management involves selecting a software subcontractor, establishing commitments with the subcontractor, and tracking and reviewing the subcontractor's performance and results. These practices cover the management of a software (only) subcontract, as well as the management of the software component of a subcontract that includes software, hardware, and possibly other system components.

The subcontractor is selected based on its ability to perform the work. Many factors contribute to the decision to subcontract a portion of the prime contractor's work. Subcontractors may be selected based on strategic business alliances, as well as technical considerations. The practices of this key process area address the traditional acquisition process associated with subcontracting a defined portion of the work to another organization.

When subcontracting, a documented agreement covering the technical and nontechnical (e.g., delivery dates) requirements is established and is used as the basis for managing the subcontract. The work to be done by the subcontractor and the plans for the work are documented. The standards that are to be followed by the subcontractor are compatible with the prime contractor's standards.

The software planning, tracking, and oversight activities for the subcontracted work are performed by the subcontractor. The prime contractor ensures that these planning, tracking, and oversight activities are performed appropriately and that the software products delivered by the subcontractor satisfy their acceptance criteria. The prime contractor works with the subcontractor to manage their product and process interfaces.

Goals

Goal 1   **The prime contractor selects qualified software subcontractors.**

Goal 2   **The prime contractor and the software subcontractor agree to their commitments to each other.**

Goal 3   **The prime contractor and the software subcontractor maintain ongoing communications.**

Goal 4

The prime contractor tracks the software subcontractor's actual results and performance against its commitments.

Commitment to Perform

Commitment 1

The project follows a written organizational policy for managing the software subcontract.

This policy typically specifies that:

1. Documented standards and procedures are used in selecting software subcontractors and managing the software subcontracts.
2. The contractual agreements form the basis for managing the subcontract.
3. Changes to the subcontract are made with the involvement and agreement of both the prime contractor and the subcontractor.

Commitment 2

A subcontract manager is designated to be responsible for establishing and managing the software subcontract.

1. The subcontract manager is knowledgeable and experienced in software engineering or has individuals assigned who have that knowledge and experience.
2. The subcontract manager is responsible for coordinating the technical scope of work to be subcontracted and the terms and conditions of the subcontract with the affected parties.

> The project's system engineering group and software engineering group define the technical scope of the work to be subcontracted.
>
> The appropriate business function groups, such as purchasing, finance, and legal, establish and monitor the terms and conditions of the subcontract.

3. The subcontract manager is responsible for:

   □ selecting the software subcontractor,
   □ managing the software subcontract, and
   □ arranging for the post-subcontract support of the subcontracted products.

Ability to Perform

Ability 1   **Adequate resources and funding are provided for select-ing the software subcontractor and managing the subcon-tract.**

1. Software managers and other individuals are assigned specific responsibilities for managing the subcontract.

2. Tools to support managing the subcontract are made available.

Examples of support tools include:

estimating models,

spreadsheet programs, and

project management and scheduling programs.

Ability 2   **Software managers and other individuals who are in-volved in establishing and managing the software subcon-tract are trained to perform these activities.**

Examples of training include:

preparing and planning for software subcontracting,

evaluating a subcontract bidder's software process capability,

evaluating a subcontract bidder's software estimates and plans,

selecting a subcontractor, and

managing a subcontract.

Ability 3   **Software managers and other individuals who are in-volved in managing the software subcontract receive ori-entation in the technical aspects of the subcontract.**

> Examples of orientation include:
>
> >application domain,
> >
> >software technologies being applied,
> >
> >software tools being used,
> >
> >methodologies being used,
> >
> >standards being used, and
> >
> >procedures being used.

Activities Performed

Activity 1

The work to be subcontracted is defined and planned according to a documented procedure.

This procedure typically specifies that:

1. The software products and activities to be subcontracted are selected based on a balanced assessment of both technical and nontechnical characteristics of the project.

   □ The functions or subsystems to be subcontracted are selected to match the skills and capabilities of potential subcontractors.

   □ The specification of the software products and activities to be subcontracted is determined based on a systematic analysis and appropriate partitioning of the system and software requirements.

2. The specification of the work to be subcontracted and the standards and procedures to be followed are derived from the project's:

   □ statement of work,

   □ system requirements allocated to software,

   □ software requirements,

   □ software development plan, and

   □ software standards and procedures.

3. A subcontract statement of work is:

□ prepared,

□ reviewed,

□ agreed to,

Examples of individuals who review and agree to the subcontract statement of work include:

the project manager,

the project software manager,

the responsible software managers,

the software configuration management manager,

the software quality assurance manager, and

the subcontract manager.

□ revised when necessary, and

□ managed and controlled.

"Managed and controlled" implies that the version of the work product in use at a given time (past or present) is known (i.e., version control) and changes are incorporated in a controlled manner (i.e., change control).

If a greater degree of control than is implied by "managed and controlled" is desired, the work product can be placed under the full discipline of configuration management, as is described in the Software Configuration Management key process area.

Refer to Ability 1 of the Software Project Planning key process area for practices covering typical contents of the statement of work.

---

4. A plan for selecting a subcontractor is prepared concurrent with the subcontract statement of work and is reviewed, as appropriate.

Activity 2 **The software subcontractor is selected, based on an evaluation of the subcontract bidders' ability to perform the work, according to a documented procedure.**

This procedure covers the evaluation of:

1. Proposals submitted for the planned subcontract.
2. Prior performance records on similar work, if available.
3. The geographic locations of the subcontract bidders' organizations relative to the prime contractor.

> Effective management of some subcontracts may require frequent face-to-face interactions.

4. Software engineering and software management capabilities.

> An example of a method to evaluate subcontractors' capabilities is the SEI Software Capability Evaluation method.

5. Staff available to perform the work.
6. Prior experience in similar applications, including software expertise on the subcontractor's software management team.
7. Available resources.

> Examples of resources include:
>
> > facilities,
> >
> > hardware,
> >
> > software, and
> >
> > training.

Activity 3

The contractual agreement between the prime contractor and the software subcontractor is used as the basis for managing the subcontract.

The contractual agreement documents:

1. The terms and conditions.
2. The statement of work.

Refer to Ability 1 of the Software Project Planning key process area for practices covering the typical contents of a statement of work.

3. The requirements for the products to be developed.

4. The list of dependencies between the subcontractor and the prime contractor.

5. The subcontracted products to be delivered to the prime contractor.

Examples of products include:

source code,

software development plan,

simulation environment,

design documentation, and

acceptance test plan.

6. The conditions under which revisions to products are to be submitted.

7. The acceptance procedures and acceptance criteria to be used in evaluating the subcontracted products before they are accepted by the prime contractor.

8. The procedures and evaluation criteria to be used by the prime contractor to monitor and evaluate the subcontractor's performance.

Activity 4   **A documented subcontractor's software development plan is reviewed and approved by the prime contractor.**

1. This software development plan covers (directly or by reference) the appropriate items from the prime contractor's software development plan.

In some cases, the prime contractor's software development plan may include the software development plan for the subcontractor, and no separate subcontractor's software development plan is needed.

> Refer to Activity 7 of the Software Project Planning key process area for practices covering content of the project's software development plan.

Activity 5

A documented and approved subcontractor's software development plan is used for tracking the software activities and communicating status.

Activity 6

Changes to the software subcontractor's statement of work, subcontract terms and conditions, and other commitments are resolved according to a documented procedure.

1. This procedure typically specifies that all affected groups of both the prime contractor and the subcontractor are involved.

Activity 7

The prime contractor's management conducts periodic status/coordination reviews with the software subcontractor's management.

1. The subcontractor is provided with visibility of the needs and desires of the product's customers and end users, as appropriate.

> The end users referred to in these practices are the customer designated end users or representatives of the end users.

2. The subcontractor's technical, cost, staffing, and schedule performance is reviewed against the subcontractor's software development plan.

3. Computer resources designated as critical for the project are reviewed; the subcontractor's contribution to the current estimates are tracked and compared to the estimates for each software component as documented in the subcontractor's software development plan.

4. Critical dependencies and commitments between the subcontractor's software engineering group and other subcontractor groups are addressed.

5. Critical dependencies and commitments between the prime contractor and the subcontractor are addressed.

     ❑ Subcontractor commitments to the prime contractor and prime contractor commitments to the subcontractor are both reviewed.

6. Nonconformance to the subcontract is addressed.

7. Project risks involving the subcontractor's work are addressed.

8. Conflicts and issues not resolvable internally by the subcontractor are addressed.

9. Action items are assigned, reviewed, and tracked to closure.

Activity 8

Periodic technical reviews and interchanges are held with the software subcontractor.

These reviews:

1. Provide the subcontractor with visibility of the customer's and end users' needs and desires, as appropriate.

2. Monitor the subcontractor's technical activities.

3. Verify that the subcontractor's interpretation and implementation of the technical requirements conform to the prime contractor's requirements.

4. Verify that commitments are being met.

5. Verify that technical issues are resolved in a timely manner.

Activity 9

Formal reviews to address the subcontractor's software engineering accomplishments and results are conducted at selected milestones according to a documented procedure.

This procedure typically specifies that:

1. Reviews are preplanned and documented in the statement of work.

2. Reviews address the subcontractor's commitments for, plans for, and status of the software activities.

3. Significant issues, action items, and decisions are identified and documented.

4. Software risks are addressed.

5. The subcontractor's software development plan is refined, as appropriate.

Activity 10

The prime contractor's software quality assurance group monitors the subcontractor's software quality assurance activities according to a documented procedure.

This procedure typically specifies that:

1. The subcontractor's plans, resources, procedures, and standards for software quality assurance are periodically reviewed to ensure they are adequate to monitor the subcontractor's performance.

2. Regular reviews of the subcontractor are conducted to ensure the approved procedures and standards are being followed.

   ◻ The prime contractor's software quality assurance group spot checks the subcontractor's software engineering activities and products.

   ◻ The prime contractor's software quality assurance group audits the subcontractor's software quality assurance records, as appropriate.

3. The subcontractor's records of its software quality assurance activities are periodically audited to assess how well the software quality assurance plans, standards, and procedures are being followed.

Activity 11

The prime contractor's software configuration management group monitors the subcontractor's activities for software configuration management according to a documented procedure.

This procedure typically specifies that:

1. The subcontractor's plans, resources, procedures, and standards for software configuration management are reviewed to ensure they are adequate.

2. The prime contractor and the subcontractor coordinate their activities on matters relating to software configuration management to ensure that the subcontractor's products can be readily integrated or incorporated into the project environment of the prime contractor.

3. The subcontractor's software baseline library is periodically audited to assess how well the standards and procedures for software configuration management

are being followed and how effective they are in managing the software baseline.

Activity 12   **The prime contractor conducts acceptance testing as part of the delivery of the subcontractor's software products according to a documented procedure.**

This procedure typically specifies that:

1. The acceptance procedures and acceptance criteria for each product are defined, reviewed, and approved by both the prime contractor and the subcontractor prior to the test.

2. The results of the acceptance tests are documented.

3. An action plan is established for any software product that does not pass its acceptance test.

Activity 13   **The software subcontractor's performance is evaluated on a periodic basis, and the evaluation is reviewed with the subcontractor.**

> Evaluation of the subcontractor's performance provides an opportunity for the subcontractor to obtain feedback on whether or not it is satisfying its customer's (i.e., the prime contractor's) needs. A mechanism such as performance award fee reviews provides this type of feedback, as opposed to the periodic coordination and technical reviews which occur throughout the project. Documentation of these evaluations also acts as input for future subcontractor selection activities.

Measurement and Analysis

Measurement 1   **Measurements are made and used to determine the status of the activities for managing the software subcontract.**

Examples of measurements include:

costs of the activities for managing the subcontract compared to the plan,

actual delivery dates for subcontracted products compared to the plan, and

actual dates of prime contractor deliveries to the subcontractor compared to the plan.

Verifying Implementation

Verification 1   **The activities for managing the software subcontract are reviewed with senior management on a periodic basis.**

The primary purpose of periodic reviews by senior management is to provide awareness of and insight into software process activities at an appropriate level of abstraction and in a timely manner. The time between reviews should meet the needs of the organization and may be lengthy, as long as adequate mechanisms for exception reporting are available.

Refer to Verification 1 of the Software Project Tracking and Oversight key process area for practices covering the typical content of senior management oversight reviews.

Verification 2   **The activities for managing the software subcontract are reviewed with the project manager on both a periodic and event-driven basis.**

Refer to Verification 2 of the Software Project Tracking and Oversight key process area for practices covering the typical content of project management oversight reviews.

Verification 3 **The software quality assurance group reviews and/or audits the activities and work products for managing the software subcontract and reports the results.**

> Refer to the Software Quality Assurance key process area.

At a minimum, the reviews and/or audits verify:

1. The activities for selecting the subcontractor.

2. The activities for managing the software subcontract.

3. The activities for coordinating configuration management activities of the prime contractor and subcontractor.

4. The conduct of planned reviews with the subcontractor.

5. The conduct of reviews that establish completion of key project milestones or stages for the subcontract.

6. The acceptance process for the subcontractor's software products.

7.5 Software Quality Assurance

a key process area for Level 2: Repeatable

The purpose of Software Quality Assurance is to provide management with appropriate visibility into the process being used by the software project and of the products being built.

Software Quality Assurance involves reviewing and auditing the software products and activities to verify that they comply with the applicable procedures and standards and providing the software project and other appropriate managers with the results of these reviews and audits.

The software quality assurance group works with the software project during its early stages to establish plans, standards, and procedures that will add value to the software project and satisfy the constraints of the project and the organization's policies. By participating in establishing the plans, standards, and procedures, the software quality assurance group helps ensure they fit the project's needs and verifies that they will be usable for performing reviews and audits throughout the software life cycle. The software quality assurance group reviews project activities and audits software work products throughout the life cycle and provides management with visibility as to whether the software project is adhering to its established plans, standards, and procedures.

Compliance issues are first addressed within the software project and resolved there if possible. For issues not resolvable within the software project, the software quality assurance group escalates the issue to an appropriate level of management for resolution.

This key process area covers the practices for the group performing the software quality assurance function. The practices identifying the specific activities and work products that the software quality assurance group reviews and/or audits are generally contained in the Verifying Implementation common feature of the other key process areas.

Goals

Goal 1   **Software quality assurance activities are planned.**

Goal 2   **Adherence of software products and activities to the applicable standards, procedures, and requirements is verified objectively.**

Goal 3   **Affected groups and individuals are informed of software quality assurance activities and results.**

Goal 4   **Noncompliance issues that cannot be resolved within the software project are addressed by senior management.**

Commitment to Perform

Commitment 1   **The project follows a written organizational policy for implementing software quality assurance (SQA).**

This policy typically specifies that:

1. The SQA function is in place on all software projects.
2. The SQA group has a reporting channel to senior management that is independent of:

   □ the project manager,
   □ the project's software engineering group, and
   □ the other software-related groups.

> Examples of other software-related groups include:
>
> software configuration management, and
>
> documentation support.

> Organizations must determine the organizational structure that will support activities that require independence, such as SQA, in the context of their strategic business goals and business environment.
>
> Independence should:
>
> provide the individuals performing the SQA role with the organizational freedom to be the "eyes and ears" of senior management on the software project;
>
> protect the individuals performing the SQA role from performance appraisal by the management of the software project they are reviewing; and
>
> provide senior management with confidence that objective information on the process and products of the software project is being reported.

3. Senior management periodically reviews the SQA activities and results.

Ability to Perform

Ability 1

A group that is responsible for coordinating and implementing SQA for the project (i.e., the SQA group) exists.

> A group is the collection of departments, managers, and individuals who have responsibility for a set of tasks or activities. A group could vary from a single individual assigned part time, to several part-time individuals assigned from different departments, to several individuals dedicated full time. Considerations when implementing a group include assigned tasks or activities, the size of the project, the organizational structure, and the organizational culture. Some groups, such as the software quality assurance group, are focused on project activities, and others, such as the software engineering process group, are focused on organization-wide activities.

Ability 2

Adequate resources and funding are provided for performing the SQA activities.

1. A manager is assigned specific responsibilities for the project's SQA activities.

2. A senior manager, who is knowledgeable in the SQA role and has the authority to take appropriate oversight actions, is designated to receive and act on software noncompliance items.

   □ All managers in the SQA reporting chain to the senior manager are knowledgeable in the SQA role, responsibilities, and authority.

3. Tools to support the SQA activities are made available.

Examples of support tools include:

workstations,

database programs,

spreadsheet programs, and

auditing tools.

Ability 3

Members of the SQA group are trained to perform their SQA activities.

Examples of training include:

software engineering skills and practices;

roles and responsibilities of the software engineering group and other software-related groups;

standards, procedures, and methods for the software project;

application domain of the software project;

SQA objectives, procedures, and methods;

involvement of the SQA group in the software activities;

effective use of SQA methods and tools; and

interpersonal communications.

Ability 4 **The members of the software project receive orientation on the role, responsibilities, authority, and value of the SQA group.**

Activities Performed

Activity 1 **A SQA plan is prepared for the software project according to a documented procedure.**

This procedure typically specifies that:

1. The SQA plan is developed in the early stages of, and in parallel with, the overall project planning.

2. The SQA plan is reviewed by the affected groups and individuals.

Examples of affected groups and individuals include:

the project software manager;

other software managers;

the project manager;

customer SQA representative;

the senior manager to whom the SQA group reports noncompliance issues; and

the software engineering group (including all subgroups, such as software design as well as the software task leaders).

---

3. The SQA plan is managed and controlled.

"Managed and controlled" implies that the version of the work product in use at a given time (past or present) is known (i.e., version control) and changes are incorporated in a controlled manner (i.e., change control).

If a greater degree of control than is implied by "managed and controlled" is desired, the work product can be placed under the full discipline of configuration management, as is described in the Software Configuration Management key process area.

Activity 2   **The SQA group's activities are performed in accordance with the SQA plan.**

The plan covers:

1. Responsibilities and authority of the SQA group.

2. Resource requirements for the SQA group (including staff, tools, and facilities).

3. Schedule and funding of the project's SQA group activities.

4. The SQA group's participation in establishing the software development plan, standards, and procedures for the project.

5. Evaluations to be performed by the SQA group.

> Examples of products and activities to be evaluated include:
>
> operational software and support software,
>
> deliverable and nondeliverable products,
>
> software and nonsoftware products (e.g., documents),
>
> product development and product verification activities (e.g., executing test cases), and
>
> the activities followed in creating the product.

6. Audits and reviews to be conducted by the SQA group.

7. Project standards and procedures to be used as the basis for the SQA group's reviews and audits.

8. Procedures for documenting and tracking noncompliance issues to closure.

> These procedures may be included as part of the plan or may be included via reference to other documents where they are contained.

9. Documentation that the SQA group is required to produce.

10. Method and frequency of providing feedback to the software engineering group and other software-related groups on SQA activities.

Activity 3

The SQA group participates in the preparation and review of the project's software development plan, standards, and procedures.

1. The SQA group provides consultation and review of the plans, standards, and procedures with regard to:

   □ compliance to organizational policy,

   □ compliance to externally imposed standards and requirements (e.g., standards required by the statement of work),

   □ standards that are appropriate for use by the project,

   □ topics that should be addressed in the software development plan, and

   □ other areas as assigned by the project.

2. The SQA group verifies that plans, standards, and procedures are in place and can be used to review and audit the software project.

Activity 4

The SQA group reviews the software engineering activities to verify compliance.

1. The activities are evaluated against the software development plan and the designated software standards and procedures.

Refer to the Verifying Implementation common feature in the other key process areas for practices covering the specific reviews and audits performed by the SQA group.

---

2. Deviations are identified, documented, and tracked to closure.

3. Corrections are verified.

Activity 5

The SQA group audits designated software work products to verify compliance.

1. The deliverable software products are evaluated before they are delivered to the customer.

2. The software work products are evaluated against the designated software standards, procedures, and contractual requirements.

3. Deviations are identified, documented, and tracked to closure.

4. Corrections are verified.

Activity 6   **The SQA group periodically reports the results of its activities to the software engineering group.**

Activity 7   **Deviations identified in the software activities and software work products are documented and handled according to a documented procedure.**

This procedure typically specifies that:

1. Deviations from the software development plan and the designated project standards and procedures are documented and resolved with the appropriate software task leaders, software managers, or project manager, where possible.

2. Deviations from the software development plan and the designated project standards and procedures not resolvable with the software task leaders, software managers, or project manager are documented and presented to the senior manager designated to receive noncompliance items.

3. Noncompliance items presented to the senior manager are periodically reviewed until they are resolved.

4. The documentation of noncompliance items is managed and controlled .

Activity 8   **The SQA group conducts periodic reviews of its activities and findings with the customer's SQA personnel, as appropriate.**

Measurement and Analysis

Measurement 1   **Measurements are made and used to determine the cost and schedule status of the SQA activities.**

> Examples of measurements include:
>
> > completions of milestones for the SQA activities compared to the plan;
> >
> > work completed, effort expended, and funds expended in the SQA activities compared to the plan; and
> >
> > numbers of product audits and activity reviews compared to the plan.

Verifying Implementation

Verification 1

The SQA activities are reviewed with senior management on a periodic basis.

> The primary purpose of periodic reviews by senior management is to provide awareness of and insight into software process activities at an appropriate level of abstraction and in a timely manner. The time between reviews should meet the needs of the organization and may be lengthy, as long as adequate mechanisms for exception reporting are available.

> Refer to Verification 1 of the Software Project Tracking and Oversight key process area for practices covering the typical content of senior management oversight reviews.

Verification 2

The SQA activities are reviewed with the project manager on both a periodic and event-driven basis.

> Refer to Verification 2 of the Software Project Tracking and Oversight key process area for practices covering the typical content of project management oversight reviews.

Verification 3

Experts independent of the SQA group periodically review the activities and software work products of the project's SQA group.

7.6 Software Configuration Management

a key process area for Level 2:   Repeatable

The purpose of Software Configuration Management is to establish and maintain the integrity of the products of the software project throughout the project's software life cycle.

Software Configuration Management involves identifying the configuration of the software (i.e., selected software work products and their descriptions) at given points in time, systematically controlling changes to the configuration, and maintaining the integrity and traceability of the configuration throughout the software life cycle. The work products placed under software configuration management include the software products that are delivered to the customer (e.g., the software requirements document and the code) and the items that are identified with or required to create these software products (e.g., the compiler).

A software baseline library is established containing the software baselines as they are developed. Changes to baselines and the release of software products built from the software baseline library are systematically controlled via the change control and configuration auditing functions of software configuration management.

This key process area covers the practices for performing the software configuration management function. The practices identifying specific configuration items/units are contained in the key process areas that describe the development and maintenance of each configuration item/unit.

Goals

Goal 1   **Software configuration management activities are planned.**

Goal 2   **Selected software work products are identified, controlled, and available.**

Goal 3   **Changes to identified software work products are controlled.**

Goal 4   **Affected groups and individuals are informed of the status and content of software baselines.**

Commitment to Perform

Commitment 1   **The project follows a written organizational policy for implementing software configuration management (SCM).**

This policy typically specifies that:

1. Responsibility for SCM for each project is explicitly assigned.

2. SCM is implemented throughout the project's life cycle.

3. SCM is implemented for externally deliverable software products, designated internal software work products, and designated support tools used inside the project (e.g., compilers).

4. The projects establish or have access to a repository for storing configuration items/units and the associated SCM records.

The contents of this repository are referred to as the "software baseline library" in these practices.

The tools and procedures for accessing this repository are referred to as the "configuration management library system" in these practices.

Work products that are placed under configuration management and treated as a single entity are referred to as configuration items.

Configuration items are typically decomposed into configuration components, and configuration components are typically decomposed into units. In a hardware/software system, all of the software may be considered as a single configuration item, or the software may be decomposed into multiple configuration items. In these practices the term "configuration items/units" is used to refer to the elements under configuration management.

---

5. The software baselines and SCM activities are audited on a periodic basis.

Ability to Perform

Ability 1

A board having the authority for managing the project's software baselines (i.e., a software configuration control board — SCCB) exists or is established.

The SCCB:

1. Authorizes the establishment of software baselines and the identification of configuration items/units.

2. Represents the interests of the project manager and all groups who may be affected by changes to the software baselines.

Examples of affected groups include:

    hardware quality assurance,

    hardware configuration management,

    hardware engineering,

    manufacturing engineering,

    software engineering (including all subgroups, such as software design),

    system engineering,

    system test,

    software quality assurance,

    software configuration management,

    contract management, and

    documentation support.

---

3. Reviews and authorizes changes to the software baselines.

4. Authorizes the creation of products from the software baseline library.

Ability 2

A group that is responsible for coordinating and implementing SCM for the project (i.e., the SCM group) exists.

A group is the collection of departments, managers, and individuals who have responsibility for a set of tasks or activities. A group could vary from a single individual assigned part time, to several part-time individuals assigned from different departments, to several individuals dedicated full time. Considerations when implementing a group include assigned tasks or activities, the size of the project, the organizational structure, and the organizational culture. Some groups, such as the software quality assurance group, are focused on project activities, and others, such as the software engineering process group, are focused on organization-wide activities.

The SCM group coordinates or implements:

1. Creation and management of the project's software baseline library.
2. Development, maintenance, and distribution of the SCM plans, standards, and procedures.
3. The identification of the set of work products to be placed under SCM.

A work product is any artifact from defining, maintaining, or using a software process.

4. Management of the access to the software baseline library.
5. Updates of the software baselines.
6. Creation of products from the software baseline library.
7. Recording of SCM actions.
8. Production and distribution of SCM reports.

Ability 3   **Adequate resources and funding are provided for performing the SCM activities.**

1. A manager is assigned specific responsibilities for SCM.
2. Tools to support the SCM activities are made available.

> Examples of support tools include:
>
> workstations,
>
> database programs, and
>
> configuration management tools.

Ability 4   **Members of the SCM group are trained in the objectives, procedures, and methods for performing their SCM activities.**

> Examples of training include:
>
> SCM standards, procedures, and methods; and
>
> SCM tools.

Ability 5   **Members of the software engineering group and other software-related groups are trained to perform their SCM activities.**

> Examples of other software-related groups include:
>
> software quality assurance, and
>
> documentation support.

> Examples of training include:
>
> the standards, procedures, and methods to be followed for SCM activities performed inside the software engineering group and other software-related groups; and
>
> the role, responsibilities, and authority of the SCM group.

Activities Performed

Activity 1   A SCM plan is prepared for each software project according to a documented procedure.

This procedure typically specifies that:

1. The SCM plan is developed in the early stages of, and in parallel with, the overall project planning.
2. The SCM plan is reviewed by the affected groups.
3. The SCM plan is managed and controlled.

> "Managed and controlled" implies that the version of the work product in use at a given time (past or present) is known (i.e., version control) and changes are incorporated in a controlled manner (i.e., change control).
>
> If a greater degree of control than is implied by "managed and controlled" is desired, the work product can be placed under the full discipline of configuration management, as is described in this key process area.

Activity 2

A documented and approved SCM plan is used as the basis for performing the SCM activities.

The plan covers:

1. The SCM activities to be performed, the schedule of activities, the assigned responsibilities, and the resources required (including staff, tools, and computer facilities).
2. The SCM requirements and activities to be performed by the software engineering group and other software-related groups.

Activity 3

A configuration management library system is established as a repository for the software baselines.

This library system:

1. Supports multiple control levels of SCM.

> Examples of situations leading to multiple levels of control include:
>
> differences in the levels of control needed at different times in the life cycle (e.g., tighter control as product matures),
>
> differences in the levels of control needed for software-only systems vs. systems which include both hardware and software.

2. Provides for the storage and retrieval of configuration items/units.

3. Provides for the sharing and transfer of configuration items/units between the affected groups and between control levels within the library.

4. Helps in the use of product standards for configuration items/units.

5. Provides for the storage and recovery of archive versions of configuration items/units.

6. Helps to ensure correct creation of products from the software baseline library.

7. Provides for the storage, update, and retrieval of SCM records.

8. Supports production of SCM reports.

9. Provides for the maintenance of the library structure and contents.

Examples of library maintenance functions include:

backup/restoring of library files, and

recovery from library errors.

Activity 4   **The software work products to be placed under configuration management are identified.**

1. The configuration items/units are selected based on documented criteria.

Examples of software work products that may be identified as configuration items/units include:

process-related documentation (e.g., plans, standards, or procedures),

software requirements,

software design,

software code units,

software test procedures,

software system build for the software test activity,

> software system build for delivery to the customer or end users,
>
> compilers, and
>
> other support tools.

2. The configuration items/units are assigned unique identifiers.

3. The characteristics of each configuration item/unit are specified.

4. The software baselines to which each configuration item/unit belongs are specified.

5. The point in its development that each configuration item/unit is placed under configuration management is specified.

6. The person responsible for each configuration item/unit (i.e., the owner, from a configuration management point of view) is identified.

Activity 5   **Change requests and problem reports for all configuration items/units are initiated, recorded, reviewed, approved, and tracked according to a documented procedure.**

Activity 6   **Changes to baselines are controlled according to a documented procedure.**

This procedure typically specifies that:

1. Reviews and/or regression tests are performed to ensure that changes have not caused unintended effects on the baseline.

2. Only configuration items/units that are approved by the SCCB are entered into the software baseline library.

3. Configuration items/units are checked in and out in a manner that maintains the correctness and integrity of the software baseline library.

> Examples of check-in/out steps include:
>
> > verifying that the revisions are authorized,
> >
> > creating a change log,
> >
> > maintaining a copy of the changes,
> >
> > updating the software baseline library, and
> >
> > archiving the replaced software baseline.

Activity 7   **Products from the software baseline library are created and their release is controlled according to a documented procedure.**

This procedure typically specifies that:

1. The SCCB authorizes the creation of products from the software baseline library.
2. Products from the software baseline library, for both internal and external use, are built only from configuration items/units in the software baseline library.

Activity 8   **The status of configuration items/units is recorded according to a documented procedure.**

This procedure typically specifies that:

1. The configuration management actions are recorded in sufficient detail so that the content and status of each configuration item/unit are known and previous versions can be recovered.
2. The current status and history (i.e., changes and other actions) of each configuration item/unit are maintained.

Activity 9   **Standard reports documenting the SCM activities and the contents of the software baseline are developed and made available to affected groups and individuals.**

> Examples of reports include:
>
> > SCCB meeting minutes,
> >
> > change request summary and status,
> >
> > trouble report summary and status (including fixes),

> summary of changes made to the software baselines,
>
> revision history of configuration items/units,
>
> software baseline status, and
>
> results of software baseline audits.

Activity 10

Software baseline audits are conducted according to a documented procedure.

This procedure typically specifies that:

1. There is adequate preparation for the audit.

2. The integrity of software baselines is assessed.

3. The structure and facilities of the configuration management library system are reviewed.

4. The completeness and correctness of the software baseline library contents are verified.

5. Compliance with applicable SCM standards and procedures is verified.

6. The results of the audit are reported to the project software manager.

7. Action items from the audit are tracked to closure.

Measurement and Analysis

Measurement 1

Measurements are made and used to determine the status of the SCM activities.

> Examples of measurements include:
>
> number of change requests processed per unit time;
>
> completions of milestones for the SCM activities compared to the plan; and
>
> work completed, effort expended, and funds expended in the SCM activities.

Verifying Implementation

Verification 1

The SCM activities are reviewed with senior management on a periodic basis.

> The primary purpose of periodic reviews by senior management is to provide awareness of and insight into software process activities at an appropriate level of abstraction and in a timely manner. The time between reviews should meet the needs of the organization and may be lengthy, as long as adequate mechanisms for exception reporting are available.

> Refer to Verification 1 of the Software Project Tracking and Oversight key process area for practices covering the typical content of senior management oversight reviews.

Verification 2   **The SCM activities are reviewed with the project manager on both a periodic and event-driven basis.**

> Refer to Verification 2 of the Software Project Tracking and Oversight key process area for practices covering the typical content of project management oversight reviews.

Verification 3   **The SCM group periodically audits software baselines to verify that they conform to the documentation that defines them.**

Verification 4   **The software quality assurance group reviews and/or audits the activities and work products for SCM and reports the results.**

> Refer to the Software Quality Assurance key process area.

At a minimum, the reviews and/or audits verify:

1. Compliance with the SCM standards and procedures by:

□ the SCM group,

□ the SCCB,

□ the software engineering group, and

□ other software-related groups.

2. Occurrence of periodic software baseline audits.

8

The Key Process Areas for Level 3: Defined

The software process for both management and engineering activities is documented, standardized, and integrated into an organization-wide software process. All projects use a documented and approved version of the organization's process for developing and maintaining software.

The key process areas for Level 3 are:

8.1   Organization Process Focus
8.2   Organization Process Definition
8.3   Training Program
8.4   Integrated Software Management
8.5   Software Product Engineering
8.6   Intergroup Coordination
8.7   Peer Reviews

8.1 Organization Process Focus

a key process area for Level 3: Defined

The purpose of Organization Process Focus is to establish the organizational responsibility for software process activities that improve the organization's overall software process capability.

Organization Process Focus involves developing and maintaining an understanding of the organization's and projects' software processes and coordinating the activities to assess, develop, maintain, and improve these processes.

The organization provides the long-term commitments and resources to coordinate the development and maintenance of the software processes across current and future software projects via a group such as a software engineering process group. This group is responsible for the organization's software process activities. It is specifically responsible for the development and maintenance of the organization's standard software process and related process assets (as described in the Organization Process Definition key process area), and it coordinates the process activities with the software projects.

Goals

Goal 1   **Software process development and improvement activities are coordinated across the organization.**

Goal 2   **The strengths and weaknesses of the software processes used are identified relative to a process standard.**

Goal 3   **Organization-level process development and improvement activities are planned.**

Commitment to Perform

Commitment 1   **The organization follows a written organizational policy for coordinating software process development and improvement activities across the organization.**

This policy typically specifies that:

1. A group is established that is responsible for the organization-level software process activities and coordinating these activities with the projects.

2. The software processes used by the projects are assessed periodically to determine their strengths and weaknesses.

3. The software processes used by the projects are appropriately tailored from the organization's standard software process.

> Refer to Activity 1 of the Integrated Software Management key process area for practices covering tailoring of the organization's standard software process.

4. Improvements to, and other useful information on, each project's software process, tools, and methods are available to other projects.

Commitment 2

Senior management sponsors the organization's activities for software process development and improvement.

Senior management:

1. Demonstrates to the organization's staff and managers its commitment to these software process activities.

2. Establishes long-term plans and commitments for funding, staffing, and other resources.

3. Establishes strategies for managing and implementing the activities for process development and improvement.

Commitment 3

Senior management oversees the organization's activities for software process development and improvement.

Senior management:

1. Ensures that the organization's standard software process supports its business goals and strategies.

2. Advises on setting priorities for software process development and improvement.

3. Participates in establishing plans for software process development and improvement.

- ❑ Senior management coordinates software process requirements and issues with higher-level staff and managers.
- ❑ Senior management coordinates with the organization's managers to secure the managers' and staff's support and participation.

Ability to Perform

Ability 1 **A group that is responsible for the organization's software process activities exists.**

> A group is the collection of departments, managers, and individuals who have responsibility for a set of tasks or activities. A group could vary from a single individual assigned part time, to several part-time individuals assigned from different departments, to several individuals dedicated full time. Considerations when implementing a group include assigned tasks or activities, the size of the project, the organizational structure, and the organizational culture. Some groups, such as the software quality assurance group, are focused on project activities, and others, such as the software engineering process group, are focused on organization-wide activities.

1. Where possible, this group is staffed by a core of software technical professionals who are assigned full time to the group, possibly supported by others, on a part-time basis.

> The most common example of this group is a software engineering process group (SEPG).

2. This group is staffed to represent the software engineering discipline and software-related disciplines.

> Examples of software engineering and software-related disciplines include:
>
> > software requirements analysis,
> >
> > software design,
> >
> > coding,
> >
> > software test,
> >
> > software configuration management, and
> >
> > software quality assurance.

Ability 2   **Adequate resources and funding are provided for the organization's software process activities.**

1. Experienced individuals who have expertise in specialized areas are committed to support this group.

> Examples of specialized areas include:
>
> > software reuse,
> >
> > computer-aided software engineering (CASE) technology,
> >
> > measurement, and
> >
> > training course development.

2. Tools to support the organization's software process activities are made available.

> Examples of support tools include:
>
> > statistical analysis tools,
> >
> > desktop publishing tools,
> >
> > database management systems, and
> >
> > process modeling tools.

Ability 3   **Members of the group responsible for the organization's software process activities receive required training to perform these activities.**

> Examples of training include:
>
>   software engineering practices;
>
>   process control techniques;
>
>   organization change management;
>
>   planning, managing, and monitoring the software process; and
>
>   technology transition.

> Refer to the Training Program key process area.

Ability 4   **Members of the software engineering group and other software-related groups receive orientation on the organization's software process activities and their roles in those activities.**

> Refer to the Training Program key process area.

Activities Performed

Activity 1   **The software process is assessed periodically, and action plans are developed to address the assessment findings.**

> Assessments are typically conducted every 1-1/2 to 3 years.
>
> Assessments look at all software processes used in the organization, but may do this by sampling process areas and projects.
>
> An example of a method to assess an organization's software process capability is the SEI Software Process Assessment method.

> The action plan identifies:
>
> which assessment findings will be addressed,
>
> guidelines for implementing the changes to address findings, and
>
> the groups or individuals responsible for implementing the changes.

Activity 2

The organization develops and maintains a plan for its software process development and improvement activities.

This plan:

1. Uses the action plans from the software process assessments and other organization improvement initiatives as primary inputs.

2. Defines the activities to be performed and the schedule for these activities.

3. Specifies the groups and individuals responsible for the activities.

4. Identifies the resources required, including staff and tools.

5. Undergoes peer review when initially released and whenever major revisions are made.

> Refer to the Peer Reviews key process area.

6. Is reviewed and agreed to by the organization's software managers and senior managers.

Activity 3

The organization's and projects' activities for developing and improving their software processes are coordinated at the organization level.

This coordination covers the development and improvement of:

1. The organization's standard software process.

> Refer to Activities 1 and 2 of the Organization Process Definition key process area for practices covering the organization's standard software process.

2. The projects' defined software processes.

> Refer to Activities 1 and 2 of the Integrated Software Management key process area for practices covering the project's defined software process.

Activity 4

The use of the organization's software process database is coordinated at the organizational level.

> The organization's software process database is used to collect information on the software processes and resulting software products of the organization and the projects.

> Refer to Activity 5 of the Organization Process Definition key process area for practices covering the organization's software process database.

Activity 5

New processes, methods, and tools in limited use in the organization are monitored, evaluated, and, where appropriate, transferred to other parts of the organization.

Activity 6

Training for the organization's and projects' software processes is coordinated across the organization.

1. Plans for training on subjects related to the organization's and projects' software processes are prepared.

2. Where appropriate, training may be prepared and conducted by the group responsible for the organization's software process activities (e.g., software engineering process group) or by the training group.

> Refer to the Training Program key process area.

Activity 7
The groups involved in implementing the software processes are informed of the organization's and projects' activities for software process development and improvement.

> Examples of means to inform and involve these people include:
>
> electronic bulletin boards on process,
>
> process advisory boards,
>
> working groups,
>
> information exchange meetings,
>
> surveys,
>
> process improvement teams, and
>
> informal discussions.

Measurement and Analysis

Measurement 1
Measurements are made and used to determine the status of the organization's process development and improvement activities.

> Examples of measurements include:
>
> work completed, effort expended, and funds expended in the organization's activities for process assessment, development, and improvement compared to the plans for these activities; and
>
> results of each software process assessment, compared to the results and recommendations of previous assessments.

Verifying Implementation

Verification 1
The activities for software process development and improvement are reviewed with senior management on a periodic basis.

> The primary purpose of periodic reviews by senior management is to provide awareness of, and insight into, software process activities at an appropriate level of abstraction and in a timely manner. The time between reviews should meet the needs of the organization and may be lengthy, as long as adequate mechanisms for exception reporting are available.

1. Progress and status of the activities to develop and improve the software process are reviewed against the plan.

2. Conflicts and issues not resolved at lower levels are addressed.

3. Action items are assigned, reviewed, and tracked to closure.

4. A summary report from each review is prepared and distributed to the affected groups and individuals.

8.2 Organization Process Definition

a key process area for Level 3: Defined

The purpose of Organization Process Definition is to develop and maintain a usable set of software process assets that improve process performance across the projects and provide a basis for cumulative, long-term benefits to the organization.

Organization Process Definition involves developing and maintaining the organization's standard software process, along with related process assets, such as descriptions of software life cycles, process tailoring guidelines and criteria, the organization's software process database, and a library of software process-related documentation.

These assets may be collected in many ways, depending on the organization's implementation of Organization Process Definition. For example, the descriptions of the software life cycles may be an integral part of the organization's standard software process or parts of the library of software process-related documentation may be stored in the organization's software process database.

The organization's software process assets are available for use in developing, implementing, and maintaining the projects' defined software processes. (The practices related to the development and maintenance of the project's defined software process are described in the Integrated Software Management key process area.)

Goals

Goal 1   **A standard software process for the organization is developed and maintained.**

Goal 2   **Information related to the use of the organization's standard software process by the software projects is collected, reviewed, and made available.**

Commitment to Perform

Commitment 1   **The organization follows a written policy for developing and maintaining a standard software process and related process assets.**

> The organization's software process assets include:
>
> the organization's standard software process,
>
> guidelines and criteria for the projects' tailoring of the organization's standard software process,
>
> descriptions of software life cycles approved for use,
>
> the organization's software process database, and
>
> a library of software process-related documentation previously developed and available for reuse.

This policy typically specifies that:

1. A standard software process is defined for the organization.

> The primary purposes of a standard software process are to maximize the sharing of process assets and experiences across the projects and to provide the ability to define and aggregate a standard set of process measurements from the projects at the organization level.

> The organization's standard software process may contain multiple software processes. Multiple software processes may be needed to address the needs of different applications, life cycles, methodologies, and tools, which the software projects may compose in multiple ways.

2. A project's defined software process is a tailored version of the organization's standard software process.

> Refer to Activity 1 of the Integrated Software Management key process area for practices covering tailoring of the organization's standard software process.

3. The organization's software process assets are maintained.

4. Information collected from the projects is organized and used to improve the organization's standard software process.

> Examples of collected information include:
>
> process and product measurements,
>
> lessons learned, and
>
> other process-related documentation.

Ability to Perform

Ability 1   **Adequate resources and funding are provided for developing and maintaining the organization's standard software process and related process assets.**

1. The development and maintenance of the organization's standard software process and related process assets is performed or coordinated by the group responsible for the organization's software process activities (e.g., software engineering process group).

> Refer to the Organization Process Focus key process area for practices covering the group responsible for the organization's software process activities.

2. Tools to support process development and maintenance are made available.

> Examples of support tools include:
>
>   desktop publishing tools,
>
>   database management systems, and
>
>   process modeling tools.

Ability 2

The individuals who develop and maintain the organization's standard software process and related process assets receive required training to perform these activities.

> Examples of training include:
>
>   software engineering practices and methods,
>
>   process analysis and documentation methods, and
>
>   process modeling.

> Refer to the Training Program key process area.

Activities Performed

Activity 1

The organizations standard software process is developed and maintained according to a documented procedure.

This procedure typically specifies that:

1. The organization's standard software process satisfies the software policies, process standards, and product standards imposed on the organization, as appropriate.

2. The organization's standard software process satisfies the software process and product standards that are

commonly imposed on the organization's projects by their customers, as appropriate.

3. State-of-the-practice software engineering tools and methods are incorporated into the organization's standard software process, as appropriate.

4. The internal process interfaces between the software disciplines are described.

> Examples of software engineering disciplines include:
>
>   software requirements analysis,
>
>   software design,
>
>   coding,
>
>   software testing,
>
>   software configuration management, and
>
>   software quality assurance.

5. The external process interfaces between the software process and the processes of other affected groups are described.

> Examples of other affected groups include:
>
>   system engineering,
>
>   system test,
>
>   contract management, and
>
>   documentation support.

6. Changes proposed for the organization's standard software process are documented, reviewed, and approved by the group responsible for the organization's software process activities (e.g., software engineering process group) before they are incorporated.

> Examples of sources for change include:
>
>   the findings and recommendations of software process assessments,

> results of the project's tailoring of the organization's standard software process,
>
> lessons learned from monitoring the organization's and projects' software process activities,
>
> changes proposed by the organization's staff and managers, and
>
> process and product measurement data that are analyzed and interpreted.

7. Plans for introducing changes to the software process of ongoing projects are defined as appropriate.

8. The description of the organization's standard software process undergoes peer review when initially developed and whenever significant changes or additions are made.

> Refer to the Peer Reviews key process area.

9. The description of the organization's standard software process is placed under configuration management.

> Refer to the Software Configuration Management key process area.

Activity 2

The organization's standard software process is documented according to established organization standards.

These standards typically specify that:

1. The process is decomposed into constituent process elements to the granularity needed to understand and describe the process.

> Each process element covers a well-defined, bounded, closely related set of activities.
>> Examples of process elements include:
>
> software estimating element,
>
> software design element,

> coding element, and
>
> peer review element.
>
> The descriptions of the process elements may be templates to be filled in, fragments to be completed, abstractions to be refined, or complete descriptions to be modified or used unmodified.

2. Each process element is described and addresses:

   □ the required procedures, practices, methods, and technologies;

   □ the applicable process and product standards;

   □ the responsibilities for implementing the process;

   □ the required tools and resources;

   □ inputs;

   □ the software work products produced;

   □ the software work products that should undergo peer review;

   □ the readiness and completion criteria; and

   □ the product and process data to be collected.

3. The relationships of the process elements are described and address:

   □ the ordering,

   □ the interfaces, and

   □ the interdependencies.

> This relationship of the process elements is sometimes referred to as a software process architecture.

Activity 3   **Descriptions of software life cycles that are approved for use by the projects are documented and maintained.**

> Examples of software life cycles include:
>
> waterfall,
>
> overlapping waterfall,

> spiral,
>
> serial build, and
>
> single prototype/overlapping waterfall.

1. The software life cycles are compatible with the organization's standard software process.

2. Changes proposed for the descriptions of software life cycles are documented, reviewed, and approved by the group responsible for the organization's software process activities (e.g., software engineering process group) before they are incorporated.

3. The descriptions of the software life cycles undergo peer review when initially documented and whenever significant changes or additions are made.

> Refer to the Peer Reviews key process area.

4. The descriptions of the software life cycles are managed and controlled.

> "Managed and controlled" implies that the version of the work product in use at a given time (past or present) is known (i.e., version control) and changes are incorporated in a controlled manner (i.e., change control).
>
> If a greater degree of control than is implied by "managed and controlled" is desired, the work product can be placed under the full discipline of configuration management, as is described in the Software Configuration Management key process area.

Activity 4

Guidelines and criteria for the projects' tailoring of the organization's standard software process are developed and maintained.

1. The tailoring guidelines and criteria cover:

   □ selecting and tailoring the software life cycle for the project,

❑ tailoring the organization's standard software process to accommodate the software life cycle and the project's characteristics, and

> Examples of tailoring include:
>
> adapting the process for a new product line or host environment,
>
> customizing the process for a specific project or class of projects, and
>
> elaborating and adding detail to the process so that the resulting project's defined software process can be enacted.

❑ standards for documenting the project's defined software process.

2. Changes proposed for the tailoring guidelines and criteria are documented, reviewed, and approved by the group responsible for the organization's software process activities (e.g., software engineering process group) before they are incorporated.

3. The tailoring guidelines and criteria are managed and controlled.

Activity 5

The organization's software process database is established and maintained.

1. The database is established to collect and make available data on the software processes and resulting software work products.

> Examples of process and work product data include:
>
> estimates of software size, effort, and cost;
>
> actual data on software size, effort, and cost;
>
> productivity data;
>
> quality measurements;
>
> peer review coverage and efficiency;
>
> test coverage and efficiency;
>
> software reliability measures;

> number and severity of defects found in the software requirements; and
>
> number and severity of defects found in the software code.

2. The data entered into the database are reviewed to ensure the integrity of the database contents.

> In addition, the database also contains or references the actual measurement data and related information and data needed to understand and interpret the measurement data and assess it for reasonableness and applicability.

3. The database is managed and controlled.

4. User access to the database contents is controlled to ensure completeness, integrity, and accuracy of the data.

> Access is limited to those who have a need to enter, change, view, analyze, or extract data.
>
> Sensitive data are protected and access to these data is appropriately controlled.

Activity 6

A library of software process-related documentation is established and maintained.

> Examples of software process-related documentation include:
>
> the description of a project's defined software process,
>
> a project's standards,
>
> a project's procedures,
>
> a project's software development plans,
>
> a project's measurement plans, and
>
> a project's process training materials.

1. Candidate documentation items are reviewed, and appropriate items that may be useful in the future are included in the library.

2. The documentation items are catalogued for easy access.

3. Revisions made to documentation items currently in the library are reviewed, and the library contents are updated as appropriate.

4. The library contents are made available for use by the software projects and other software-related groups.

> Examples of software-related groups include:
>
> software quality assurance
>
> software configuration management,
>
> software test, and
>
> documentation support.

5. The use of each documentation item is reviewed periodically, and the results are used to maintain the library contents.

6. The library contents are managed and controlled.

Measurement and Analysis

Measurement 1 **Measurements are made and used to determine the status of the organization's process definition activities.**

> Examples of measurements include:
>
> status of the schedule milestones for process development and maintenance and
>
> costs for the process definition activities.

Verifying Implementation

Verification 1   **The software quality assurance group reviews and/or audits the organization's activities and work products for developing and maintaining the organization's standard software process and related process assets and reports the results.**

> Refer to the Software Quality Assurance key process area.

At a minimum, these reviews and/or audits verify that:

1. The appropriate standards are followed in developing, documenting, and maintaining the organization's standard software process and related process assets.

2. The organization's standard software process and related process assets are controlled and used appropriately.

8.3 Training Program

a key process area for Level 3: Defined

The purpose of the Training Program key process area is to develop the skills and knowledge of individuals so they can perform their roles effectively and efficiently.

Training Program involves first identifying the training needed by the organization, projects, and individuals, then developing or procuring training to address the identified needs.

Each software project evaluates its current and future skill needs and determines how these skills will be obtained. Some skills are effectively and efficiently imparted through informal vehicles (e.g., on-the-job training and informal mentoring), whereas other skills need more formal training vehicles (e.g., classroom training and guided self-study) to be effectively and efficiently imparted. The appropriate vehicles are selected and used.

This key process area covers the practices for the group performing the training function. The practices identifying the specific training topics (i.e., knowledge or skill needed) are contained in the Ability to Perform common feature of the individual key process areas.

Goals

Goal 1   **Training activities are planned.**

Goal 2   **Training for developing the skills and knowledge needed to perform software management and technical roles is provided.**

Goal 3   **Individuals in the software engineering group and software-related groups receive the training necessary to perform their roles.**

Commitment to Perform

Commitment 1   **The organization follows a written policy for meeting its training needs.**

                  This policy typically specifies that:

                  1. The needed skills and knowledge for each software management and technical role are identified.

                  2. Training vehicles for imparting skills and knowledge are identified and approved.

                  > Examples of approved training vehicles include:
                  >
                  > classroom training,
                  >
                  > computer-aided instruction,
                  >
                  > guided self-study,
                  >
                  > formal apprenticeship and mentoring programs, and
                  >
                  > facilitated videos.

                  3. Training is provided to build the skill base of the organization, to fill the specific needs of the projects, and to develop the skills of individuals.

                  4. Training is developed within the organization or obtained from outside the organization when appropriate.

Examples of external sources of training include:

> customer-provided training,
>
> commercially available training courses,
>
> academic programs,
>
> professional conferences, and
>
> seminars.

Ability to Perform

Ability 1

A group responsible for fulfilling the training needs of the organization exists.

The members of the training group may include full-time or part-time instructors drawn from the organization; the members may also be drawn from external sources.

A group is the collection of departments, managers, and individuals who have responsibility for a set of tasks or activities. A group could vary from a single individual assigned part time, to several part-time individuals assigned from different departments, to several individuals dedicated full time. Considerations when implementing a group include assigned tasks or activities, the size of the project, the organizational structure, and the organizational culture. Some groups, such as the software quality assurance group, are focused on project activities, and others, such as the software engineering process group, are focused on organization-wide activities.

Ability 2

Adequate resources and funding are provided for implementing the training program.

Examples of training program elements include:

> the organization's training plan,
>
> training materials,
>
> development or procurement of training,

> conduct of training,
>
> training facilities,
>
> evaluation of training, and
>
> maintenance of training records.

1. A manager is designated to be responsible for implementing the organization's training program.
2. Tools to support the training program activities are made available.

> Examples of support tools include:
>
> workstations,
>
> instructional design tools,
>
> database programs, and
>
> packages for developing presentation materials.

3. Appropriate facilities are made available to conduct training.

> Classroom training facilities should be separated from the students' work environment to eliminate interruptions.
>
> Where appropriate, training is conducted in settings that closely resemble actual performance conditions and includes activities to simulate actual work situations.

Ability 3   **Members of the training group have the necessary skills and knowledge to perform their training activities.**

> Examples of ways to provide these skills and knowledge include:
>
> training in instructional techniques, and
>
> refresher training in the subject matter.

Ability 4   **Software managers receive orientation on the training program.**

Activities Performed

Activity 1   **Each software project develops and maintains a training plan that specifies its training needs.**

The plan covers:

1. The set of skills needed and when those skills are needed.

2. The skills for which training is required and the skills that will be obtained via other vehicles.

> Some skills are effectively and efficiently imparted through informal vehicles (e.g., informal training and presentations, reading books and journals, "chalk talks," brown-bag lunch seminars, on-the-job training, and informal mentoring); while other skills, to be effectively and efficiently imparted, need to be based on more formal training vehicles (e.g., classroom training, computer-aided instructions, guided self-study, facilitated video, and formal apprenticeship and mentoring programs).

3. The training that is required, for whom it is required, and when it is required.

> Refer to the Ability to Perform common feature in all other key process areas for examples of specific training needs.

> Where appropriate, training for individuals is tied to their work responsibilities so that on-the-job activities or other outside experiences will reinforce the training within a reasonable time after the training.

4. How training will be provided.

> Training may be provided by the software project, by the organization's training group, or by an external organization.

> Examples of training appropriately done by the software project include:
>
> > training in specific applications and requirements of the project,
> >
> > training in the project's software architecture, and
> >
> > other training more effectively or efficiently performed at the project level.

Activity 2

The organization's training plan is developed and revised according to a documented procedure.

This procedure typically specifies that:

1. The plan uses the software projects' training needs identified in their training plans.

2. The specific training to be provided is identified based on the skills needed by the organization and when those skills are needed.

3. The organization's training plan is revised, as appropriate, to incorporate changes.

4. The organization's training plan is reviewed by the affected individuals when it is initially released and whenever major revisions are made.

> Examples of affected individuals include:
>
> > senior management,
> >
> > software managers, and
> >
> > managers of software-related groups.

5. The organization's training plan is managed and controlled.

"Managed and controlled" implies that the version of the work product in use at a given time (past or present) is known (i.e., version control) and changes are incorporated in a controlled manner (i.e., change control).

If a greater degree of control than is implied by "managed and controlled" is desired, the work product can be placed under the full discipline of configuration management, as is described in the Software Configuration Management key process area.

6. The organization's training plan is readily available to the affected groups and individuals.

Examples of affected groups and individuals include:

senior management,

the training group,

the managers of software-related groups,

software engineering (including all subgroups, such as software design),

software estimating,

system engineering,

system test,

software quality assurance,

software configuration management,

contract management, and

documentation support.

Activity 3

The training for the organization is performed in accordance with the organization's training plan.

The plan covers:

1. The specific training needed within the organization and when it is needed.

2. The training that will be obtained from external sources and training that will be provided by the training group.

3. The funding and resources (including staff, tools, and facilities) needed to prepare and conduct or procure the training.

4. Standards for instructional materials used in training courses developed by the training group.

5. The schedule for developing and revising the training courses that will be developed by the training group.

6. The schedule for conducting the training, based on the projected need dates and the projected number of students.

7. The procedures for:

   ▫ selecting the individuals who will receive the training,

   ▫ registering and participating in the training,

   ▫ maintaining records of the training provided, and

   ▫ collecting, reviewing, and using training evaluations and other training feedback.

Activity 4   **Training courses prepared at the organization level are developed and maintained according to organization standards.**

These standards require that:

1. A description of each training course is developed.

> Examples of the topics addressed by the description include:
>
> intended audience,
>
> preparation for participating,
>
> training objectives,
>
> length of the training,
>
> lesson plans,
>
> criteria for determining the students' satisfactory completion,
>
> procedures for periodically evaluating the effectiveness of the training, and
>
> special considerations, such as piloting and field testing the training course, needs for refresher training, and opportunities for follow-up training.

2. The materials for the training course are reviewed.

> Examples of individuals who review the training materials include:
>
>> instructional experts,
>>
>> subject matter experts, and
>>
>> representative students from pilot sessions of the training course being reviewed.

3. The materials for the training courses are managed and controlled.

Activity 5

A waiver procedure for required training is established and used to determine whether individuals already possess the knowledge and skills required to perform in their designated roles.

Activity 6

Records of training are maintained.

1. Records are kept of all students who successfully complete each training course or other approved training activity.
2. Records are kept of all students who successfully complete their designated required training.
3. Records of successfully completed training are made available for consideration in assignments of the staff and managers.

Measurement and Analysis

Measurement 1

Measurements are made and used to determine the status of the training program activities.

> Examples of measurements include:
>
>> actual attendance at each training course compared to the projected attendance,
>>
>> progress in providing training courses compared to the organization's and projects' training plans, and
>>
>> number of training waivers approved over time.

Measurement 2   **Measurements are made and used to determine the quality of the training program.**

Examples of measurements include:

results of post-training tests,

reviews of the courses from the students, and

feedback from the software managers.

Verifying Implementation

Verification 1   **The training program activities are reviewed with senior management on a periodic basis.**

The primary purpose of periodic reviews by senior management is to provide awareness of, and insight into, software process activities at an appropriate level of abstraction and in a timely manner. The time between reviews should meet the needs of the organization and may be lengthy, as long as adequate mechanisms for exception reporting are available.

Refer to Verification 1 of the Software Project Tracking and Oversight key process area for practices covering the typical content of senior management oversight reviews.

Verification 2   **The training program is independently evaluated on a periodic basis for consistency with, and relevance to, the organization's needs.**

Verification 3   **The training program activities and work products are reviewed and/or audited and the results are reported.**

At a minimum, the reviews and/or audits verify that:

1. The process for developing and revising the organization's training plan is followed.

2. The process for developing and revising a training course is followed.

3. Training records are properly maintained.

4. Individuals designated as requiring specific training complete that training.

5. The organization's training plan is followed.

8.4 Integrated Software Management

a key process area for Level 3: Defined

The purpose of Integrated Software Management is to integrate the software engineering and management activities into a coherent, defined software process that is tailored from the organization's standard software process and related process assets, which are described in Organization Process Definition.

Integrated Software Management involves developing the project's defined software process and managing the software project using this defined software process. The project's defined software process is tailored from the organization's standard software process to address the specific characteristics of the project.

The software development plan is based on the project's defined software process and describes how the activities of the project's defined software process will be implemented and managed. The management of the software project's size, effort, cost, schedule, staffing, and other resources is tied to the tasks of the project's defined software process.

Since the projects' defined software processes are all tailored from the organization's standard software process, the software projects can share process data and lessons learned.

The basic practices for estimating, planning, and tracking a software project are described in the Software Project Planning and Software Project Tracking and Oversight key process areas. They focus on recognizing problems when they occur and adjusting the plans and/or performance to address the problems. The practices of this key process area build on, and are in addition to, the practices of those two key process areas. The emphasis of Integrated Software Management shifts to anticipating problems and acting to prevent or minimize the effects of these problems.

Goals

Goal 1   **The project's defined software process is a tailored version of the organization's standard software process.**

Goal 2   **The project is planned and managed according to the project's defined software process.**

Commitment to Perform

Commitment 1   **The project follows a written organizational policy requiring that the software project be planned and managed using the organization's standard software process and related process assets.**

> Refer to the Organization Process Definition key process area for practices covering the organization's standard software process and related process assets.

This policy typically specifies that:

1. Each project documents the project's defined software process by tailoring the organization's standard software process.

2. The project's deviations from the organization's standard software process are documented and approved.

3. Each project performs its software activities in accordance with the project's defined software process.

4. Each project collects and stores appropriate project measurement data in the organization's software process database.

> Refer to Activity 5 of the Organization Process Definition key process area for practices covering the organization's software process database.

Ability to Perform

Ability 1   **Adequate resources and funding are provided for managing the software project using the project's defined software process.**

> Refer to Ability 3 of the Software Project Planning key process area and Ability 3 of the Software Project Tracking and Oversight key process area for practices covering resources and funding for software project planning, tracking, and oversight.

Ability 2

The individuals responsible for developing the project's defined software process receive required training in how to tailor the organization's standard software process and use the related process assets.

> Examples of training include:
>
> using the software process database,
>
> using the organization's standard software process, and
>
> using the guidelines and criteria for tailoring the organization's standard software process to meet the needs of the software project.

> Refer to the Training Program key process areas.

Ability 3

The software managers receive required training in managing the technical, administrative, and personnel aspects of the software project based on the project's defined software process.

> Refer to Ability 4 of the Software Project Planning key process area and Ability 4 of the Software Project Tracking and Oversight key process area for practices covering training for software project planning, tracking, and oversight.

> Examples of training include:
>
> methods and procedures for software estimating, planning, and tracking based on the project's defined software process; and

> methods and procedures for identifying, managing, and communicating software risks.

> Refer to the Training Program key process area.

Activities Performed

Activity 1

The project's defined software process is developed by tailoring the organization's standard software process according to a documented procedure.

> Refer to Activity 2 of Organization Process Definition key process area for practices covering the contents of the organization's standard software process.

This procedure typically specifies that:

1. A software life cycle is:
   - selected from among those approved by the organization, to satisfy the project's contractual and operational constraints;

> Refer to Activity 3 of the Organization Process Definition key process area for practices covering approved software life cycles.

   - modified, if necessary, in ways permitted by the organization's tailoring guidelines and criteria; and
   - documented according to the organization's standards.

> Refer to Activity 4 of the Organization Process Definition key process area for practices covering the organization's tailoring guidelines and criteria.

2. The description of the project's defined software process is documented.

> Refer to Activity 2 of the Organization Process Definition key process area for practices covering the expected contents of a process definition.

> The tailoring uses the organization's process assets as appropriate.

3. Tailoring of the organization's standard software process for the project is reviewed by the group responsible for coordinating the organization's software process activities (e.g., software engineering process group) and approved by senior management.

> Refer to Activity 6 of the Organization Process Definition key process area for practices covering the library of software process-related documentation.

  ▫ Waivers for deviations from the organization's standard software process are documented and are reviewed and approved by senior management.

4. Waivers for deviations from contractual software process requirements are documented and are reviewed and approved by senior management and the software project's customer, as appropriate.

5. The description of the project's defined software process is managed and controlled.

> "Managed and controlled" implies that the version of the work product in use at a given time (past or present) is known (i.e., version control) and changes are incorporated in a controlled manner (i.e., change control).
>
> If a greater degree of control than is implied by "managed and controlled" is desired, the work product can be placed under the full discipline of configuration management, as is described in the Software Configuration Management key process area.

Activity 2

Each project's defined software process is revised according to a documented procedure.

This procedure typically specifies that:

1. Changes derived from the following are documented and systematically reviewed:

   □ lessons learned from monitoring the software activities of the organization's projects,

   □ changes proposed by the software project, and

   □ process and work product measurement data.

2. Changes to the project's defined software process are reviewed and approved before they are incorporated.

Examples of individuals who review the changes include:

members of the groups responsible for the organization's software process activities (e.g., software engineering process group),

the software managers, and

the project software manager.

Examples of individuals who approve the changes include:

the project software manager and

the project manager.

Activity 3

The project's software development plan, which describes the use of the project's defined software process, is developed and revised according to a documented procedure.

Refer to Activities 6 and 7 of the Software Project Planning key process area and Activities 1 and 2 of the Software Project Tracking and Oversight key process area for practices covering the software development plan.

Activity 4

The software project is managed in accordance with the project's defined software process.

> Refer to the Software Project Planning and the Software
> Project Tracking and Oversight key process areas for
> basic practices covering managing a software project.

The project's defined software process typically specifies
that:

1. Provisions are made for gathering, analyzing, and reporting measurement data needed to manage the software project.

2. The activities for software estimating, planning, and
   tracking are tied to the key tasks and work products of
   the project's defined software process.

3. Readiness and completion criteria are established,
   documented, and used to authorize initiation and determine completion of key tasks.

4. Documented criteria are defined to indicate when to
   replan the software project.

5. Technical and management lessons learned are documented and stored in the organization's library of
   software process-related documentation.

> Refer to Activity 6 of the Organization Process Definition
> key process area for practices covering the organization's
> library of software process-related documentation.

6. Technical and management lessons learned from
   monitoring the activities of other projects in the organization are systematically reviewed and used to
   estimate, plan, track, and replan the software project.

7. The staffing plan addresses the software project's
   needs for individuals with special skills and application domain knowledge.

8. Training needs are identified and documented to fit the
   specific needs of the software project.

> Refer to Activity 1 of the Training Program key process
> area for practices covering the identification of the pro-
> ject's training needs.

9. The software plans and processes followed in interacting with other groups are adjusted to account for disparities with these groups and for other potential problems.

Examples of disparities and problems include:

  differences in process maturity,

  process incompatibility, and

  various business factors.

Activity 5

The organization's software process database is used for software planning and estimating.

Refer to Activity 5 of the Organization Process Definition key process area for practices covering the organization's software process database.

---

1. The database is used as a source of data to estimate, plan, track, and replan a software project; data for similar software projects are used when possible.

Examples of data contained in the organization's software process database include:

  size of the software work products,

  software effort,

  software cost,

  schedule,

  staffing, and

  technical activities.

---

2. Parameter values used to derive estimates for software size, effort, cost, schedule, and use of critical computer resources are compared to those of other software projects to assess their validity.

- ▢ Similarities and differences to the other projects in terms of application domain and design approach are assessed and recorded.
- ▢ Rationales for similarities and differences between the parameter values are recorded.
- ▢ The reasoning used to judge the credibility of the project's estimates is recorded.

3. The software project provides appropriate software planning data, replanning data, and actual measured data for storage in the organization's software process database.

> Examples of data recorded by the software project include:
>
> the task description,
>
> the assumptions,
>
> the estimates,
>
> the revised estimates,
>
> the actual measured data, and
>
> the associated information needed to reconstruct the estimates, assess their reasonableness, and derive estimates for new work.

Activity 6

The size of the software work products (or size of changes to the software work products) is managed according to a documented procedure.

> Refer to Activity 9 of the Software Project Planning key process area and Activity 5 of the Software Project Tracking and Oversight key process area for basic practices covering planning and tracking size of software work products.

This procedure typically specifies that:

1. A group that is independent of the software engineering group reviews the procedures for estimating the size of the software work products and provides guidance in using historical data from the organization's

software process database to establish credible estimates.

> An example of an independent group is a software estimating group.
>
> An example of a method to evaluate the credibility of software size estimates is a function-by-function comparison to a completed system.

□ The individuals who prepare the size estimates ensure that the procedures and data used in the estimates are appropriate.

□ When the validity of a size estimate is questioned, a team of peers and experts reviews the estimate.

2. A contingency factor is applied to the size estimate for each software element identified as a software risk.

□ The rationale for the contingency is documented.

□ The risks associated with reducing or eliminating the contingency are assessed and documented.

3. Off-the-shelf or reusable software components are identified.

□ Reuse measurements account for the reuse of requirements, design, code, test plan, and test procedures, etc.

□ The effort to modify and incorporate reusable components is factored into the size estimates.

4. Factors which could significantly affect the size of the software work products are identified and monitored closely.

5. A size threshold is established for each managed software element which, when projected to be exceeded, requires action.

Activity 7   **The project's software effort and costs are managed according to a documented procedure.**

> Refer to Activity 10 of the Software Project Planning key process area and Activity 6 of the Software Project Tracking and Oversight key process area for basic practices covering planning and tracking software efforts and costs.

This procedure typically specifies that:

1. Software effort, cost, and staffing profile models, if used, are adapted to the project and use available historical data where appropriate.

2. Referenced productivity and cost data are adjusted to incorporate project variables.

> Examples of project variables include:
>
> the geographic locations of the project's groups and organizations (e.g., subcontractor),
>
> the size and complexity of the system,
>
> the stability of the requirements,
>
> the host environment for development,
>
> the target environment of the system,
>
> the developers' familiarity and experience with the application,
>
> the availability of resources, and
>
> other special constraints.

3. The overall software effort and cost is allocated to individually managed tasks or stages as needed to manage the effort and cost effectively.

4. When the software effort and cost status is reviewed and the estimates are revised, actual expenditures over time and against work completed are compared to the software development plan and used to refine the effort and cost estimates for remaining work.

   □ Parameter values of the models used in estimating software effort and costs are updated whenever major changes are made to the software requirements.

   □ Actual data on project productivity and other new software costs are used where appropriate.

5. An effort and cost threshold is established for each individually managed software task or stage which, when projected to be exceeded, requires action.

Activity 8

The project's critical computer resources are managed according to a documented procedure.

> Refer to Activity 11 of the Software Project Planning key process area and Activity 7 of the Software Project Tracking and Oversight key process area for basic practices covering planning and tracking critical computer resources.

This procedure typically specifies that:

1. Estimates for the project's critical computer resources are derived based on historical experience, simulations, prototyping, or analysis, as appropriate.

   □ Sources and rationale for estimates are documented.

   □ Similarities and differences between the project and the sources for historical data in terms of application domain and design approach are assessed and recorded.

   □ The reasoning used to judge the credibility of the estimates is recorded.

2. The planned computer resources, the system requirements allocated to software, the software requirements, and/or the software design are adjusted to achieve the project's critical computer resource requirements.

3. The available computer resources are allocated to the software components.

4. The available capacity for the critical computer resources provides for a specified reserve capacity when the initial estimates are made.

5. A threshold is established for each critical computer resource which, when projected to be exceeded, requires action.

Activity 9

The critical dependencies and critical paths of the project's software schedule are managed according to a documented procedure.

> Refer to Activity 12 of the Software Project Planning key process area, Activity 8 of the Software Project Tracking and Oversight key process area, and Activity 4 of the Intergroup Coordination key process area for practices covering negotiating and tracking critical dependencies.

This procedure typically specifies that:

1. Milestones, tasks, commitments, critical dependencies, staffing, costs, and reviews are allocated in the schedule consistent with the project's defined software process.

   □ The software schedule identifies specific tasks and milestones whose completion can be objectively determined (i.e., a binary or yes/no determination).

   > Different levels of schedule detail, appropriately tied to each other, are developed to accommodate the needs of different groups and individuals.

2. Critical dependencies are defined, negotiated, and reflected in the software schedule.

   > Critical dependencies include both those within the software engineering group (i.e., between subgroups) and between the software engineering group and other affected groups.

3. Schedule critical paths are defined and reflected in the software schedule.

4. The software project's critical dependencies and schedule critical paths are tracked on a regular basis.

5. Specific documented threshold criteria are established for each critical path which, when projected to be exceeded, require action.

Examples of actions include:

conducting analyses and simulations to tradeoff function, quality, cost, schedule, staffing, and other resources;

allocating contingencies and schedule slack, if available;

evaluating the effects of contemplated actions on all critical paths; and

making decisions visible to the affected groups.

Activity 10

The project's software risks are identified, assessed, documented, and managed according to a documented procedure.

Refer to Activity 13 of the Software Project Planning key process area and Activity 10 of the Software Project Tracking and Oversight key process area for basic practices covering identifying and tracking risk.

Examples of software risks that are to be managed include significant possibilities that the software project could fail to meet its objectives in areas such as:

schedule,

cost,

functionality,

throughput or real-time performance,

reliability or availability, and

use of critical computer resources.

> Examples of activities to manage risks include:
>
> > early identification of high-risk project objectives;
> >
> > identification of events that could introduce or increase risks;
> >
> > prototyping or early implementation of high-risk modules; and
> >
> > close monitoring of key project risk indicators.

This procedure typically specifies that:

1. A software risk management plan is documented and used to identify and manage the software risks.

> Examples of items in a software risk management plan include:
>
> > resources required (including staff and tools);
> >
> > risk management methods (e.g., identification, analysis, prioritization, planning, monitoring, and resolution);
> >
> > list of identified risks (including assessment, prioritization, status, and plans);
> >
> > risk management schedule;
> >
> > responsibilities and authorities;
> >
> > method and frequency of communicating risk status and activities; and
> >
> > measurements.

2. Contingency planning is based on the project's defined software process and is performed throughout the project's software life cycle.

> Examples of areas covered by contingency planning activities include:
>
> > identification of options,
> >
> > impact assessment of options,
> >
> > technical feasibility of options,

> allocation of management reserves, and
>
> decision criteria on when to pursue an option.

3. Alternatives for each software risk are defined, where possible, along with criteria for selecting among the alternatives.

4. The initial release and major revisions to the software risk management plan undergo peer review.

> Refer to the Peer Reviews key process area.

5. The software risk management plan is managed and controlled.

6. Software risks are tracked, reassessed, and replanned at selected project milestones, at designated risk checkpoints, and during the planning of significant changes that affect the software project.

   □ Risk priorities and software risk management plans are reviewed and revised at these reassessment points.

   □ Information obtained from monitoring the risks is used to refine the risk assessments and software risk management plans.

7. The software engineering group and other affected groups and individuals are included in the communications on the software risks, the software risk management plans, and the results of risk mitigation.

> Examples of affected groups and individuals include:
>
>> customer,
>>
>> subcontractors,
>>
>> end users,
>>
>> software estimating,
>>
>> system engineering,
>>
>> system test,

> software quality assurance,
>
> software configuration management,
>
> contract management, and
>
> documentation support.

Activity 11   **Reviews of the software project are periodically performed to determine the actions needed to bring the software project's performance and results in line with the current and projected needs of the business, customer, and end users, as appropriate.**

> Examples of actions include:
>
> accelerating the schedule,
>
> changing the system requirements in response to a change in market opportunities or customer and end user needs, and
>
> terminating the project.

> The end users referred to in these practices are the customer-designated end users or representatives of the end users.

Measurement and Analysis

Measurement 1   **Measurements are made and used to determine the effectiveness of the integrated software management activities.**

> Examples of measurements include:
>
> effort expended over time to manage the software project, compared to the plan;
>
> frequency, causes, and magnitude of replanning effort;
>
> for each identified software risk, the realized adverse impact compared to the estimated loss; and

> the number and magnitude of unanticipated major adverse impacts to the software project, tracked over time.

Verifying Implementation

Verification 1

The activities for managing the software project are reviewed with senior management on a periodic basis.

> Refer to Verification 1 of the Software Project Tracking and Oversight key process area for practices covering the typical content of senior management oversight reviews.

Verification 2

The activities for managing the software project are reviewed with the project manager on both a periodic and event-driven basis.

> Refer to Verification 2 of the Software Project Tracking and Oversight key process area for practices covering the typical content of project management oversight reviews.

Verification 3

The software quality assurance group reviews and/or audits the activities and work products for managing the software project and reports the results.

> Refer to the Software Quality Assurance key process area.

At a minimum, the reviews and/or audits verify:

1. The process for developing and revising the project's defined software process.

2. The process for preparing the project's software development plan and software risk management plan.

3. The processes for managing the project in accordance with the project's defined software process.

4. The processes for collecting and providing appropriate data to the organization's software process database.

5. The process for using the organization's software process database to support the software project's planning, estimating, and tracking activities.

8.5 Software Product Engineering

a key process area for Level 3: Defined

The purpose of Software Product Engineering is to consistently perform a well-defined engineering process that integrates all the software engineering activities to produce correct, consistent software products effectively and efficiently.

Software Product Engineering involves performing the engineering tasks to build and maintain the software using the project's defined software process (which is described in the Integrated Software Management key process area) and appropriate methods and tools.

The software engineering tasks include analyzing the system requirements allocated to software (these system requirements are described in the Requirements Management key process area), developing the software requirements, developing the software architecture, designing the software, implementing the software in the code, integrating the software components, and testing the software to verify that it satisfies the specified requirements (i.e., the system requirements allocated to software and the software requirements).

Documentation needed to perform the software engineering tasks (e.g., software requirements document, software design document, test plan, and test procedures) is developed and reviewed to ensure that each task addresses the results of predecessor tasks and the results produced are appropriate for the subsequent tasks (including the tasks of operating and maintaining the software). When changes are approved, affected software work products, plans, commitments, processes, and activities are revised to reflect the approved changes.

Goals

Goal 1   **The software engineering tasks are defined, integrated, and consistently performed to produce the software.**

Goal 2   **Software work products are kept consistent with each
                            other.**

Commitment to Perform

Commitment 1   **The project follows a written organizational policy for
                            performing the software engineering activities.**

                            This policy typically specifies that:

                            1. The software engineering tasks are performed in ac-
                               cordance with the project's defined software process.

                            > Refer to Activities 1 and 2 of the Integrated Software
                            > Management key process area for practices covering the
                            > project's defined software process.

                            2. Appropriate methods and tools are used to build and
                               maintain the software products.
                            3. The software plans, tasks, and products are traceable
                               to the system requirements allocated to software.

                            > The system requirements allocated to the software are
                            > referred to as "allocated requirements" in these practices.
                            >   Refer to the Requirements Management key process
                            > area for practices covering the system requirements allo-
                            > cated to software.

Ability to Perform

Ability 1   **Adequate resources and funding are provided for per-
                            forming the software engineering tasks.**

                            1. Skilled individuals are available to perform the differ-
                               ent software engineering tasks, including:
                               □ software requirements analysis,
                               □ software design,
                               □ coding,

□ testing, and

□ software maintenance.

2. Tools to support the software engineering tasks are made available.

Examples of general support tools include:

workstations,

database management systems,

on-line help aids,

graphics tools,

interactive documentation tools, and

word processing systems.

Examples of support tools for software requirements analysis include:

requirements tracking tools,

specification tools,

prototyping tools,

modeling tools, and

simulation tools.

Examples of support tools for software design include:

specification tools,

prototyping tools,

simulation tools, and

program design languages.

Examples of support tools for coding include:

editors,

compilers,

cross-reference generators, and

pretty printers.

Examples of support tools for software testing include:

test management tools,

test generators,

test drivers,

test profilers,

symbolic debuggers, and

test coverage analyzers.

Ability 2

Members of the software engineering technical staff receive required training to perform their technical assignments.

The members of the software engineering technical staff should receive training in the application domain.

Examples of training in software requirements analysis include:

principles of analyzing software requirements;

the existing software requirements for any existing software to be maintained;

skills to interview end users and application domain experts in order to establish the software requirements (i.e., requirements elicitation); and

the use of the tools, methods, conventions, and standards selected by the project for analyzing software requirements.

Examples of training in software design include:

design concepts;

the existing design for any existing software to be maintained; and

use of the tools, methods, conventions, and standards selected by the project for designing software.

Examples of training in coding include:

    the selected programming language(s);

    reviewing the existing source code for any existing code to be maintained;

    use of the tools, methods, conventions, and standards selected by the project for programming; and

    unit testing techniques.

Examples of training in software testing and other verification techniques include:

    verification methods (analysis, demonstration, and inspection as well as test);

    test planning;

    use of the tools, methods, conventions, and standards selected by the project for testing and verifying the software;

    criteria for test readiness and completion; and

    measuring test coverage.

Refer to the Training Program key process area.

Ability 3

Members of the software engineering technical staff receive orientation in related software engineering disciplines.

Examples of related software engineering disciplines include:

    software requirements analysis,

    software design,

    coding,

    testing,

    software configuration management, and

    software quality assurance.

> Refer to the Training Program key process area.

Ability 4 | **The project manager and all software managers receive orientation in the technical aspects of the software project.**

> Examples of orientation include:
>
> > software engineering methods and tools,
> >
> > the application domain,
> >
> > deliverable and nondeliverable software and associated work products, and
> >
> > guidelines on how to manage the project using the chosen methods and tools.

> Refer to the Training Program key process area.

Activities Performed

Activity 1 | **Appropriate software engineering methods and tools are integrated into the project's defined software process.**

> Refer to Activities 1 and 2 of the Integrated Software Management key process area for practices covering the project's defined software process.

1. The software engineering tasks are integrated according to the project's defined software process.
2. Methods and tools appropriate for use on the software project are selected.

> Candidate methods and tools are selected based on their applicability to the organization's standards, the project's defined software process, the existing skill base, availability of training, contractual requirements, power, ease of use, and support services.

      □ The rationale for selecting a particular tool or method is documented.

3. Configuration management models appropriate to the software project are selected and used.

> Examples of configuration management models include:
>
>   check-out/check-in models,
>
>   composition models,
>
>   transaction models, and
>
>   change set models.

4. The tools used to develop and maintain the software products are placed under configuration management.

> Refer to the Software Configuration Management key process area.

Activity 2

The software requirements are developed, maintained, documented, and verified by systematically analyzing the allocated requirements according to the project's defined software process.

1. The individuals involved in developing the software requirements review the allocated requirements to ensure that issues affecting the software requirements analysis are identified and resolved.

> Software requirements cover the software functions and performance, the interfaces to both hardware and software, and other system components (e.g., humans).

2. Effective methods for requirements analysis are used to identify and derive the software requirements.

Examples of methods for requirements analysis include:

> functional decomposition,
>
> object-oriented decomposition,
>
> tradeoff studies,
>
> simulations,
>
> modeling,
>
> prototyping, and
>
> scenario generation.

3. The results of the requirements analysis and the rationale for the selected alternative are documented.

4. The software requirements are analyzed to ensure they are feasible and appropriate to implement in software, clearly stated, consistent with each other, testable, and complete (when considered as a set).

   □ Problems with the software requirements are identified and reviewed with the group responsible for the system requirements; appropriate changes are made to the allocated requirements and to the software requirements.

Refer to the Requirements Management key process area.

5. The software requirements are documented.

6. The group responsible for system and acceptance testing of the software analyzes each software requirement to verify it can be tested.

7. The methods for verifying and validating that each software requirement is satisfied are identified and documented.

Examples of verification and validation methods include:

> demonstration,
>
> system testing,
>
> acceptance testing,

analysis, and

inspection.

8. The software requirements document undergoes peer review before it is considered complete.

Refer to the Peer Reviews key process area.

9. The software requirements document is reviewed and approved.

Examples of individuals who review and approve the software requirements document include:

the project manager,

the system engineering manager,

the project software manager, and

the software test manager.

10. The software requirements document is reviewed with the customer and end users, as appropriate.

The end users referred to in these practices are the customer-designated end users or representatives of the end users.

11. The software requirements document is placed under configuration management.

Refer to the Software Configuration Management key process area.

12. The software requirements are appropriately changed whenever the allocated requirements change.

> Refer to the Requirements Management key process area.

Activity 3   **The software design is developed, maintained, documented, and verified, according to the project's defined software process, to accommodate the software requirements and to form the framework for coding.**

> The software design consists of the software architecture and the detailed software design.

1. Design criteria are developed and reviewed.

> Examples of design criteria include:
>
> verifiability,
>
> adherence to design standards,
>
> ease of construction,
>
> simplicity, and
>
> ease of planning.

2. The individuals involved in the software design review the software requirements to ensure that issues affecting the software design are identified and resolved.

3. Application standards are used where appropriate.

> Examples of application standards include:
>
> standards for operating system interfaces,
>
> standards for computer–human interfaces, and
>
> standards for networking interfaces.

4. Effective methods are used to design the software.

Examples of software design methods include:

  prototyping,

  structural models,

  design reuse,

  object-oriented design, and

  essential systems analysis.

5. The software architecture is developed early, within the constraints of the software life cycle and technology being used.

The software architecture establishes the top-level software framework with well-defined internal and external interfaces.

6. The software architecture is reviewed to ensure that architecture issues affecting the software detailed design are identified and resolved.

7. The software detailed design is developed based on the software architecture.

8. The software design (i.e., the software architecture and detailed design) is documented.

   □ The documentation of the software design covers the software components; the internal interfaces between software components; and the software interfaces to other software systems, to hardware, and to other system components (e.g., humans).

9. The software design document undergoes peer review before the design is considered complete.

Refer to the Peer Reviews key process area.

10. The software design document is placed under configuration management.

> Refer to the Software Configuration Management key process area.

11. The software design document is appropriately changed whenever the software requirements change.

Activity 4

The software code is developed, maintained, documented, and verified, according to the project's defined software process, to implement the software requirements and software design.

1. The individuals involved in coding review the software requirements and software design to ensure that issues affecting the coding are identified and resolved.

2. Effective programming methods are used to code the software.

> Examples of programming methods include:
>
>   structured programming and
>   code reuse.

3. The sequence in which code units are developed is based on a plan that accounts for factors such as criticality, difficulty, integration and test issues, and needs of the customer and end users, as appropriate.

4. Each code unit undergoes peer review and is unit tested before the unit is considered complete.

> Refer to the Peer Reviews key process area.

5. The code is placed under configuration management.

> Refer to the Software Configuration Management key process area.

6. The code is appropriately changed whenever the software requirements or software design changes.

Activity 5   **Software testing is performed according to the project's defined software process.**

1.   Testing criteria are developed and reviewed with the customer and the end users, as appropriate.

2.   Effective methods are used to test the software.

3.   The adequacy of testing is determined based on:

   □ the level of testing performed,

Examples of levels of testing include:

   unit testing,

   integration testing,

   system testing, and

   acceptance testing.

   □ the test strategy selected, and

Examples of test strategies include:

   functional (black-box),

   structural (white-box), and

   statistical.

   □ the test coverage to be achieved.

Examples of test coverage approaches include:

   statement coverage,

   path coverage,

   branch coverage, and

   usage profile.

---

4.   For each level of software testing, test readiness criteria are established and used.

> Examples of criteria to determine test readiness include:
>
> > software units have successfully completed a code peer review and unit testing before they enter integration testing,
> >
> > the software has successfully completed integration testing before it enters system testing, and
> >
> > a test readiness review is held before the software enters acceptance testing.

5. Regression testing is performed, as appropriate, at each test level whenever the software being tested or its environment changes.

6. The test plan, test procedures, and test cases undergo peer review before they are considered ready for use.

> Refer to the Peer Reviews key process area.

7. The test plans, test procedures, and test cases are managed and controlled.

> "Managed and controlled" implies that the version of the work product in use at a given time (past or present) must be known and changes must be incorporated in a controlled manner.
>
> If a greater degree of formality than is implied by "managed and controlled" is desired, the work product can be placed under configuration management, as is described in the Software Configuration Management key process area.

8. Test plans, test procedures, and test cases are appropriately changed whenever the allocated requirements, software requirements, software design, or code being tested changes.

Activity 6   **Integration testing of the software is planned and performed according to the project's defined software process.**

1. The plans for integration testing are documented and based on the software development plan.

2. The integration test cases and test procedures are reviewed with the individuals responsible for the software requirements, software design, and system and acceptance testing.

3. Integration testing of the software is performed against the designated version of the software requirements document and the software design document.

Activity 7

System and acceptance testing of the software are planned and performed to demonstrate that the software satisfies its requirements.

> System testing is performed to ensure the software satisfies the software requirements.
>
> Acceptance testing is performed to demonstrate to the customer and end users that the software satisfies the allocated requirements.

1. Resources for testing the software are assigned early enough to provide for adequate test preparation.

> Examples of activities required to prepare for testing include:
>
> preparing testing documentation,
>
> scheduling testing resources,
>
> developing test drivers, and
>
> developing simulators.

2. System and acceptance testing are documented in a test plan, which is reviewed with, and approved by, the customer and end users, as appropriate. The test plan covers:

   □ the overall testing and verification approach;

   □ responsibilities of the developing organization, subcontractors, customer, and end users, as appropriate;

□ test facility, test equipment, and test support requirements; and

□ acceptance criteria.

3. The test cases and test procedures are planned and prepared by a test group that is independent of the software developers.

4. The test cases are documented and are reviewed with, and approved by, the customer and end users, as appropriate, before the testing begins.

5. Testing of the software is performed against baselined software and the baselined documentation of the allocated requirements and the software requirements.

6. Problems identified during testing are documented and tracked to closure.

> Refer to Activity 9 of the Software Project Tracking and Oversight key process area and Activity 5 of the Software Configuration Management key process area for practices covering documenting and tracking problems.

7. Test results are documented and used as the basis for determining whether the software satisfies its requirements.

8. The test results are managed and controlled.

Activity 8

The documentation that will be used to operate and maintain the software is developed and maintained according to the project's defined software process.

1. Appropriate methods and tools are used to develop the documentation.

> Examples of methods and tools include:
>
> word processing,
>
> case studies, and
>
> documentation reuse.

2. Documentation specialists actively participate in planning, developing, and maintaining documentation.

3. Preliminary versions of the documentation are developed and made available early in the software life cycle for the customer, end users, and software maintainers, as appropriate, to review and provide feedback.

Examples of documentation include:

   training documentation,

   on-line documentation,

   the user's manual,

   the operator's manual, and

   the maintenance manual.

---

4. Final versions of the documentation are verified against the software baselined for software acceptance testing.

5. The documentation undergoes peer review.

Refer to the Peer Reviews key process area.

---

6. The documentation is managed and controlled.

7. The final documentation is reviewed and approved by the customer, end users, and software maintainers, as appropriate.

Activity 9

Data on defects identified in peer reviews and testing are collected and analyzed according to the project's defined software process.

Examples of the kinds of data to be collected and analyzed include:

   defect description,

   defect category,   —

   severity of the defect,

   units containing the defect,

units affected by the defect,

activity where the defect was introduced,

peer review or test cases that identified the defect,

description of the scenario being run that identified the defect, and

expected result and actual results that identified the defect.

Activity 10

Consistency is maintained across software products, including the software plans, process descriptions, allocated requirements, software requirements, software design, code, test plans, and test procedures.

1. Software work products are documented, and the documentation is readily available.

2. The software requirements, design, code, and test cases are traced to the source from which they were derived and to the products of the subsequent software engineering activities.

3. The documentation tracing the allocated requirements through the software requirements, design, code, and test cases is managed and controlled.

4. As understanding of the software improves, changes to the software work products, plans, process descriptions, and activities are proposed, analyzed, and incorporated as appropriate.

   □ The project determines the impact of the change before the change is made.

   □ Where changes to the allocated requirements are needed, they are approved and incorporated before any software work products or activities are changed.

   □ Changes to all software products, plans, process descriptions, and activities are coordinated.

   □ Changes are negotiated with and communicated to the affected groups.

> Examples of affected groups include:
>
> > software engineering,
> >
> > software estimating,
> >
> > system test,
> >
> > software quality assurance,
> >
> > software configuration management,
> >
> > contract management, and
> >
> > documentation support.

> ☐ Changes are tracked to completion.

Measurement and Analysis

Measurement 1   **Measurements are made and used to determine the functionality and quality of the software products.**

> Examples of measurements include:
>
> > numbers, types, and severity of defects identified in the software products tracked cumulatively and by stage; and
> >
> > allocated requirements summarized by category (e.g., security, system configuration, performance, and reliability) and traced to the software requirements and system test cases.

Measurement 2   **Measurements are made and used to determine the status of the software product engineering activities.**

> Examples of measurements include:
>
> > status of each allocated requirement throughout the life of the project;
> >
> > problem reports by severity and length of time they are open;
> >
> > change activity for the allocated requirements;
> >
> > effort to analyze proposed changes for each proposed change and cumulative totals;

> number of changes incorporated into the software baseline by category (e.g., interface, security, system configuration, performance, and usability); and
>
> size and cost to implement and test incorporated changes, including initial estimate and actual size and cost.

Verifying Implementation

Verification 1

The activities for software product engineering are reviewed with senior management on a periodic basis.

> Refer to Verification 1 of the Software Project Tracking and Oversight key process area for practices covering the typical content of senior management oversight reviews.

Verification 2

The activities for software product engineering are reviewed with the project manager on both a periodic and event-driven basis.

> Refer to Verification 2 of the Software Project Tracking and Oversight key process area for practices covering the typical content of project management oversight reviews.

Verification 3

The software quality assurance group reviews and/or audits the activities and work products for software product engineering and reports the results.

> Refer to the Software Quality Assurance key process area.

At a minimum, the reviews and/or audits verify that:

1. The software requirements are reviewed to ensure that they are:

   □ complete,

   □ correct,

    ▫ consistent,

    ▫ feasible, and

    ▫ testable.

2. Readiness and completion criteria for each software engineering task are satisfied.

3. Software products comply with the standards and requirements specified for them.

4. Required testing is performed.

5. System and acceptance testing of the software are performed according to documented plans and procedures.

6. Tests satisfy their acceptance criteria, as documented in the software test plan.

7. Tests are satisfactorily completed and recorded.

8. Problems and defects detected are documented, tracked, and addressed.

9. Tracing of the allocated requirements through the software requirements, design, code, and test cases is performed.

10. The documentation used to operate and maintain the software is verified against the software baseline and any applicable allocated requirements before the software product is released to the customer or end users.

8.6 Intergroup Coordination

a key process area for Level 3: Defined

The purpose of Intergroup Coordination is to establish a means for the software engineering group to participate actively with the other engineering groups so the project is better able to satisfy the customer's needs effectively and efficiently.

Intergroup Coordination involves the software engineering group's participation with other project engineering groups to address system-level requirements, objectives, and issues. Representatives of the project's engineering groups participate in establishing the system-level requirements, objectives, and plans by working with the customer and end users, as appropriate. These requirements, objectives, and plans become the basis for all engineering activities.

The technical working interfaces and interactions between groups are planned and managed to ensure the quality and integrity of the entire system. Technical reviews and interchanges are regularly conducted with representatives of the project's engineering groups to ensure that all engineering groups are aware of the status and plans of all the groups and that system and intergroup issues receive appropriate attention.

The software-specific practices related to these engineering tasks are described in the Requirements Management and Software Product Engineering key process areas.

Goals

Goal 1   **The customer's requirements are agreed to by all affected groups.**

Goal 2   **The commitments between the engineering groups are agreed to by the affected groups.**

Goal 3   **The engineering groups identify, track, and resolve intergroup issues.**

Commitment to Perform

Commitment 1   **The project follows a written organizational policy for establishing interdisciplinary engineering teams.**

This policy typically specifies that:

1. The system requirements and project-level objectives for the project are defined and reviewed by all affected groups.

> Examples of affected groups include:
>
> software engineering,
>
> software estimating,
>
> system test,
>
> software quality assurance,
>
> software configuration management,
>
> contract management, and
>
> documentation support.

2. The engineering groups coordinate their plans and activities.

3. Managers are responsible for establishing and maintaining an environment to facilitate interaction, coordination, support, and teamwork between the project's engineering groups, between the project and the customer or end users, as appropriate, and throughout the organization.

The end users referred to in these practices are the customer-designated end users or representatives of the end users.

Ability to Perform

Ability 1   **Adequate resources and funding are provided for coordinating the software engineering activities with other engineering groups.**

Ability 2   **The support tools used by the different engineering groups are compatible to enable effective communication and coordination.**

Examples of support tools that should be compatible include:

    word processing systems,

    database systems,

    graphics tools,

    spreadsheet programs,

    problem tracking packages, and

    library management tools.

Ability 3   **All managers in the organization receive required training in teamwork.**

Examples of training include:

   building teams;

   managing teams;

   establishing, promoting, and facilitating teamwork; and

   group dynamics.

Refer to the Training Program key process area.

Ability 4   **All task leaders in each engineering group receive orientation in the processes, methods, and standards used by the other engineering groups.**

Refer to the Training Program key process area.

Ability 5   **The members of the engineering groups receive orientation in working as a team.**

Refer to the Training Program key process area.

Activities Performed

Activity 1   **The software engineering group and the other engineering groups participate with the customer and end users, as appropriate, to establish the system requirements.**

Specifically, these groups:

1. Define the critical characteristics of the customer's and end users' requirements, as appropriate.

2. Negotiate critical dependencies.

3. Document the acceptance criteria for each product delivered to the customer or end user, as appropriate.

Activity 2   **Representatives of the project's software engineering group work with representatives of the other engineering**

groups to monitor and coordinate technical activities and resolve technical issues.

1. The representatives of these groups monitor and coordinate technical activities by:

   □ coordinating the specification and providing the technical review and approval of the system requirements and system design;

The system requirements and system design are typically the responsibility of the system engineering group, but representatives of the other engineering groups are expected to have significant involvement in these tasks.
The system requirements and system design include:

   the overall system requirements,

   the system configuration (i.e., hardware, software, and other system components),

   the allocation and tracing of requirements to these system components, and

   the definitions of the interfaces between these system components.

   □ providing the project-level technical review and analysis needed to manage and control changes to the system requirements and project-level objectives throughout the project's life cycle;

   □ tracking and reviewing the design and development activities for hardware, software, and other system components; and

   □ assessing, developing recommendations for, and tracking technical risks that involve more than one engineering group.

Refer to Activity 10 of the Integrated Software Management key process area for practices covering risk management.

---

2. The representatives of the groups handle technical issues by:

- □ resolving project-level conflicts and clarifying system requirements and design issues;

- □ developing joint recommendations to resolve problems; and

- □ addressing process issues that span the engineering groups of the project.

Activity 3

A documented plan is used to communicate intergroup commitments and to coordinate and track the work performed.

This plan is:

1. The baseline for:

   - □ the project schedule,

   - □ the contractual and technical aspects of the project, and

   - □ the assignment of responsibilities to the engineering groups.

2. Used to coordinate activities between the different engineering groups.

3. Readily available to the members of all engineering groups.

4. Updated to incorporate all intergroup commitments and changes to these commitments.

5. Updated as the work progresses to reflect progress and plan changes at the project level, particularly when major project milestones are completed and when plans change significantly.

6. Reviewed and agreed to by all engineering groups and the project manager.

Activity 4

Critical dependencies between engineering groups are identified, negotiated, and tracked according to a documented procedure.

Refer to Activity 9 of the Integrated Software Management key process area for practices covering management of critical dependencies.

This procedure typically specifies that:

1. Each critical dependency is explicitly defined, including:

   □ the item to be provided,

   □ who will provide it,

   □ when it will be provided, and

   □ the criteria for acceptance.

2. Critical dependencies are negotiated between the software engineering group and other engineering groups in the project and organization.

3. Need dates and availability dates of critical dependency items are tied to the project schedule and the software schedule.

4. The agreement for each critical dependency is documented, reviewed, and approved by both the receiving group and the group responsible for providing the critical dependency item.

5. Critical dependencies are tracked on a regular basis, and corrective actions are taken when appropriate.

   □ Status and actual or projected completion are compared to the plan used to coordinate intergroup commitments.

   □ Effects of late and early completions are evaluated for impacts on future activities and milestones.

   □ Actual and potential problems are reported to the appropriate managers.

Activity 5

Work products produced as input to other engineering groups are reviewed by representatives of the receiving groups to ensure that the work products meet their needs.

Activity 6

Intergroup issues not resolvable by the individual representatives of the project engineering groups are handled according to a documented procedure.

Examples of intergroup issues include:

incompatible schedules,

inadequate funding,

> technical risks,
>
> system-level design and requirements defects, and
>
> system-level problems.

Activity 7

Representatives of the project engineering groups conduct periodic technical reviews and interchanges.

In these meetings, the participants:

1. Provide visibility of the needs and desires of the customer and end users, as appropriate.
2. Monitor the technical activities of the project.
3. Ensure that the groups' interpretation and implementation of the technical requirements conform to the system requirements.
4. Review the commitments to determine whether they are being met.

> Refer to the Software Project Tracking and Oversight key process area for practices covering reviews.

5. Review the technical risks and other technical issues.

> Refer to Activity 10 of the Integrated Software Management key process area for practices covering risk management.

Measurement and Analysis

Measurement 1

Measurements are made and used to determine the status of the intergroup coordination activities.

> Examples of measurements include:
>
> actual effort and other resources expended by the software engineering group for support to other engineering groups;

> actual effort and other resources expended by the other engineering groups in support of the software engineering group;
>
> actual completion of specific tasks and milestones by the software engineering group to support the activities of other engineering groups; and
>
> actual completion of specific tasks and milestones by the other engineering groups to support the activities of the software engineering group.

Verifying Implementation

Verification 1

The activities for intergroup coordination are reviewed with senior management on a periodic basis.

> Refer to Verification 1 of the Software Project Tracking and Oversight key process area for practices covering the typical content of the senior management oversight reviews.

Verification 2

The activities for intergroup coordination are reviewed with the project manager on both a periodic and event-driven basis.

> Refer to Verification 2 of the Software Project Tracking and Oversight key process area for practices covering the typical content of the project management oversight reviews.

Verification 3

The software quality assurance group reviews and/or audits the activities and work products for intergroup coordination and reports the results.

> Refer to the Software Quality Assurance key process area.

> The software quality assurance responsibilities for this key process area may be subsumed into a quality assurance function that covers all the project engineering groups.

At a minimum, the reviews and/or audits verify:

1. The procedure for identifying, negotiating, and tracking critical dependencies between the project engineering groups.
2. The handling of intergroup issues.

8.7 Peer Reviews

a key process area for Level 3: Defined

The purpose of Peer Reviews is to remove defects from the software work products early and efficiently. An important corollary effect is to develop a better understanding of the software work products and of defects that might be prevented.

Peer Reviews involve a methodical examination of software work products by the producers' peers to identify defects and areas where changes are needed. The specific products that will undergo a peer review are identified in the project's defined software process and scheduled as part of the software project planning activities, as described in Integrated Software Management.

This key process area covers the practices for performing peer reviews. The practices identifying the specific software work products that undergo peer review are contained in the key process areas that describe the development and maintenance of each software work product.

Goals

Goal 1   **Peer review activities are planned.**

Goal 2   **Defects in the software work products are identified and removed.**

Commitment to Perform

Commitment 1   **The project follows a written organizational policy for performing peer reviews.**

This policy typically specifies that:

1. The organization identifies a standard set of software work products that will undergo peer review.

2. Each project identifies the software work products that will undergo peer review.

> Refer to Activity 1 of the Integrated Software Management key process area and Activity 2 of the Organization Process Definition key process area for practices covering the identification of software products that undergo peer review.

> Examples of software work products include:
>
> operational software and support software,
>
> deliverable and nondeliverable software work products,
>
> software (e.g., source code) and nonsoftware work products (e.g., documents), and
>
> process descriptions.

3. Peer reviews are led by trained peer review leaders.

4. Peer reviews focus on the software work product being reviewed and not on the producer.

5. Results of the peer reviews are not used by management to evaluate the performance of individuals.

Ability to Perform

Ability 1   **Adequate resources and funding are provided for performing peer reviews on each software work product to be reviewed.**

Resources and funding are provided to:

1. Prepare and distribute the peer review materials.
2. Lead the peer review.
3. Review the materials.
4. Participate in the peer review and any follow-up reviews required based on the defects identified in the peer review.
5. Monitor the rework of the software work product based on the defects identified in the peer review.
6. Collect and report the data resulting from the peer reviews.

Ability 2   **Peer review leaders receive required training in how to lead peer reviews.**

> Examples of training include:
>
> the objectives, principles, and methods of peer reviews;
>
> planning and organizing a peer review;
>
> evaluating readiness and completion criteria for a peer review;
>
> conducting and facilitating a peer review;
>
> reporting the results of a peer review;
>
> tracking and confirming rework to address the actions identified in a peer review; and
>
> collecting and reporting the data required for the peer reviews.

> Refer to the Training Program key process area.

Ability 3   **Reviewers who participate in peer reviews receive required training in the objectives, principles, and methods of peer reviews.**

> Examples of training include:
>
> types of peer reviews (e.g., reviews of software requirements, software design, code, and software test procedures);

the objectives, principles, and methods of peer reviews;

roles of reviewers; and

estimating the effort for preparing and participating
in peer reviews.

Refer to the Training Program key process area.

Activities Performed

Activity 1

Peer reviews are planned, and the plans are documented.

These plans:

1. Identify the software work products that will undergo
   peer review.

   ▫ The software work products selected include the set
     identified in the organization's standard software
     process.

   Refer to Activity 2 of the Organization Process Definition
   key process area for practices covering the organization's
   standard software process.

2. Specify the schedule of peer reviews.

   For peer reviews that are scheduled to occur in the near
   future, the trained peer review leaders and the other reviewers for each peer review are identified.

Activity 2

**Peer reviews are performed according to a documented
procedure.**

This procedure typically specifies that:

1. Peer reviews are planned and led by trained peer
   review leaders.

2. Review materials are distributed to the reviewers in advance so they can adequately prepare for the peer review.

The review materials should include the relevant inputs to the development of the software work product undergoing peer review.

Examples of relevant input include:

the objectives of the software work product,

the applicable standards,

the relevant requirements for a design module, or

the relevant detailed design for a code module.

---

3. Reviewers have assigned roles in peer reviews.

4. Readiness and completion criteria for the peer reviews are specified and enforced.

   □ Issues in satisfying these criteria are reported to the appropriate managers.

5. Checklists are used to identify criteria for the review of the software work products in a consistent manner.

   □ The checklists are tailored to the specific type of work product and peer review.

Examples of items addressed by tailoring the checklist include:

compliance with standards and procedures,

completeness,

correctness,

rules of construction, and

maintainability.

   □ The checklists are reviewed by the checklist developers' peers and potential users.

6. Actions identified in the peer reviews are tracked until they are resolved.

7. The successful completion of peer reviews, including the rework to address the items identified in the peer reviews, is used as a completion criterion for the associated task.

Activity 3

Data on the conduct and results of the peer reviews are recorded.

Examples of data include:

    identification of the software work product reviewed,

    size of the software work product,

    size and composition of the review team,

    preparation time per reviewer,

    length of the review meeting,

    types and number of defects found and fixed, and

    rework effort.

Measurement and Analysis

Measurement 1

Measurements are made and used to determine the status of the peer review activities.

Examples of measurements include:

    number of peer reviews performed compared to the plan,

    overall effort expended on peer reviews compared to the plan, and

    number of work products reviewed compared to the plan.

Verifying Implementation

Verification 1

The software quality assurance group reviews and/or audits the activities and work products for peer reviews and reports the results.

> Refer to the Software Quality Assurance key process area.

At a minimum, the reviews and/or audits verify that:

1. The planned peer reviews are conducted.
2. The peer review leaders are adequately trained for their roles.
3. The reviewers are properly trained or experienced in their roles.
4. The process for preparing for the peer reviews, conducting the peer reviews, and performing the follow-up actions are followed.
5. Reporting of peer review data is complete, accurate, and timely.

9

The Key Process Areas for Level 4: Managed

Detailed measures of the software process and product quality are collected. Both the software process and products are quantitatively understood and controlled using detailed measured.

The key process areas for Level 4 are:

9.1   Quantitative Process Management
9.2   Software Quality Management

9.1 Quantitative Process Management

a key process area for Level 4: Managed

The purpose of Quantitative Process Management is to control the process performance of the software project quantitatively. Software process performance represents the actual results achieved from following a software process.

Quantitative Process Management involves establishing goals for the performance of the project's defined software process, which is described in the Integrated Software Management key process area, taking measurements of the process performance, analyzing these measurements, and making adjustments to maintain process performance within acceptable limits. When the process performance is stabilized within acceptable limits, the project's defined software process, the associated measurements, and the acceptable limits for the measurements are established as a baseline and used to control process performance quantitatively.

The organization collects process performance data from the software projects and uses these data to characterize the process capability (i.e., the process performance a new project can expect to attain) of the organization's standard software process, which is described in the Organization Process Definition key process area. Process capability describes the range of expected results from following a software process (i.e., the most likely outcomes that are expected from the next software project the organization undertakes). These process capability data are, in turn, used by the software projects to establish and revise their process performance goals and to analyze the performance of the projects' defined software processes.

Goals

Goal 1   **The quantitative process management activities are planned.**

Goal 2   **The process performance of the project's defined software process is controlled quantitatively.**

Goal 3   **The process capability of the organization's standard software process is known in quantitative terms.**

Commitment to Perform

Commitment 1 **The project follows a written organizational policy for measuring and quantitatively controlling the performance of the project's defined software process.**

This policy typically specifies that:

1. Each project implements a documented plan to bring the project's defined software process under quantitative control.

> The term "quantitative control" implies any quantitative or statistically based technique appropriate to analyze a software process, identify special causes of variations in the performance of the software process, and bring the performance of the software process within well-defined limits.
>
> A special cause of variation is some transient circumstance (such as a specific local condition, a single machine, a single individual, or a small group of people performing in an unexpected way) that causes an unexpected, transient change in the process performance.

2. Sensitive data relating to individuals' performances are protected, and access to these data is appropriately controlled.

> Use of measurement data to evaluate individuals will negatively affect the correctness and usefulness of the measurement data that are reported.

Commitment 2 **The organization follows a written policy for analyzing the process capability of the organization's standard software process.**

This policy typically specifies that:

1. The project's measurements of process performance are analyzed to establish and maintain a process capability baseline for the organization's standard software process.

> The process capability baseline includes:
>
> > the description of the organization's standard software process,
> >
> > the standard definitions of the measurements, and
> >
> > the expected range of values for the measurements.

2. The process capability baseline for the organization's standard software process is used by the software projects in establishing their process performance goals.

Ability to Perform

Ability 1

A group that is responsible for coordinating the quantitative process management activities for the organization exists.

> A group is the collection of departments, managers, and individuals who have responsibility for a set of tasks or activities. A group could vary from a single individual assigned part time, to several part-time individuals assigned from different departments, to several individuals dedicated full time. Considerations when implementing a group include assigned tasks or activities, the size of the project, the organizational structure, and the organizational culture. Some groups, such as the software quality assurance group, are focused on project activities, and others, such as the software engineering process group, are focused on organization-wide activities.

1. Either this group is part of the group responsible for the organization's software process activities (e.g., software engineering process group) or its activities are closely coordinated with that group.

Ability 2   **Adequate resources and funding are provided for the quantitative process management activities.**

1. The managers and task leaders of the software engineering groups and other software-related groups perform the project's quantitative process management activities.

Examples of software-related groups include:

software quality assurance,

software configuration management, and

documentation support.

---

2. An organization-wide measurement program exists.

The organization's measurement program includes:

the definition of the organization-wide measurements,

the collection of the organization's measurement data,

the analysis of the organization's measurement data, and

the quantitative measurement goals for the organization.

---

3. Tools to support quantitative process management are made available.

Examples of support tools include:

software source code analyzers,

automated test coverage analyzers,

database systems,

quantitative analysis packages, and

problem-tracking packages.

Ability 3   **Support exists for collecting, recording, and analyzing data for selected process and product measurements.**

> The product data referred to in these practices are product measurements used in analyzing the software process.

Ability 4   **The individuals implementing or supporting quantitative process management receive required training to perform these activities.**

> Examples of training include:
>
>   modeling and analyzing the software process;
>
>   selecting, collecting, and validating process measurement data; and
>
>   applying basic quantitative methods and analysis techniques (e.g., estimation models, Pareto diagrams, and control charts).

> Refer to the Training Program key process area.

Ability 5   **The members of the software engineering group and other software-related groups receive orientation on the goals and value of quantitative process management.**

> Refer to the Training Program key process area.

Activities Performed

Activity 1   **The software project's plan for quantitative process management is developed according to a documented procedure.**

This procedure typically specifies that:

1. The quantitative process management plan is based on:

   □ the organization's strategic goals for product quality, productivity, and product development cycle time;

   □ the organization's measurement program;

   □ the organization's standard software process;

   □ the project's goals for the software product's quality, productivity, and product development cycle time;

   □ the measured performance of other projects' defined software processes; and

   □ the description of the project's defined software process.

2. The plan undergoes peer review.

Refer to the Peer Reviews key process area.

---

3. The plan is reviewed by the group responsible for the organization's software process activities (e.g., the software engineering process group).

4. The plan is managed and controlled .

"Managed and controlled" implies that the version of the work product in use at a given time (past or present) is known (i.e., version control) and changes are incorporated in a controlled manner (i.e., change control).

If a greater degree of formality than is implied by "managed and controlled" is desired, the work product can be placed under the full discipline of configuration management, as is described in the Software Configuration Management key process area.

Activity 2   **The software project's quantitative process management activities are performed in accordance with the project's quantitative process management plan.**

The plan covers:

1. The goals and objectives of the quantitative process management activities.

2. The software tasks or other software activities that will be measured and analyzed.

3. The instrumentation of the project's defined software process.

> The instrumentation is based on the organization's measurement program, the description of the organization's standard software process, and the description of the project's defined software process.

4. The quantitative process management activities to be performed and the schedule for these activities.

> In addition to current organizational and project needs, measurements that may be useful to future efforts are included.

5. The groups and individuals responsible for the quantitative process management activities.

6. The resources required to perform the quantitative process management activities, including staff and tools.

7. The procedures to be followed in performing the quantitative process management activities.

Activity 3   **The strategy for the data collection and the quantitative analyses to be performed are determined based on the project's defined software process.**

The attributes of the project's defined software process that are considered include:

1. The tasks, the activities, and their relationships to each other.

2. The software work products and their relationships to each other and to the project's defined software process.

3. The process control points and data collection points.

Activity 4   **The measurement data used to control the project's defined software process quantitatively are collected according to a documented procedure.**

This procedure typically specifies that:

1. The measurement data collected support the organization's and the software project's measurement goals and objectives.

2. The specific measurement data to be collected, their precise definitions, the intended use and analysis of each measurement, and the process control points at which they will be collected are defined.

Examples of measurement data include:

estimated/planned versus actual data on software size, cost, and schedule;

productivity data;

quality measurements as defined in the software quality plan;

coverage and efficiency of peer reviews;

effectiveness of training;

test coverage and efficiency;

software reliability measures;

number and severity of defects found in the software requirements;

number and severity of defects found in the software code; and

number and rate of closure on action items.

---

3. The measurements are chosen from the entire software life cycle (e.g., both the development and post-development stages).

4. The measurements cover the properties of the key software process activities and major software work products.

5. The measurement data that relate to the organization's standard software process are uniformly collected across the software projects.

6. The measurements to be controlled are a natural result of the software activities where possible.

7. The measurements are selected to support predefined analysis activities.

> In some cases, measurements may be research oriented and should be explicitly designated as such.

8. The validity of the measurement data is independently assessed.

9. The collected measurement data are stored in the organization's software process database, as appropriate.

> Refer to Activity 5 of the Organization Process Definition key process area for practices covering the organization's software process database.

Activity 5

The project's defined software process is analyzed and brought under quantitative control according to a documented procedure.

This procedure typically specifies that:

1. The specific data analysis activities are predefined.

> The description of the data analysis activities covers:
>
> > input data required,
> >
> > tools used,
> >
> > data manipulations performed,
> >
> > information to be derived, and
> >
> > decision criteria used in performing the analysis and deciding what actions to take as a result of the analysis.

> Examples of analysis techniques include:
>
> > Pareto diagrams,
> >
> > control charts,
> >
> > trend diagrams, and
> >
> > scatter diagrams.

2. Measurement data on the process activities throughout the project's defined software process are identified, collected, and analyzed.

3. The selected measurements appropriately characterize the process they represent.

4. The expected values for mean and variance are specified for each measurement.

5. The acceptable limits for each measurement are defined, and the project's process performance baseline is established.

> An example of establishing acceptable limits is to calculate the historical deviation from the mean performance of the process.

6. The actual values of each measurement are compared to the expected values of the mean and variance.

> Examples of comparing actual process performance to defined acceptable limits include:
>
> > comparing the peer review hours spent per thousand lines of source code to upper and lower limits determined by analyzing historical data; and
> >
> > comparing the expansion ratio of software requirements (e.g., number of "shalls") into the number of lines of source code to upper and lower limits determined by analyzing historical data.

7. Adjustments are made to bring the actual process performance in line with the defined acceptable limits, as appropriate.

8. When the project's defined software process is controlled quantitatively, baselines are established for:

   □ the definition of the measurements,

   □ the actual measurement data, and

   □ the acceptable limits for the measurements.

9. The process performance baseline for the software project is managed and controlled.

Activity 6   **Reports documenting the results of the software project's quantitative process management activities are prepared and distributed.**

1. The results of the data analysis are reviewed with those affected by the data before they are reported to anyone else.

2. The software managers, software task leaders, and senior management receive regular reports appropriate for their needs.

3. The software quality assurance group receives regular reports appropriate to its needs.

4. The project manager, senior managers, software managers, and software task leaders receive specialized reports on request.

Activity 7   **The process capability baseline for the organization's standard software process is established and maintained according to a documented procedure.**

This procedure typically specifies that:

1. The project's software process data, as summarized in its process performance baseline, are recorded in the organization's software process database.

Refer to Activity 5 of the Organization Process Definition key process area for practices covering the organization's software process database.

---

2. The process performance baseline for each project's defined software process is incorporated, as appropriate, into the process capability baseline for the organization's standard software process.

3. The process capability baseline for the organization's standard software process is documented.

4. Process capability trends for the organization's standard software process are examined to predict likely problems or opportunities for improvements.

Examples of using capability trends include:

predicting the occurrence of software defects and comparing the predictions to actuals, and

predicting the distribution and characteristics of defects remaining in a product based on the data from peer reviews and/or test.

Examples of areas that are likely sources of defects include:

items for estimating and planning,

activities performed early in the software life cycle such as requirements analysis,

major documentation items,

items and activities that have been prone to defect insertion in the past,

activities for implementing changes and fixing defects, and

labor-intensive activities.

Examples of areas that are likely opportunities for improvement include:

activities that other projects and organizations have successfully automated,

nondeliverable and support items and activities such as training and tools,

> quality-oriented activities such as peer reviews and testing, and
>
> labor-intensive activities.

5. The process capability baseline for the organization's standard software process is managed and controlled.

6. When a software project that is substantially different from past projects is undertaken, a new process performance baseline is established for that project as part of tailoring the organization's standard software process.

> Refer to Activity 1 of the Integrated Software Management key process area for practices covering the project's tailoring of the organization's standard software process.

> Examples of substantial differences include:
>
> new application domains,
>
> use of radically different technologies, and
>
> significant change in the size of the application.

7. Changes to the organization's standard software process are tracked and analyzed to assess their effects on the process capability baseline.

Measurement and Analysis

Measurement 1   **Measurements are made and used to determine the status of the activities for quantitative process management.**

> Examples of measurements include:
>
> the cost over time for the quantitative process management activities, compared to the plan; and

> the accomplishment of schedule milestones for quantitative process management activities, compared to the approved plan (e.g., establishing the process measurements to be used on the project, determining how the process data will be collected, and collecting the process data).

Verifying Implementation

Verification 1

The activities for quantitative process management are reviewed with senior management on a periodic basis.

> Refer to Verification 1 of the Organization Process Focus key process area and Verification 1 of the Software Project Tracking and Oversight key process area for practices covering the typical content of senior management oversight reviews.

Verification 2

The software project's activities for quantitative process management are reviewed with the project manager on both a periodic and event-driven basis.

> Refer to Verification 2 of the Software Project Tracking and Oversight key process area for practices covering the typical content of project management oversight reviews.

Verification 3

The software quality assurance group reviews and/or audits the activities and work products for quantitative process management and reports the results.

> Refer to the Software Quality Assurance key process area.

At a minimum, the reviews and/or audits verify that:

1. The plans for the quantitative process management activities are followed.

2. The procedures for quantitative process management are followed.

3. The collection and analysis of quantitative process management data are performed as required, including verification that:

   □ the needed data exist,

   □ the needed data are collected,

   □ the data collected are needed,

   □ the data collected support the goals and objectives of the organization's measurement program,

   □ the cost of collecting the data is justified by the usefulness of the data,

   □ the data are collected at the correct point in the software life cycle,

   □ the data are accurate and correct,

   □ the data are timely, and

   □ the confidentiality of the data is properly protected.

9.2 Software Quality Management

a key process area for Level 4: Managed

The purpose of Software Quality Management is to develop a quantitative understanding of the quality of the project's software products and achieve specific quality goals.

Software Quality Management involves defining quality goals for the software products, establishing plans to achieve these goals, and monitoring and adjusting the software plans, software work products, activities, and quality goals to satisfy the needs and desires of the customer and end user for high-quality products.

The practices of Software Quality Management build on the practices of the Integrated Software Management and Software Product Engineering key process areas, which establish and implement the project's defined software process, and the Quantitative Process Management key process area, which establishes a quantitative understanding of the ability of the project's defined software process to achieve the desired results.

Quantitative goals are established for the software products based on the needs of the organization, the customer, and the end users. So that these goals may be achieved, the organization establishes strategies and plans, and the project specifically adjusts its defined software process, to accomplish the quality goals.

Goals

Goal 1
The project's software quality management activities are planned.

Goal 2
Measurable goals for software product quality and their priorities are defined.

Goal 3
Actual progress toward achieving the quality goals for the software products is quantified and managed.

Commitment to Perform

Commitment 1
The project follows a written organizational policy for managing software quality.

This policy typically specifies that:

1. The project's software quality management activities support the organization's commitment to improve the quality of the software products.

> Improvements to the process that increase software product quality are a top priority of the organization.
>
> Each new software product release should be measurably better than its predecessor or leading competitor.

2. The project defines and collects the measurements used for software quality management based on the project's defined software process.

3. The project defines the quality goals for the software products and monitors its progress toward them.

4. Responsibilities for software quality management are defined and assigned to the software engineering group and other software-related groups.

Examples of software-related groups include:

software quality assurance,

software configuration management, and

documentation support.

□ Criteria are established to enable the groups to determine their success in achieving the quality goals for the software products.

Ability to Perform

Ability 1

Adequate resources and funding are provided for managing the quality of the software products.

1. Specialty engineers in areas such as safety and reliability are available to help set the software quality goals and review progress toward the goals.

2. Tools to support predicting, measuring, tracking, and analyzing software quality are made available.

Examples of support tools include:

data collection tools,

database systems,

spreadsheet programs,

software life-cycle simulators,

quantitative analysis tools, and

code audit tools.

Ability 2

The individuals implementing and supporting software quality management receive required training to perform their activities.

Examples of training include:

planning quality commitments and goals for the product,

measuring product and process quality, and

> controlling product quality using the defined software process.

> Refer to the Training Program key process area.

Ability 3   **The members of the software engineering group and other software-related groups receive required training in software quality management.**

> Examples of training include:
>
>> understanding the goals and benefits of quantitatively managing product quality,
>>
>> collecting measurement data,
>>
>> understanding the quality measurements for the software process and product, and
>>
>> planning and controlling the quality of the software product.

> Refer to the Training Program key process area.

Activities Performed

Activity 1   **The project's software quality plan is developed and maintained according to a documented procedure.**

This procedure typically specifies that:

1. An understanding of the software quality needs of the organization, customer, and end users is developed, as appropriate.

> The end users referred to in these practices are the customer-designated end users or representatives of the end users.

> Examples of ways to measure the customer's and end users' software quality needs include:
>
> surveys,
>
> focus groups, and
>
> product evaluations by users.

2. The software quality needs and priorities of the organization, customer, and end users are traceable to the system requirements allocated to software and the software quality goals.

> An example of a method to trace these needs and priorities is Quality Function Deployment (QFD).
>
> An example of tracing needs and priorities to the software quality goals for the product is establishing targets for the number of post-delivery defects and performing predictive exercises as the product matures to assess the likelihood of meeting those goals.

> The system requirements allocated to the software are referred to as "allocated requirements" in these practices.
>
> Refer to the Requirements Management key process area for practices covering the system requirements allocated to software.

3. The capability of the project's defined software process to satisfy the software quality goals is assessed and documented.

> Techniques such as Quality Function Deployment and Taguchi's method for robust design can be used to relate the quality goals of a product to the process capability.

4. The software quality plan satisfies the quality plans of the organization, as appropriate.
5. The software quality plan is based on plans for previous or current projects in the organization, as appropriate.

6. The software quality plan is updated at the start of the project, at major project milestones, and whenever the allocated requirements change significantly.

7. The software quality plan undergoes peer review.

Refer to the Peer Reviews key process area.

---

8. The software quality plan is reviewed by affected groups and individuals.

Examples of affected groups and individuals include:

    the customer,

    the end user,

    software engineering (including all subgroups, such as software design),

    software estimating,

    system engineering,

    system test,

    software quality assurance,

    software configuration management,

    contract management, and

    documentation support.

---

9. Senior management reviews the software quality plans.

10. The software quality plan is managed and controlled.

"Managed and controlled" implies that the version of the work product in use at a given time (past or present) is known (i.e., version control) and changes are incorporated in a controlled manner (i.e., change control).

If a greater degree of formality than is implied by "managed and controlled" is desired, the work product can be placed under the full discipline of configuration management, as is described in the Software Configuration Management key process area.

---

11. The software quality plan is available to all affected groups and individuals.

Activity 2   **The project's software quality plan is the basis for the project's activities for software quality management.**

The plan covers:

1. The points in the process where software quality is measured.

2. The high-leverage quality goals for the software products.

> High-leverage quality goals for the software products are those that provide the greatest customer satisfaction at the least cost, or the "must haves" from the customer or end user.

3. The actions that the software project will implement to improve on past quality performance.

4. The activities to measure software product quality.

> Examples of software activities to measure software product quality include:
>
> peer reviews,
>
> prototype development,
>
> product simulation, and
>
> testing.

5. Quality goals for software work products, as appropriate.

> Examples of quality goals for software products that are appropriate to document in the project's software quality plan include:
>
> the characteristics that are planned to be met; and
>
> the critical characteristics that, if not met, would make the product undesirable or not needed by the customers or end users.

6. The actions that will be taken when the software product quality is projected not to meet the quality goals.

Activity 3

The project's quantitative quality goals for the software products are defined, monitored, and revised throughout the software life cycle.

1. Characteristics of product quality that describe how well the software product will perform or how well it can be developed and maintained are identified.

Examples of software product quality characteristics include:

functionality,

reliability,

maintainability, and

usability.

---

2. The measurements used to quantify the characteristics of software product quality are identified.

Examples of activities to identify measurements for software product quality include:

reviewing prior performance data and customer requirements,

developing prototypes,

expressing intermediate software products in formal representations,

using formal software engineering methods, and

conducting tests.

---

3. For each characteristic of software product quality, measurable, numeric values, based on the required and desired values, are selected as quality goals for the product.

> Examples of possible quality goals for the software product's reliability include:
>
> > the mean time between failure as specified in the requirements,
> >
> > the mean time between failure that must be achieved (as determined by analysis and experimentation), and
> >
> > the mean time between failure that is planned to be achieved.

4. Quality goals for the software products are documented in the project's software quality plan.

> Examples of quality goals for software products that are appropriate to document in the project's software quality plan include:
>
> > the characteristics that are planned to be met; and
> >
> > the critical characteristics that, if not met, would make the product undesirable or not needed by the customers or end users.

5. Quality goals for each software life-cycle stage are defined and documented.

> Examples of software life-cycle stages include:
>
> > software requirements,
> >
> > software design,
> >
> > coding, and
> >
> > software test.

> Examples of quality goals related to software life-cycle stages include:
>
> > product defects related to each software life-cycle stage will be reduced from the previous product release by some predetermined percentage, and
> >
> > a predetermined percentage of predicted defects will be found by the end of the test cycle.

6. Quality goals for the software products and software life-cycle stages are revised as understanding of the products and understanding of the organization's, customer's, and end users' needs evolve.

Activity 4

The quality of the project's software products is measured, analyzed, and compared to the products' quantitative quality goals on an event-driven basis.

> Refer to the Quantitative Process Management key process area for practices covering use of measurement data.

1. The software tasks are planned and performed to address the project's software quality goals. At the beginning of a software task, the team performing the task:

   □ reviews the quality goals for the software product,

   □ determines the quality goals applicable to the software task,

   □ identifies its plans to achieve the software quality goals, and

   □ reviews changes made to the process to meet the software quality goals.

> An example of a change is revising a peer review checklist to address defects that have been found to escape peer reviews.

2. The quality of the software work products of each software life-cycle stage is measured.

> Examples of methods to measure the quality of work products include:
>
>   peer reviews,
>
>   simulation, and
>
>   testing.

3. The quality measurements are analyzed and compared to the software quality goals to determine whether the quality goals are satisfied.

4. Appropriate actions, consistent with the software quality plan, are taken to bring the quality measures of the products in line with the software quality goals.

5. When it is determined that the software quality goals conflict (that is, one goal cannot be achieved without compromising another goal), actions are taken to resolve the conflict.

   ❑ The cost for achieving the software quality goals is analyzed.

   ❑ Alternative software quality goals are considered in light of long-term business strategies as well as short-term priorities.

   ❑ The customer and end users participate in quality tradeoff decisions, as appropriate.

   ❑ The software work products and plans are revised, as appropriate, to reflect the results of the tradeoffs.

Activity 5

The software project's quantitative quality goals for the products are allocated appropriately to the subcontractors delivering software products to the project.

> Refer to Activity 1 of the Software Subcontract Management key process area.

Measurement and Analysis

Measurement 1

Measurements are made and used to determine the status of the software quality management activities.

> Examples of measurements include:
>
> the cost of poor quality (based on the known quality measurements to whatever degree of accuracy they can be collected) and
>
> the costs for achieving the quality goals.

Verifying Implementation

Verification 1   **The activities for software quality management are reviewed with senior management on a periodic basis.**

> Refer to Verification 1 of the Software Project Tracking
> and Oversight key process area for practices covering the
> typical content of senior management oversight reviews.

Verification 2   **The activities for software quality management are reviewed with the project manager on both a periodic and
event-driven basis.**

> Refer to Verification 2 of the Software Project Tracking
> and Oversight key process area for practices covering the
> typical content of project management oversight reviews.

Verification 3   **The software quality assurance group reviews and/or audits
the activities and work products for software quality management and reports the results.**

> Refer to the Software Quality Assurance key process area.

At a minimum, the reviews and/or audits verify:

1. The preparation of the project's software quality plan.
2. The process for establishing and tracking the software
   quality goals.

10

The Key Process Areas for Level 5: Optimizing

Continuous process improvement is enabled by quantitative feedback from the process and from testing innovative ideas and technologies.

The key process areas for Level 5 are:

10.1   Defect Prevention
10.2   Technology Change Management
10.3   Process Change Management

10.1 Defect Prevention

a key process area for Level 5: Optimizing

The purpose of Defect Prevention is to identify the cause of defects and prevent them from recurring.

Defect Prevention involves analyzing defects that were encountered in the past and taking specific actions to prevent the occurrence of those types of defects in the future. The defects may have been identified on other projects as well as in earlier stages or tasks of the current project. Defect prevention activities are also one mechanism for spreading lessons learned between projects.

Trends are analyzed to track the types of defects that have been encountered and to identify defects that are likely to recur. Based on an understanding of the project's defined software process and how it is implemented (as described in the Integrated Software Management and Software Product Engineering key process areas), the root causes of the defects and the implications of the defects for future activities are determined.

Both the project and the organization take specific actions to prevent recurrence of the defects. Some of the organizational actions may be handled as described in the Process Change Management key process area.

Goals

Goal 1   **Defect prevention activities are planned.**

Goal 2   **Common causes of defects are sought out and identified.**

Goal 3   **Common causes of defects are prioritized and systematically eliminated.**

Commitment to Perform

Commitment 1   **The organization follows a written policy for defect prevention activities.**

This policy typically specifies that:

1. Long-term plans and commitments are established for funding, staffing, and other resources for defect prevention.

2. The resources needed are allocated for the defect prevention activities.

3. Defect prevention activities are implemented across the organization to improve the software processes and products.

4. The results of the defect prevention activities are reviewed to ensure the effectiveness of those activities.

5. Management and technical actions identified as a result of the defect prevention activities are addressed.

Commitment 2 **The project follows a written organizational policy for defect prevention activities.**

This policy typically specifies that:

1. Defect prevention activities are included in each project's software development plan.

2. The resources needed are allocated for the defect prevention activities.

3. Project management and technical actions identified as a result of the defect prevention activities are addressed.

Ability to Perform

Ability 1 **An organization-level team to coordinate defect prevention activities exists.**

1. This team is either part of the group responsible for the organization's software process activities (e.g., software engineering process group) or its activities are closely coordinated with that group.

Refer to the Organization Process Focus key process area.

Ability 2 **A team to coordinate defect prevention activities for the software project exists.**

1. This team is closely tied to the team responsible for developing and maintaining the project's defined software process.

> Members of the team coordinating defect prevention activities are usually assigned to this team on a part-time basis and have other software engineering activities as their primary responsibility.

> Refer to Activities 1 and 2 of the Integrated Software Management key process area for practices covering developing and maintaining the project's defined software process.

Ability 3

Adequate resources and funding are provided for defect prevention activities at the project and organization levels.

1. Defect prevention activities are planned into each person's responsibilities, as appropriate.

> Examples of defect prevention activities include:
>
>   task kick-off meetings,
>
>   causal analysis meetings,
>
>   reviewing and planning of proposed actions, and
>
>   implementing actions.

2. Management participation in the defect prevention activities is planned.

3. Each software project is represented on the team coordinating defect prevention activities for the organization, as appropriate.

4. Tools to support defect prevention activities are made available.

> Examples of support tools include:
>
>   statistical analysis tools and
>
>   database systems.

Ability 4   **Members of the software engineering group and other software-related groups receive required training to perform their defect prevention activities.**

> Examples of software-related groups include:
>
> > software quality assurance,
> >
> > software configuration management, and
> >
> > documentation support.

> Examples of training include:
>
> > defect prevention methods,
> >
> > conduct of task kick-off meetings,
> >
> > conduct of causal analysis meetings, and
> >
> > statistical methods (e.g., cause/effect diagrams and Pareto analysis).

> Refer to the Training Program key process area.

Activities Performed

Activity 1   **The software project develops and maintains a plan for its defect prevention activities.**

This plan:

1. Identifies the defect prevention activities (e.g., task kick-off and causal analysis meetings) that will be held.
2. Specifies the schedule of defect prevention activities.
3. Covers the assigned responsibilities and resources required, including staff and tools.
4. Undergoes peer review.

> Refer to the Peer Reviews key process area.

Activity 2   **At the beginning of a software task, the members of the team performing the task meet to prepare for the activities of that task and the related defect prevention activities.**

> Kick-off meetings are held to familiarize the members of the team with the details of the implementation of the process, as well as any recent changes to the process.

These kick-off meetings cover:

1. The software process, standards, procedures, methods, and tools applicable to the task, with an emphasis on recent changes.

> Changes may be implemented as an experiment to evaluate a recommendation from a previous causal analysis meeting.

2. The inputs required and available for the task.
3. The outputs to be produced with examples, if available.
4. The methods to be used to evaluate the outputs.
5. The methods to be used to verify adherence to the software process.
6. A list of errors that are commonly made or introduced during the current stage and recommended preventive actions for these errors.
7. The team assignments.
8. The task schedule.
9. The software product quality goals for the task and software project.

> Refer to the Software Quality Management key process area.

Activity 3   **Causal analysis meetings are conducted according to a documented procedure.**

This procedure typically specifies that:

1. Each team that performs a software task conducts causal analysis meetings.

   □ A causal analysis meeting is conducted shortly after the task is completed.

   □ Meetings are conducted during the software task if and when the number of defects uncovered warrants the additional meetings.

   □ Periodic causal analysis meetings are conducted after software products are released to the customer, as appropriate.

   □ For software tasks of long duration, periodic in-process defect prevention meetings are conducted, as appropriate.

   An example of a long-duration task is a level-of-effort, customer-support task.
   ---

2. The meetings are led by a person trained in conducting causal analysis meetings.

3. Defects are identified and analyzed to determine their root causes.

   An example of a method to determine root causes is cause/effect diagrams.
   ---

4. The defects are assigned to categories of root causes.

   Examples of defect root cause categories include:

       inadequate training,

       breakdown in communications,

       unidentified details of the problem, and

       mistakes in manual procedures (e.g., typing).
   ---

5. Proposed actions to prevent the future occurrence of identified defects and similar defects are developed and documented.

Examples of proposed actions include modifications to:

the process,

training,

tools,

methods,

communications, and

software work products.

---

6. Common causes of defects are identified and documented.

Examples of common causes include:

frequent errors made in invoking a certain system function, and

frequent errors made in a related group of software units.

---

7. The results of the meeting are recorded for use by the organization and other projects.

Activity 4   **Each of the teams assigned to coordinate defect prevention activities meets on a periodic basis to review and coordinate implementation of action proposals from the causal analysis meetings.**

The teams involved may be at the organization or project level.

The teams:

1. Review the output from the causal analysis meetings and select action proposals that will be addressed.

2. Review action proposals that have been assigned to them by other teams coordinating defect prevention activities in the organization and select action proposals that will be addressed.

3. Review actions taken by the other teams in the organization to assess whether these actions can be applied to their activities and processes.

4. Perform a preliminary analysis of the action proposals and set their priorities.

Priority is usually nonrigorous and is based on an understanding of:

the causes of defects,

the implications of not addressing the defects,

the cost to implement process improvements to prevent the defects, and

the expected impact on software quality.

An example of a technique used to set priorities for the action proposals is Pareto analysis.

---

5. Reassign action proposals to teams at another level in the organization, as appropriate.

6. Document their rationale for decisions and provide the decision and the rationale to the submitters of the action proposals.

7. Assign responsibility for implementing the action items resulting from the action proposals.

   ▫ Implementation of the action items includes making immediate changes to the activities that are within the purview of the team and arranging for other changes.

   ▫ Members of the team usually implement the action items, but, in some cases, the team can arrange for someone else to implement an action item.

8. Review results of defect prevention experiments and take actions to incorporate the results of successful experiments into the rest of the project or organization, as appropriate.

Examples of defect prevention experiments include:

> using a temporarily modified process, and
> using a new tool.

---

9. Track the status of the action proposals and action items.

10. Document software process improvement proposals for the organization's standard software process and the project's defined software processes as appropriate.

The submitters of the action proposal are designated as the submitters of the software process improvement proposals.

Refer to Activity 5 of the Process Change Management key process area for practices covering handling of software process improvement proposals.

---

11. Review and verify completed action items before they are closed.

12. Ensure that significant efforts and successes in preventing defects are recognized.

Activity 5 **Defect prevention data are documented and tracked across the teams coordinating defect prevention activities.**

1. Action proposals identified in causal analysis meetings are documented.

Examples of data that are in the description of an action proposal include:

    originator of the action proposal,

    description of the defect,

    description of the defect cause,

    defect cause category,

    stage when the defect was injected,

    stage when the defect was identified,

    description of the action proposal, and

    action proposal category.

---

2. Action items resulting from action proposals are documented.

Examples of data that are in the description of an action item include:

    the person responsible for implementing it,

    a description of the areas affected by it,

    the individuals who are to be kept informed of its status,

    the next date its status will be reviewed,

    the rationale for key decisions,

    a description of implementation actions,

    the time and cost for identifying the defect and correcting it, and

    the estimated cost of not fixing the defect.

---

3. The defect prevention data are managed and controlled.

> "Managed and controlled" implies that the version of the work product in use at a given time (past or present) is known (i.e., version control) and changes are incorporated in a controlled manner (i.e., change control).
>
> If a greater degree of control than is implied by "managed and controlled" is desired, the work product can be placed under the full discipline of configuration management, as is described in the Software Configuration Management key process area.

Activity 6

Revisions to the organization's standard software process resulting from defect prevention actions are incorporated according to a documented procedure.

> Refer to Activity 1 of the Organization Process Definition key process area for practices covering the organization's standard software process.

Activity 7

Revisions to the project's defined software process resulting from defect prevention actions are incorporated according to a documented procedure.

> Refer to Activity 2 of the Integrated Software Management key process area for practices covering the project's defined software process.

Activity 8

Members of the software engineering group and software-related groups receive feedback on the status and results of the organization's and project's defect prevention activities on a periodic basis.

The feedback provides:

1. A summary of the major defect categories.

2. The frequency distribution of defects in the major defect categories.

3. Significant innovations and actions taken to address the major defect categories.

4. A summary status of the action proposals and action items.

> Examples of means to provide this feedback include:
>
> electronic bulletin boards,
>
> newsletters, and
>
> information flow meetings.

Measurement and Analysis

Measurement 1   **Measurements are made and used to determine the status of the defect prevention activities.**

> Examples of measurements include:
>
> the costs of defect prevention activities (e.g., holding causal analysis meetings and implementing action items), cumulatively;
>
> the time and cost for identifying the defects and correcting them, compared to the estimated cost of not correcting the defects;
>
> profiles measuring the number of action items proposed, open, and completed;
>
> the number of defects injected in each stage, cumulatively, and overreleases of similar products; and
>
> the number of defects.

Verifying Implementation

Verification 1   **The organization's activities for defect prevention are reviewed with senior management on a periodic basis.**

> The primary purpose of periodic reviews by senior management is to provide awareness of, and insight into, software process activities at an appropriate level of abstraction and in a timely manner. The time between reviews should meet the needs of the organization and may be lengthy, as long as adequate mechanisms for exception reporting are available.

These reviews cover:

1. A summary of the major defect categories and the frequency distribution of defects in these categories.

2. A summary of the major action categories and the frequency distribution of actions in these categories.

3. Significant actions taken to address the major defect categories.

4. A summary status of the proposed, open, and completed action items.

5. A summary of the effectiveness of and savings attributable to the defect prevention activities.

6. The actual cost of completed defect prevention activities and the projected cost of planned defect prevention activities.

Verification 2 **The software project's activities for defect prevention are reviewed with the project manager on both a periodic and event-driven basis.**

> Refer to Verification 2 of the Software Project Tracking and Oversight key process area for practices covering the typical content of project management oversight reviews.

Verification 3 **The software quality assurance group reviews and/or audits the activities and work products for defect prevention and reports the results.**

> Refer to the Software Quality Assurance key process area.

At a minimum, the reviews and/or audits verify that:

1. The software engineering managers and technical staff are trained for their defect prevention roles.

2. The task kick-off meetings and causal analysis meetings are properly conducted.

3. The process for reviewing action proposals and implementing action items is followed.

10.2 Technology Change Management

a key process area for Level 5: Optimizing

The purpose of Technology Change Management is to identify new technologies (i.e., tools, methods, and processes) and transition them into the organization in an orderly manner.

Technology Change Management involves identifying, selecting, and evaluating new technologies and incorporating effective technologies into the organization. The objective is to improve software quality, increase productivity, and decrease the cycle time for product development.

The organization establishes a group (such as a software engineering process group or a technology support group) that works with the software projects to introduce and evaluate new technologies and manage changes to existing technologies. Particular emphasis is placed on technology changes that are likely to improve the capability of the organization's standard software process (as described in the Organization Process Definition key process area).

By maintaining an awareness of software-related technology innovations and systematically evaluating and experimenting with them, the organization selects appropriate technologies to improve the quality of its software and the productivity of its software activities. Pilot efforts are performed to assess new and unproven technologies before they are incorporated into normal practice. With appropriate sponsorship of the organization's management, the selected technologies are incorporated into the organization's standard software process and current projects, as appropriate.

Changes to the organization's standard software process (as described in the Organization Process Definition key process area) and the projects' defined software processes (as described in the Integrated Software Management key process area) resulting from these technology changes are handled as described in the Process Change Management key process area.

Goals

Goal 1   **Incorporation of technology changes is planned.**

Goal 2   **New technologies are evaluated to determine their effect on quality and productivity.**

Goal 3   **Appropriate new technologies are transferred into normal practice across the organization.**

Commitment to Perform

Commitment 1   **The organization follows a written policy for improving its technology capability.**

This policy typically specifies that:

1. Objectives for technology change management are established and documented.
2. A documented plan addresses the objectives for technology change management.

Commitment 2   **Senior management sponsors the organization's activities for technology change management.**

Senior management:

1. Helps to define a strategy that addresses the organization's goals for product quality, productivity, and cycle time for product development.
2. Helps to define a strategy that addresses the customer's and end users' needs and desires, as appropriate.

> The end users referred to in these practices are the customer-designated end users or representatives of the end users.

3. Coordinates with the organization's managers in defining their goals and approaches for accomplishing the organization's strategy.
4. Makes a commitment to the effort for technology change management that is visible throughout the organization.
5. Establishes long-term plans and commitments for funding, staffing, and other resources.

Commitment 3   **Senior management oversees the organization's technology change management activities.**

Senior management:

1. Helps to establish policies for technology change management and reviews and approves these policies.
2. Allocates resources for technology change management activities.

3. Helps relate organizational strategies and objectives to strategies for technology change management.

4. Participates in establishing the plans for technology change management.

  □ Senior management coordinates requirements and issues for technology change management at all appropriate levels of the organization.

  □ Senior management coordinates with the organization's managers to secure the managers' and staff's support and participation.

Ability to Perform

Ability 1   **A group responsible for the organization's technology change management activities exists.**

> A group is the collection of departments, managers, and individuals who have responsibility for a set of tasks or activities. A group could vary from a single individual assigned part time, to several part-time individuals assigned from different departments, to several individuals dedicated full time. Considerations when implementing a group include assigned tasks or activities, the size of the project, the organizational structure, and the organizational culture. Some groups, such as the software quality assurance group, are focused on project activities, and others, such as the software engineering process group, are focused on organization-wide activities.

1. The group is either part of the group responsible for the organization's software process activities (e.g., software engineering process group) or its activities are closely coordinated with that group.

2. The group coordinates and helps to:

  □ explore potential areas for applying new technology;

  □ select and plan for new technologies;

  □ acquire, install, and customize new technologies;

> □ communicate and coordinate with related research and development activities within the organization; and
>
> □ communicate with the technology suppliers on problems and enhancements.

Ability 2   **Adequate resources and funding are provided to establish and staff a group responsible for the organization's technology change management activities.**

1. Experienced staff members with expertise in specialized areas are available to this group to help in evaluating, planning, and supporting initiatives for technology change management.

> Examples of specialized areas include:
>
> workstations,
>
> computer hardware,
>
> software reuse,
>
> computer-aided software engineering (CASE) technology,
>
> software measurement,
>
> formal methods, and
>
> programming languages.

2. Tools to support technology change management are made available.

> Examples of support tools include:
>
> workstations,
>
> database programs, and
>
> subscriptions to on-line technology databases.

Ability 3   **Support exists for collecting and analyzing data needed to evaluate technology changes.**

This support includes the ability to:

1. Record selected process and product data automatically.
2. Support data analysis.
3. Display selected data.

> The results of data analysis are presented in formats that appropriately convey the information content, e.g., graphical displays.

Ability 4

Appropriate data on the software processes and software work products are available to support analyses performed to evaluate and select technology changes.

> Examples of process and product data include:
>
> resource expenditures and productivity by project, process stage, tools and methods used, program category, degree of program modification, etc.;
>
> schedule time by project, process stage of each project, program category, program size, degree of program modification, etc.;
>
> peer-review data, including defect data and review efficiencies;
>
> defect data showing stage introduced, stage removed, type, cause, severity, and time and effort to fix;
>
> change activity, including amount of code produced, amount of documentation produced, etc.;
>
> data on the activities to fix defects, including the identification of the defects, the product version where the defect fix was implemented, and identification of defects introduced in implementing each defect fix; and
>
> density of defects by project, product type, specific product, and specific subproduct (e.g., program modules).

Ability 5

Members of the group responsible for the organization's technology change management activities receive required training to perform these activities.

> Examples of training include:
>
>> the organization's standard software process,
>>
>> technology transfer and change management,
>>
>> software process improvement,
>>
>> tools and methods used by the organization,
>>
>> analytical and support facilities available to the organization, and
>>
>> principles of statistical quality control.

> Refer to the Training Program key process area.

Activities Performed

Activity 1

The organization develops and maintains a plan for technology change management.

This plan:

1. Covers the assigned responsibilities and resources required, including staff and tools.

2. Defines the long-term technical strategy for automating and improving the organization's standard software process and enhancing the organization's market position.

3. Identifies the procedures to be followed in performing the organization's technology change management activities.

4. Describes the approach for introducing new technologies to address specific needs of the organization and projects.

   □ Process areas that are potential areas for technology changes are identified.

   □ Approaches for identifying opportunities for technology changes are identified.

   □ The specific planned or candidate technologies are identified.

- ❏ Where appropriate, the life span for the planned technologies is estimated, from introduction to replacement.

- ❏ The make/buy tradeoff studies are documented.

- ❏ Approaches for assessing unproven candidate technologies are defined.

- ❏ The acquisition and installation procedures are defined.

- ❏ The initial training, continuing training, and consultation support are defined.

5. Undergoes peer review.

> Refer to the Peer Reviews key process area.

6. Is reviewed by the affected managers.

Activity 2

The group responsible for the organization's technology change management activities works with the software projects in identifying areas of technology change.

This group:

1. Solicits suggestions for technology changes.

2. Identifies available new technologies that may be appropriate to the organization's and projects' needs.

   - ❏ A periodic search is made to identify commercially available technologies that meet identified and anticipated needs.

   - ❏ Systematic efforts are made to maintain awareness of leading relevant technical work and trends of new technologies.

   - ❏ Systematic efforts are made to review the technologies used externally and to compare these technologies to those used within the organization.

   - ❏ Areas where new technologies have been used successfully are identified, and data and documentation of experience with using them are collected and reviewed.

3. Evaluates new technologies to determine their applicability to the organization's and projects' current and future needs.

Activity 3

Software managers and technical staff are kept informed of new technologies.

1. Information on new technologies is disseminated, as appropriate.
2. Information on advanced technologies already in use in parts of the organization is disseminated, as appropriate.
3. Information on the status of technologies being transferred into the organization is disseminated, as appropriate.

Activity 4

The group responsible for the organization's technology change management systematically analyzes the organization's standard software process to identify areas that need or could benefit from new technology.

This group:

1. Analyzes the organization's standard software process to determine areas where new technologies would be most helpful.
2. Identifies helpful technology changes and determines the economics of those changes.
3. Defines the relationship of the identified technology to the organization's standard software process.
4. Defines the expected outcomes of the technology change qualitatively and quantitatively, as appropriate.
5. Determines the need for piloting each potential technology change.
6. Determines the priority of the candidate new technologies.
7. Documents results of the analysis activities.

Activity 5

Technologies are selected and acquired for the organization and software projects according to a documented procedure.

This procedure typically specifies that:

1. Requests for the acquisition of new technologies are documented.

   □ Management approval is required for technologies with projected expenses above a predefined level.

2. Preliminary cost/benefit analyses are performed for the potential technology changes.

3. Predefined and approved selection criteria are used to identify the highest potential benefits.

4. Requirements and plans for the selected technology changes are defined and documented.

   □ Where practical, the expected life span and plans for replacement/upgrade are estimated.

   □ Where appropriate, tradeoff studies are performed, reviewed, and documented to determine whether the technology should be developed internally or procured externally.

   □ Where appropriate, the plan provides for installing the new technology on a pilot basis to determine its effectiveness and economic benefits.

   □ The requirements and plans are reviewed by the managers of the affected groups and the group responsible for technology change management activities.

Activity 6   **Pilot efforts for improving technology are conducted, where appropriate, before a new technology is introduced into normal practice.**

1. These pilot efforts are conducted to determine the feasibility and economics of untried or advanced technologies.

2. The plans for the pilot effort are documented.

   □ The plan covers the objectives, evaluation criteria, and activities for the pilot effort.

3. The plan for conducting the pilot effort is reviewed and approved by the managers of the affected groups.

> Examples of affected groups include:
>
> > software engineering (including all subgroups),
> >
> > software estimating,
> >
> > system engineering,
> >
> > system test,
> >
> > software quality assurance,
> >
> > software configuration management,
> >
> > contract management, and
> >
> > documentation support.

4. The group responsible for technology change management activities provides consultation and assistance to the project implementing the pilot effort.

5. The pilot effort is performed in an environment that is relevant to the development or maintenance environment.

6. The results of the pilot effort are collected, analyzed, and documented.

   □ Lessons learned and problems encountered during the effort are documented.

   □ The benefits and impacts of broader use in the organization are estimated. The uncertainty in these estimates is assessed.

   □ A decision is made whether to terminate the effort, proceed with broad-scale implementation of the technology, or replan and continue the pilot effort.

Activity 7

Appropriate new technologies are incorporated into the organization's standard software process according to a documented procedure.

> Refer to Activity 1 of the Organization Process Definition key process area and Activity 5 of the Process Change Management key process area for practices covering changes to the organization's standard software process.

Activity 8   **Appropriate new technologies are incorporated into the
                            projects' defined software processes according to a docu-
                            mented procedure.**

> Refer to Activity 2 of the Integrated Software Management
> key process area for practices covering revision of the
> project's defined software process.

Measurement and Analysis

Measurement 1   **Measurements are made and used to determine the status
                            of the organization's activities for technology change
                            management.**

> Examples of measurements include:
>
>   the overall technology change activity, including
>   number, type, and size of changes; and
>
>   the effect of implementing the technology change,
>   compared to the goals.

Verifying Implementation

Verification 1   **The organization's activities for technology change man-
                            agement are reviewed with senior management on a peri-
                            odic basis.**

> The primary purpose of periodic reviews by senior man-
> agement is to provide awareness of, and insight into,
> software process activities at an appropriate level of ab-
> straction and in a timely manner. The time between re-
> views should meet the needs of the organization and may
> be lengthy, as long as adequate mechanisms for exception
> reporting are available.

These reviews:

   1. Summarize the activities for technology change man-
      agement.

    2. Identify needed strategy changes.

    3. Result in the resolution of issues.

    4. Result in the approval of revisions to the plans for technology change management, as appropriate.

Verification 2   **The software quality assurance group reviews and/or audits the activities and work products for technology change management and reports the results.**

Refer to the Software Quality Assurance key process area.

At a minimum, the reviews and/or audits verify:

1. The plans for technology change management.

2. The process for selecting, procuring, and installing new technologies.

10.3 Process Change Management

a key process area for Level 5: Optimizing

The purpose of Process Change Management is to continually improve the software processes used in the organization with the intent of improving software quality, increasing productivity, and decreasing the cycle time for product development.

Process Change Management involves defining process improvement goals and, with senior management sponsorship, proactively and systematically identifying, evaluating, and implementing improvements to the organization's standard software process and the projects' defined software processes on a continuous basis.

Training and incentive programs are established to enable and encourage everyone in the organization to participate in process improvement activities. Improvement opportunities are identified and evaluated for potential payback to the organization. Pilot efforts are performed to assess process changes before they are incorporated into normal practice.

When software process improvements are approved for normal practice, the organization's standard software process and the projects' defined software processes are revised as appropriate. The practices for revising the organization's standard software process are found in the Organization Process Definition key process area, and the practices for revising the projects' defined software processes are found in the Integrated Software Management key process area.

Goals

Goal 1 **Continuous process improvement is planned.**

Goal 2 **Participation in the organization's software process improvement activities is organization-wide.**

Goal 3 **The organization's standard software process and the projects' defined software processes are improved continuously.**

Commitment to Perform

Commitment 1 **The organization follows a written policy for implementing software process improvements.**

This policy typically specifies that:

1. The organization has quantitative, measurable goals for software process improvement and tracks performance against these goals.

2. The organization's process improvements are directed toward improving product quality, increasing productivity, and decreasing the cycle time for product development.

3. All of the organization's staff and managers are expected to participate in improving the software processes.

> Skilled and motivated people are recognized as the principal process improvement resource.

Commitment 2 **Senior management sponsors the organization's activities for software process improvement.**

Senior management:

1. Establishes the organization's long-term goals and plans for process improvement.

2. Allocates resources for process improvement activities.

3. Coordinates with the software managers to ensure they have reasonable, yet aggressive, process improvement goals and effective process improvement plans to meet these goals.

4. Monitors process improvement performance against goals.

5. Maintains a consistent priority focus on process improvement in the face of product crises.

6. Ensures that process improvement issues are promptly resolved.

7. Rewards employee participation in the process improvement activities.

Ability to Perform

Ability 1   **Adequate resources and funding are provided for software process improvement activities.**

1. Resources are allocated to:

   □ lead, guide, and support the process improvement activities;

   □ maintain the process improvement records;

   □ develop, control, and disseminate process changes; and

   □ establish and operate the administrative and human resources functions to conduct the communications, motivation, and recognition activities needed to maintain a high level of employee participation.

2. Experienced individuals who have expertise in defining and analyzing software processes are available to help the organization's staff and managers in its process improvement activities.

3. Tools to support process improvement are made available.

> Examples of support tools include:
>
> > statistical analysis tools,
> >
> > database systems,
> >
> > process automation tools, and
> >
> > process modeling tools.

Ability 2   **Software managers receive required training in software process improvement.**

> Examples of training include:
>
> > managing technological and organizational change,
> >
> > team building, and
> >
> > teamwork skills as applied to continuous process improvement.

> Refer to the Training Program key process area.

Ability 3   **The managers and technical staff of the software engineering group and other software-related groups receive required training in software process improvement.**

> Examples of software-related groups include:
>
> > software quality assurance,
> >
> > software configuration management, and
> >
> > documentation support.

> Examples of training include:
>
> > the principles of quality and process improvement, and
> >
> > the procedures for proposing process improvements.

> Refer to the Training Program key process area.

Ability 4   **Senior management receives required training in software process improvement.**

> Examples of training include:
>
> benchmarking and comparative evaluation,
>
> principles of process improvement,
>
> setting and tracking goals for process improvement, and
>
> motivation and team building in an environment of continuous process improvement.

Activities Performed

Activity 1   **A software process improvement program is established which empowers the members of the organization to improve the processes of the organization.**

Activity 2   **The group responsible for the organization's software process activities (e.g., software engineering process group) coordinates the software process improvement activities.**

> Refer to the Organization Process Focus key process area for practices covering the group responsible for the organization's software process improvement activities.

This group:

1. Defines organizational goals and measurement plans for software process performance.

2. Reviews the organizational goals for process performance with senior management for their endorsement.

3. Participates in the effort to define the organization's training needs for process improvement and supports the development and presentation of training course materials.

> Refer to the Training Program key process area.

4. Defines and maintains the procedures for handling process improvement proposals.

5. Reviews software process improvement proposals and coordinates the actions for these proposals.

6. Tracks status, accomplishments, and participation in the process improvement activities and periodically reports the results to senior management.

7. Coordinates and tracks changes to the organization's standard software process.

8. Defines, establishes, and maintains the process improvement records.

Activity 3   **The organization develops and maintains a plan for software process improvement according to a documented procedure.**

Refer to Activity 2 of the Organization Process Focus key process area for other practices covering the organization's software process improvement plan.

This procedure typically specifies that:

1. The software process improvement plan is based on:

   □ the organization's business and strategic operating plans, and

   □ customer satisfaction indicators.

2. The software process improvement plan undergoes peer review.

Refer to the Peer Reviews key process area.

3. The software process improvement plan is reviewed by the affected managers.

4. The software process improvement plan is managed and controlled.

Activity 4   **The software process improvement activities are performed in accordance with the software process improvement plan.**

> "Managed and controlled" implies that the version of the work product in use at a given time (past or present) is known (i.e., version control) and changes are incorporated in a controlled manner (i.e., change control).
>
> If a greater degree of control than is implied by "managed and controlled" is desired, the work product can be placed under the full discipline of configuration management, as is described in the Software Configuration Management key process area.

The plan covers:

1. The resources required, including staff and tools.
2. The highest priority process areas for improvement.
3. Measurable short-term and long-term goals for software process performance and improvement.
4. Teams and their assignments for addressing improvements for specific process areas.

> Examples of teams include:
>
>   working groups,
>
>   process action teams, and
>
>   technical committees.

5. The procedures for:

   □ the senior managers overseeing the software process improvement activities;

   □ the software managers planning and coordinating the software process improvement activities;

   □ individuals and teams identifying, evaluating, and introducing appropriate software process improvements; and

   □ the teams developing software process improvements for assigned process areas.

6. The administrative and support plans required to maintain continuous process improvement.

      □ Appropriate administrative procedures are included to encourage participation in and facilitate the software process improvement activities.

      □ Administrative personnel are included in oversight and review of the software process improvement activities.

      □ The roles and contributions of employees to continuous process improvement are recognized.

Activity 5

Software process improvement proposals are handled according to a documented procedure.

This procedure typically specifies that:

  1. Software process improvement proposals are submitted.

The software process improvement proposals can be submitted at any time and can address any area of the software processes.

Examples of sources for software process improvement proposals include:

    the findings and recommendations of software process assessments,

    the organization's software process improvement goals,

    analysis of data on customer problems and customer satisfaction,

    analysis of data on project performance compared to software quality and productivity goals,

    the results of process benchmarks,

    the potential for process/task automation,

    analysis of data on defect causes,

    the measured effectiveness of the software process activities,

    examples of software process improvement proposals that were successfully adopted, and

    feedback on previously submitted software process improvement proposals, as appropriate.

2. Each software process improvement proposal is evaluated; a decision is made whether to implement the proposal, and the decision rationale is documented.

3. The expected benefits of each software process improvement proposal are determined.

Examples of expected benefit areas include:

    productivity,

    quality,

    cycle time,

    other indicators of customer or end user satisfaction, and

    any other internal factors.

---

4. The priority of software process improvement proposals selected for implementation is determined.

   □ Focus on high-priority software process improvement proposals is maintained.

5. Implementation of the software process improvement actions resulting from the proposals is assigned and planned.

6. Software process improvement actions that require a substantial effort are assigned to a team responsible for implementation.

Examples of substantial efforts include improvements requiring piloting of new technologies and other large changes.

Teams to focus on specific software process areas are established.

    Actions that are appropriate for piloting are coordinated.

> Examples of teams include:
>
> > working groups,
> >
> > process action teams, and
> >
> > technical committees.

7. The status of each software process improvement proposal is tracked.

8. Software process improvement proposals for which the response has been unusually long are identified and acted upon.

9. Software process changes that are judged to have a major impact on product quality or productivity or that will significantly alter satisfaction of the customer and end users are reviewed and approved by appropriate management before they are implemented.

10. Completed software process improvement actions are reviewed, verified, and approved before they are closed.

11. Submitters of the software process improvement proposals receive:

   □ prompt acknowledgment of their proposals, and

   □ notification of the disposition of their proposals.

Activity 6   **Members of the organization actively participate in teams to develop software process improvements for assigned process areas.**

1. Each of these process improvement teams is funded and the activities are planned and scheduled.

2. Goals are established for each process improvement effort; where possible, these goals are defined quantitatively.

3. The plans are approved by the managers of the affected groups and the group that defines and maintains the affected process descriptions.

> Examples of affected groups include:
>
> > software engineering (including all subgroups, such as software design, as well as the software task leaders),

> software estimating,
>
> system engineering,
>
> system test,
>
> software quality assurance,
>
> software configuration management,
>
> contract management, and
>
> documentation support.

Activity 7

Where appropriate, the software process improvements are installed on a pilot basis to determine their benefits and effectiveness before they are introduced into normal practice.

1. Adjustments to the proposed process improvement are made and documented during the pilot effort to optimize its implementation.

2. Lessons learned and problems encountered are documented.

3. The benefits, risks, and impacts of the process improvement's broader use in the organization are estimated, and the uncertainty in these estimates is assessed.

4. A decision is made whether to terminate the effort, proceed with broad-scale implementation of the improvement, or replan and continue the pilot effort.

Activity 8

When the decision is made to transfer a software process improvement into normal practice, the improvement is implemented according to a documented procedure.

This procedure typically specifies that:

1. The resources needed to support major changes to the software process are established and funded.

2. The strategy for collecting data to measure and track the change in software process performance is documented, reviewed, and agreed to.

   □ This strategy is agreed to by the individuals responsible for implementing the software processes affected by the change.

□ The support tools are instrumented, as appropriate, to record the desired data automatically.

3. Training courses are updated to reflect the current software process, and training is provided before installing the process change for general use.

> Refer to the Training Program key process area.

4. Consultation support, appropriate to the expected needs, is established before installing the process change for broad-scale use and is continued as needed.

5. Appropriate process changes are incorporated into the organization's standard software process.

> Refer to Activity 1 of the Organization Process Definition key process area for practices covering the organization's standard software process.

6. Appropriate process changes are incorporated into the projects' defined software processes.

> Refer to Activity 2 of the Integrated Software Management key process area for practices covering the project's defined software process.

Activity 9

Records of software process improvement activities are maintained.

1. Information about the initiation, status, and implementation of software process improvement proposals is maintained.

2. Ready access is provided to the software process improvement records.

3. Historical data are maintained and reports are produced on software process improvements.

> Examples of records and reports include:
>
> > the project's productivity, quality, and schedule performance;
> >
> > the program's defect history;
> >
> > the organizational software quality and productivity trends; and
> >
> > the cost, schedule, and productivity of software process development and improvement.

> Refer to Activity 5 of the Organization Process Definition key process area for practices covering the organization's software process database, which is one of the possible mechanisms for maintaining process improvement records.

Activity 10

Software managers and technical staff receive feedback on the status and results of the software process improvement activities on an event-driven basis.

The feedback provides:

1. A summary of the major software process improvement activities.

2. Significant innovations and actions taken to address software process improvement.

3. A summary status of the software process improvement proposals that are submitted, open, and completed.

> Examples of means to provide this feedback include:
>
> > electronic bulletin boards,
> >
> > newsletters, and
> >
> > information flow meetings.

Measurement and Analysis

Measurement 1

Measurements are made and used to determine the status of the software process improvement activities.

Examples of measurements include:

the number of software process improvement proposals submitted and implemented for each process area;

the number of software process improvement proposals submitted by each of the projects, groups, and departments;

the number and types of awards and recognitions received by each of the projects, groups, and departments;

the response time for handling software process improvement proposals;

the percentage of software process improvement proposals accepted per reporting period;

the overall change activity, including number, type, and size of changes;

the effect of implementing each process improvement compared to its defined goals;

overall performance of the organization's and project's processes, including effectiveness, quality, and productivity compared to their defined goals;

overall productivity and software quality trends for each project; and

process measurements that relate to the indicators of the customer's satisfaction.

Verifying Implementation

Verification 1   **The activities for software process improvement are reviewed with senior management on a periodic basis.**

The primary purpose of periodic reviews by senior management is to provide awareness of, and insight into, software process activities at an appropriate level of abstraction and in a timely manner. The time between reviews should meet the needs of the organization and may be lengthy, as long as adequate mechanisms for exception reporting are available.

These reviews are held to:

1. Summarize participation in the process improvement activities.
2. Assess process performance.
3. Identify needed goal changes.
4. Resolve issues.
5. Approve revisions to the software process improvement plan as appropriate.

Verification 2

The software quality assurance group reviews and/or audits the activities and work products for software process improvement and reports the results.

Refer to the Software Quality Assurance key process area.

At a minimum, the reviews and/or audits verify:

1. The preparation of the organization's software process improvement plan.
2. The process of initiating, submitting, reviewing, approving, and planning implementation of software process improvement proposals.
3. The degree to which the process measurements conform to the software process descriptions and reflect actual performance.
4. The process for documenting, reviewing, approving, controlling, and disseminating changes to the organization's standard software process and projects' defined software processes.
5. The degree to which software process improvement activities are consistently measured and tracked.
6. The degree to which actual software process improvement performance achieves the plans and goals.

Appendix A

References

Armitage93   James W. Armitage, Marc I. Kellner, and Richard W. Phillips, *Software Process Definition Guide: Content of Enactable Software Process Definitions,* CMU/SEI-93-SR-18, August 1993.

Billings94   C. Billings, J. Clifton, B. Kolkhorst, E. Lee, and W.B. Wingert, "Journey to a Mature Software Process," IBM Systems Journal, Vol. 33, No. 1, 1994, pp. 46–61.

Boehm81   B.W. Boehm, *Software Engineering Economics*, Prentice-Hall, Englewood Cliffs, NJ, 1981.

Coallier94   Francois Coallier, "How ISO 9001 Fits into the Software World," *IEEE Software*, vol. 11, no. 1, January 1994, pp. 98–100.

Cooper93   Kenneth G. Cooper and Thomas W. Mullen, *Swords & Plowshares: The Rework Cycles of Defense and Commercial Software Development Projects*, PA Consulting Group, 1993.

Dion93   Raymond Dion, "Process Improvement and the Corporate Balance Sheet," *IEEE Software*, vol. 10, no. 4, July 1993, pp. 28–35.

DoD87   *Report of the Defense Science Board Task Force on Military Soft-*
                 ware, Office of the Under Secretary of Defense for Acquisition,
                 Department of Defense, Washington, D.C., September 1987.

Dorling91   Alec Dorling and Peter Simms, *ImproveIT*, U.K. Ministry of De-
                 fense, June 1991.

Durand93   Ian G. Durand, Donald W. Marquardt, et al., "Updating the ISO
                 9000 Quality Standards: Responding to Marketplace Needs," *ASQC*
                 Quality Progress, vol. 26, no. 7, July 1993, pp. 23–30.

Fowler90   P. Fowler and S. Rifkin, *Software Engineering Process Group*
                 Guide, Software Engineering Institute, CMU/SEI-90-TR-24, DTIC
                 Number ADA235784, September 1990.

GAO-93-13   *Mission-Critical Systems—Defense Attempting to Address Major*
                 Software Changes, General Accounting Office, GAO/IMTEC-93-
                 13, December 1992, pp. 1–29.

Humphrey87a   W.S. Humphrey, *Characterizing the Software Process: A Maturity*
                 Framework, Software Engineering Institute, CMU/SEI-87-TR-11,
                 DTIC Number ADA182895, June 1987. A revised version of this report
                 was published in *IEEE Software*, vol. 5, no. 2, March 1988, pp. 73–79.

Humphrey87b   W.S. Humphrey and W.L. Sweet, *A Method for Assessing the Software*
                 Engineering Capability of Contractors, Software Engineering Institute,
                 CMU/SEI-87-TR-23, DTIC Number ADA187320, September 1987.

Humphrey89a   W.S. Humphrey, *Managing the Software Process*, Addison-Wesley,
                 Reading, MA, 1989.

Humphrey89b   Watts S. Humphrey, David H. Kitson, and T. Kasse, "The State of
                 Software Engineering Practice: A Preliminary Report," Software
                 Engineering Institute, CMU/SEI-89-TR-1, DTIC Number
                 ADA206573, February 1989.

Humphrey89c   Watts S. Humphrey, David H. Kitson, and Julia Gale, "A Compari-
                 son of U.S. and Japanese Software Process Maturity," *Proceedings*
                 of the 13th International Conference on Software Engineering,
                 Austin, TX, 13–17 May 1991, pp. 38–49.

Humphrey91a   W.S. Humphrey, D.H. Kitson, and J. Gale, "A Comparison of U.S.
                 and Japanese Software Process Maturity," *Proceedings of the 13th*
                 International Conference on Software Engineering, Austin, TX,
                 13–17 May 1991, pp. 38–49.

Humphrey91b   Watts S. Humphrey, T.R. Snyder, and Ronald R. Willis, "Software
                 Process Improvement at Hughes Aircraft," *IEEE Software*, vol. 8,
                 no. 4, July 1991, pp. 11–23.

ISO-N944R   *Study Report: The Need and Requirements for a Software Process*
                 Assessment Standard, ISO/IEC JTC1/SC7, Document N944R, Issue
                 2.0, 11 June 1992.

ISO-N017R   *Requirements Specification for a Software Process Assessment Standard*,
                 ISO/IEC JTC1/SC7/WG10, Document WG10/N017R, 3 June 1993.

Kitson89   David H. Kitson and Watts S. Humphrey, "The Role of Assessment
              in Software Process Improvement," Software Engineering Institute,
              CMU/SEI-89-TR-3, DTIC Number ADA227426, December 1989.

Koch93   G.R. Koch, "Process Assessment: the 'BOOTSTRAP' Approach,"
              Information and Software Technology, vol. 35, no. 6/7, June/July
              1993, pp. 387–403.

Lipke92   W.H. Lipke and K.L. Butler, "Software Process Improvement: A
              Success Story," *Crosstalk: The Journal of Defense Software Engi-
              neering*, no. 38, November 1992, pp. 29–31.

Lloyd's94   *Lloyd's Register TickIT Auditor's Course,* Issue 1.4, Lloyd's Regis-
              ter, March 1994.

Marquardt91   Donald Marquardt et al., "Vision 2000: The Strategy for the ISO
              9000 Series Standards in the '90s," *ASQC Quality Progress*, vol. 24,
              no. 5, May 1991, pp. 25–31.

Paulk91   M.C. Paulk, B. Curtis, M.B. Chrissis, et al., *Capability Maturity
              Model for Software*, Software Engineering Institute, CMU/SEI-91-
              TR-24, DTIC Number ADA240603, August 1991.

Paulk93a   M.C. Paulk, B. Curtis, M.B. Chrissis, and C.V. Weber, *Capability
              Maturity Model for Software, Version 1.1*, Software Engineering
              Institute, CMU/SEI-93-TR-24, DTIC Number ADA263403, Febru-
              ary 1993.

Paulk93b   M.C. Paulk, C.V. Weber, S. Garcia, M.B. Chrissis, and M. Bush,
              Key Practices of the Capability Maturity Model, Version 1.1, Soft-
              ware Engineering Institute, CMU/SEI-93-TR-25, DTIC Number
              ADA263432, February 1993.

Paulk93c   Mark C. Paulk, Bill Curtis, Mary Beth Chrissis, and Charles V.
              Weber, "Capability Maturity Model, Version 1.1," *IEEE Software*,
              vol. 10, no. 4, July 1993, pp. 18–27.

Paulk93d   Mark C. Paulk, "Comparing ISO 9001 and the Capability Maturity
              Model for Software," *Software Quality Journal*, vol. 2, no. 4,
              December 1993, pp. 245–256.

Paulk94a   Mark C. Paulk and Michael D. Konrad, "An Overview of ISO's
              SPICE Project," *American Programmer*, vol. 7, no. 2, February
              1994, pp. 16–20.

Paulk94b   Mark C. Paulk, *A Comparison of ISO 9001 and the Capability
              Maturity Model for Software*, Software Engineering Institute,
              CMU/SEI-94-TR-12, August 1994.

TickIT   *TickIT: A Guide to Software Quality Management System Construc-
              tion and Certification Using EN29001, Issue 2.0*, U.K. Department
              of Trade and Industry and the British Computer Society, 28 February
              1992.

Trillium   *Trillium: Telecom Software Product Development Process Capabil-
              ity Assessment Model*, Draft 2.2, Bell Canada, July 1992.

Weber91   C.V. Weber, M.C. Paulk, C.J. Wise, and J.V. Withey, *Key Practices of the Capability Maturity Model*, Software Engineering Institute, CMU/SEI-91-TR-25, DTIC Number ADA240604, August 1991.

Whitney94   Roselyn Whitney, Elise Nawrocki, Will Hayes, and Jane Siegel, *Instant Profile: Development and Trial of a Method to Measure Software Engineering Maturity Status*, CMU/SEI-94-TR-04, Software Engineering Institute, March 1994.

Wohlwend93   H. Wohlwend and S. Rosenbaum, "Software Improvements in an International Company," *Proceedings of the 15th International Conference of Software Engineering*, Washington D.C, May 1993.

Appendix B

Acronyms

AB	ability to perform (CMM KPA common feature)
AC	activities performed (CMM KPA common feature)
AI	Assessment Instrument (ISO SPICE)
ATQG	Assessor Training and Qualification Guide (ISO SPICE)
BPG	Baseline Practices Guide (ISO SPICE)
CCB	configuration control board
CDG	Capability Determination Guide (ISO SPICE)
CM	[Software] Configuration Management (CMM Level 2 KPA) configuration management
CMM	capability maturity model
CMU	Carnegie Mellon University
CO	commitment to perform (CMM KPA common feature)
DoD	Department of Defense
DP	Defect Prevention (CMM Level 5 KPA)

DTIC	Defense Technical Information Center
GAO	General Accounting Office
IC	Intergroup Coordination (CMM Level 3 KPA)
IDEAL	initiating, diagnosing, establishing, acting, leveraging
IG	Introductory Guide (ISO SPICE)
IM	Integrated [Software] Management (CMM Level 3 KPA)
ISM	Integrated Software Management (CMM Level 3 KPA)
ISO	International Organization for Standardization
JTC1	Joint Technical Committee 1 (ISO/IEC joint technical committee on information technology)
KP	key practice
KPA	key process area
KSLOC	thousand source lines of code
ME	measurement and analysis (CMM KPA common feature)
MQ	maturity questionnaire
OPD	Organization Process Definition (CMM Level 3 KPA)
OPF	Organization Process Focus (CMM Level 3 KPA)
PAG	Process Assessment Guide (ISO SPICE)
PAT	process action team
PC	Process Change [Management] (CMM Level 5 KPA)
PCM	Process Change Management (CMM Level 5 KPA)
PD	[Organization] Process Definition (CMM Level 3 KPA)
PE	[Software] Product Engineering (CMM Level 3 KPA)
PF	[Organization] Process Focus (CMM Level 3 KPA)
PIG	Process Improvement Guide (ISO SPICE)
PP	[Software] Project Planning (CMM Level 2 KPA)
PR	Peer Reviews (CMM Level 3 KPA)
PT	[Software] Project Tracking [and Oversight] (CMM Level 2 KPA)
PTO	[Software] Project Tracking and Oversight (CMM Level 2 KPA)
QA	[Software] Quality Assurance (CMM Level 2 KPA)
QFD	quality function deployment
QM	[Software] Quality Management (CMM Level 4 KPA)
QP	Quantitative Process [Management] (CMM Level 4 KPA)
QPM	Quantitative Process Management (CMM Level 4 KPA)
RAI	Research Access Inc.
RM	Requirements Management (CMM Level 2 KPA)
ROI	return on investment

SC7   Subcommittee 7 (ISO JTC1 subcommittee on software engineering)

SCCB   software configuration control board

SCE   Software Capability Evaluation (SEI project; now CBA)
software capability evaluation (method)

SCM   Software Configuration Management (CMM Level 2 KPA)
software configuration management

SDF   software development file

SDP   software development plan

SEI   Software Engineering Institute

SEPG   Software Engineering Process Group

SLOC   source lines of code

SM   [Software] Subcontract Management (CMM Level 2 KPA)

SOW   statement of work

SPA   Software Process Assessment (SEI project; now CBA)
software process assessment (method)

SPE   Software Product Engineering (CMM Level 3 KPA)

SPIN   Software Process Improvement Network

SPM   Software Process Measurement (SEI project)

SPP   Software Process Program
Software Project Planning (CMM Level 2 KPA)

SQA   Software Quality Assurance (CMM Level 2 KPA)

SQM   Software Quality Management (CMM Level 4 KPA)

SSM   Software Subcontract Management (CMM Level 2 KPA)

TC176   Technical Committee 176 (ISO technical committee on quality management systems)

TCM   Technology Change Management (CMM Level 5 KPA)

TM   Technology [Change] Management (CMM Level 5 KPA)

TP   Training Program (CMM Level 3 KPA)

TQM   Total Quality Management

VE   verifying implementation (CMM KPA common feature)

WBS   work breakdown structure

WG10   Working Group 10 (ISO/IEC JTC1/SC7 Working Group on software process assessment)

WG7   Working Group 7 (ISO/IEC JTC1/SC7 Working Group on software life cycle processes)

Appendix C

Glossary

ability to perform See *common features*.

acceptance criteria The criteria that a system or component must satisfy in order to be accepted by a user, a customer, or other authorized entity. [IEEE-STD-610]

acceptance testing Formal testing conducted to determine whether a system satisfies its acceptance criteria and to enable the customer to determine whether to accept the system. [IEEE-STD-610]

acting phase See *IDEAL approach*.

action item (1) A unit in a list that has been assigned to an individual or group for disposition. (2) An action proposal that has been accepted.

action proposal A documented suggestion for change to a process or process-related item that will prevent the future occurrence of defects identified as a result of defect-prevention activities. (See also *software process improvement proposal*.)

activities performed   See *common features*.

activity   Any step taken or function performed, both mental and physical, toward achieving some objective. Activities include all the work the managers and technical staff do to perform the tasks of the project and organization. (See *task* for contrast.)

allocated requirements   See *system requirements allocated to software*.

application domain   A bounded set of related systems (i.e., systems that address a particular type of problem). Development and maintenance in an application domain usually requires special skills and/or resources. Examples include payroll and personnel systems, command and control systems, compilers, and expert systems.

appraisal   a generic term for either software process assessment or software capability evaluation.

assessment   See *software process assessment*.

audit   An independent examination of a work product or set of work products to assess compliance with specifications, standards, contractual agreements, or other criteria. [IEEE-STD-610]

baseline   A specification or product that has been formally reviewed and agreed upon, that thereafter serves as the basis for further development, and that can be changed only through formal change control procedures. [IEEE-STD-610]

baseline configuration management   The establishment of baselines that are formally reviewed and agreed on and serve as the basis for further development. Some software work products, e.g., the software design and the code, should have baselines established at predetermined points, and a rigorous change control process should be applied to these items. These baselines provide control and stability when interacting with the customer. (See also *baseline management*.)

baseline management   In configuration management, the application of technical and administrative direction to designate the documents and changes to those documents that formally identify and establish baselines at specific times during the life cycle of a configuration item. [IEEE-STD-610]

benchmark   A standard against which measurements or comparisons can be made. [IEEE-STD-610]

bidder   An individual, partnership, corporation, or association that has submitted a proposal and is a candidate to be awarded a contract to design, develop, and/or manufacture one or more products.

capability maturity model   A description of the stages through which software organizations evolve as they define, implement, measure, control, and improve their software processes. This model provides a guide for selecting process improvement strategies by facilitating the determination of current process capabilities and the identification of the issues most critical to software quality and process improvement.

causal analysis   The analysis of defects to determine their underlying root cause.

causal analysis meeting   A meeting, conducted after completing a specific task, to analyze defects uncovered during the performance of that task.

commitment   A pact that is freely assumed, visible, and expected to be kept by all parties.

commitment to perform   See *common features*.

common cause (of a defect)   A cause of a defect that is inherently part of a process or system. Common causes affect every outcome of the process and everyone working in the process. (See *special cause* for contrast.)

common features   The subdivision categories of the CMM key process areas. The common features are attributes that indicate whether the implementation and institutionalization of a key process area are effective, repeatable, and lasting. The CMM common features are the following:

- **commitment to perform**   The actions the organization must take to ensure that the process is established and will endure. Commitment to perform typically involves establishing organizational policies and leadership.

- **ability to perform**   The preconditions that must exist in the project or organization to implement the software process competently. Ability to perform typically involves resources, organizational structures, and training.

- **activities performed**   A description of the activities, roles, and procedures necessary to implement a key process area. Activities performed typically involve establishing plans and procedures, performing and tracking the work, and taking corrective actions as necessary.

- **measurement and analysis**   A description of the basic measurement practices that are necessary to determine status related to the process. These measurements are used to control and improve the process. Measurement and analysis typically includes examples of the measurements that could be taken.

- **verifying implementation**   The steps to ensure that the activities are performed in compliance with the process that has been established. Verification typically encompasses reviews and audits by management and software quality assurance.

configuration   In configuration management, the functional and physical characteristics of hardware or software as set forth in technical documentation or achieved in a product. [IEEE-STD-610]

configuration control   An element of configuration management, consisting of the evaluation, coordination, approval or disapproval, and implementation of changes to configuration items after formal establishment of their configuration identification. [IEEE-STD-610]

configuration identification   An element of configuration management, consisting of selecting the configuration items for a system and recording their functional and physical characteristics in technical documentation. [IEEE-STD-610]

configuration item   An aggregation of hardware, software, or both that is designated for configuration management and treated as a single entity in the configuration management process. [IEEE-STD-610]

configuration management   A discipline applying technical and administrative direction and surveillance to identify and document the functional and physical characteristics of a configuration item, control changes to those characteristics, record and report change processing and implementation status, and verify compliance with specified requirements. [IEEE-STD-610]

configuration management library system   The tools and procedures to access the contents of the software baseline library.

configuration unit   The lowest-level entity of a configuration item or component that can be placed into, and retrieved from, a configuration management library system.

consistency   The degree of uniformity, standardization, and freedom from contradiction among the documents or parts of system or component. [IEEE-STD-610]

contingency factor   An adjustment (increase) of a size, cost, or schedule plan to account for likely underestimates of these parameters due to incomplete specification, inexperience in estimating the application domain, and so on.

contract terms and conditions   The stated legal, financial, and administrative aspects of a contract.

critical computer resource   The parameters of the computing resources deemed to be a source of risk to the project because the potential need for those resources may exceed the amount that is available. Examples include target computer memory and host computer disk space.

critical path   A series of dependent tasks for a project that must be completed as planned to keep the entire project on schedule.

customer   The individual or organization responsible for accepting the product and authorizing payment to the developing organization.

defect   A flaw in a system or system component that causes the system or component to fail to perform its required function. A defect, if encountered during execution, may cause a failure of the system.

defect density   The number of defects identified in a product divided by the size of the product component (expressed in standard measurement terms for that product).

defect prevention   The activities involved in identifying defects or potential defects and preventing them from being introduced into a product.

defect root cause   The underlying reason (e.g., process deficiency) that allowed a defect to be introduced.

defined level   See *maturity level.*

defined software process   See *project's defined software process.*

dependency item   A product, action, piece of information, and the like, that must be provided by one individual or group to a second individual or group so that the latter can perform a planned task.

developmental configuration management   The application of technical and administrative direction to designate and control software and associated technical documentation that define the evolving configuration of a software work product during development. Developmental configuration management is under the direct control of the developer. Items under developmental configuration management are not baselines, although they may be baselined and placed under baseline configuration management at some point in their development.

deviation   A noticeable or marked departure from the appropriate norm, plan, standard, procedure, or variable being reviewed.

diagnosing phase   See *IDEAL approach.*

documented procedure   See *procedure.*

effective process   A process that can be characterized as practiced, documented, enforced, trained, measured, and able to improve. (See also *well-defined process.*)

end user   The individual or group who will use the system for its intended operational purpose when it is deployed in its environment.

end user representatives   A selected sample of end users who represent the total population of end users.

engineering group   A collection of individuals (both managers and technical staff) representing an engineering discipline. Examples of engineering disciplines include systems engineering, hardware engineering, system test, software engineering, software configuration management, and software quality assurance.

establishing phase   See *IDEAL approach.*

evaluation   See *software capability evaluation.*

event-driven review/activity   A review or activity whose performance is based on the occurrence of an event within the project (e.g., a formal review or the completion of a life cycle stage). (See *periodic review/activity* for contrast.)

findings   The conclusions of an assessment, evaluation, audit, or review that identify the most important issues, problems, or opportunities within the area of investigation.

first-line software manager   A manager who has direct management responsibility (including providing technical direction and administering the personnel and salary functions) for the staffing and activities of a single organizational unit (e.g., a department or project team) of software engineers and other related staff.

formal review   A formal meeting at which a product is presented to the end user, customer, or other interested parties for comment and approval. It can also be a review of the management and technical activities and of the progress of the project.

function   A set of related actions, undertaken by individuals or tools that are specifically assigned or fitted for their roles, to accomplish a set purpose or end.

goals   A summary of the key practices of a key process area that can be used to determine whether an organization or project has effectively implemented the key process area. The goals signify the scope, boundaries, and intent of each key process area.

group   The collection of departments, managers, and individuals who have responsibility for a set of tasks or activities. A group could vary from a single individual assigned part time, to several part-time individuals assigned from different departments, to several individuals dedicated full time.

host computer   A computer used to develop software. (See *target computer* for contrast.)

IDEAL approach   The SEI approach to the cycle of software process improvement, based on initiating an improvement effort, diagnosing the software process, establishing mechanisms for improving the process, acting to implement the improvements, and leveraging them across the organization. The five phases of the IDEAL approach are:

□ **initiating phase**   The first phase, when sponsorship and the software process improvement infrastructure are defined and established.

□ **diagnosing phase**   The second phase, when appraisals are conducted to establish the software process maturity baseline of the organization and a set of recommendations for improvement are communicated to the organization.

□ **establishing phase**   The third phase, when a software process improvement infrastructure is built, including the formation of process action teams and the definition of software process improvement strategic and tactical plans.

- □ **acting phase** The fourth phase, when the improvements are implemented.

- □ **leveraging phase** The final phase, when lessons learned from the software process improvement effort are analyzed, resulting in updates to the software process improvement process. Sponsorship is renewed and new goals are set for the next improvement cycle.

infrastructure The underlying framework of an organization or system, including organizational structures, policies, standards, training, facilities, and tools, that supports its ongoing performance.

initial level See *maturity level*.

initiating phase See *IDEAL approach*.

institutionalization The building of infrastructure and culture that support methods, practices, and procedures so that they are the ongoing way of doing business, even after those who originally defined them are gone.

integrated software management The unification and integration of the software engineering and management activities into a coherent defined software process based on the organization's standard software process and related process assets.

integration See *software integration*.

key practices The infrastructure and activities that contribute most to the effective implementation and institutionalization of a key process area.

key process area A cluster of related activities that, when performed collectively, achieve a set of goals considered to be important for establishing process capability. The key process areas have been defined to reside at a single maturity level. They are the areas identified by the SEI to be the principal building blocks to help determine the software process capability of an organization and understand the improvements needed to advance to higher maturity levels. The Level 2 key process areas in the CMM are Requirements Management, Software Project Planning, Software Project Tracking and Oversight, Software Subcontract Management, Software Quality Assurance, and Software Configuration Management. The Level 3 key process areas in the CMM are Organization Process Focus, Organization Process Definition, Training Program, Integrated Software Management, Software Product Engineering, Intergroup Coordination, and Peer Reviews. The Level 4 key process areas are Quantitative Process Management and Software Quality Management. The Level 5 key process areas are Defect Prevention, Technology Change Management, and Process Change Management.

leveraging phase See *IDEAL approach*.

life cycle   See *software life cycle.*

maintenance   The process of modifying a software system or component after delivery to correct faults, improve performance or other attributes, or adapt to a changed environment. [IEEE-STD-610]

managed and controlled   The process of identifying and defining software work products that are not part of a baseline and therefore are not placed under configuration management but that must be controlled for the project to proceed in a disciplined manner. "Managed and controlled" implies that the version of the work product in use at a given time (past or present) is known (i.e., version control), and changes are incorporated in a controlled manner (i.e., change control).

managed level   See *maturity level.*

manager   A role that encompasses providing technical and administrative direction and control to individuals performing tasks or activities within the manager's area of responsibility. The traditional functions of a manager include planning, resourcing, organizing, directing, and controlling work within an area of responsibility.

maturity level   A well-defined evolutionary plateau toward achieving a mature software process. The five maturity levels in the SEI's Capability Maturity Model are:

- **initial**   The software process is characterized as ad hoc, and occasionally even chaotic. Few processes are defined, and success depends on individual effort.

- **repeatable**   Basic project management processes are established to track cost, schedule, and functionality. The necessary process discipline is in place to repeat earlier successes on projects with similar applications.

- **defined**   The software process for both management and engineering activities is documented, standardized, and integrated into a standard software process for the organization. All projects use an approved, tailored version of the organization's standard software process for developing and maintaining software.

- **managed**   Detailed measures of the software process and product quality are collected. Both the software process and products are quantitatively understood and controlled.

- **optimizing**   Continuous process improvement is enabled by quantitative feedback from the process and from piloting innovative ideas and technologies.

maturity questionnaire   See *software process maturity questionnaire.*

measure   A unit of measurement (such as source lines of code or document pages of design).

measurement   The dimension, capacity, quantity, or amount of something (e.g., 300 source lines of code or 7 document pages of design).

method   A reasonably complete set of rules and criteria that establish a precise and repeatable way of performing a task and arriving at a desired result.

methodology   A collection of methods, procedures, and standards that defines an integrated synthesis of engineering approaches to the development of a product.

milestone   A scheduled event for which some individual is accountable and that is used to measure progress.

nontechnical requirements   Agreements, conditions, and/or contractual terms that affect and determine the management activities of a software project.

operational software   The software that is intended to be used and operated in a system when it is delivered to its customer and deployed in its intended environment.

optimizing level   See *maturity level*.

organization   A unit within a company or other entity within which many projects are managed as a whole. All projects within an organization share a common top-level manager and common policies.

organization's measurement program   The set of related elements for addressing an organization's measurement needs. It includes the definition of organization-wide measurements, methods and practices for collecting organizational measurement data, methods and practices for analyzing organizational measurement data, and measurement goals for the organization.

organization's software process assets   A collection of entities, maintained by an organization, for use by projects in developing, tailoring, maintaining, and implementing their software processes. These software process assets typically include:

- the organization's standard software process,
- descriptions of the software life cycles approved for use,
- the guidelines and criteria for tailoring the organization's standard software process,
- the organization's software process database, and
- a library of software process-related documentation.

Any entity that the organization considers useful in performing the activities of process definition and maintenance could be included as a process asset.

organization's software process database   A database established to collect and make available data on the software processes and resulting software work products, particularly as they relate to the organization's standard software process. The database contains or references both the actual measurement data and the related information needed to understand the measurement data and assess it for reasonableness and applicability. Examples of process and work product data include estimates of software size, effort, and cost; actual data on software size, effort, and cost; productivity data; peer review coverage and efficiency; and number and severity of defects found in the software code.

organization's standard software process   The operational definition of the basic process that guides the establishment of a common software process across the software projects in an organization. It describes the fundamental software process elements that each software project is expected to incorporate into its defined software process. It also describes the relationships (e.g., ordering and interfaces) between these software process elements.

orientation   An overview or introduction to a topic for those overseeing or interfacing with the individuals responsible for performing in the topic area. (See *train* for contrast.)

Pareto analysis   The analysis of defects by ranking causes from most significant to least significant. Pareto analysis is based on the principle, named after the nineteenth-century economist Vilfredo Pareto, that most effects come from relatively few causes, that is, 80% of the effects come from 20% of the possible causes.

peer review   A review of a software work product, following defined procedures, by peers of the producers of the product for the purpose of identifying defects and improvements.

peer review leader   An individual specifically trained and qualified to plan, organize, and lead a peer review.

periodic review/activity   A review or activity that occurs at specified, regular time intervals. (See *event-driven review/activity* for contrast.)

policy   A guiding principle, typically established by senior management, that is adopted by an organization or project to influence and determine decisions.

prime contractor   An individual, a partnership, a corporation, or an association that administers a subcontract to design, develop, and/or manufacture one or more products.

procedure   A written description of a course of action to be taken to perform a given task. [IEEE-STD-610]

process   A sequence of steps performed for a given purpose, for example, the software development process. [IEEE-STD-610]

process capability   The range of expected results that can be achieved by following a process. (See *process performance* for contrast.)

process capability baseline　A documented characterization of the range of expected results that would normally be achieved by following a specific process under typical circumstances. A process capability baseline is typically established at an organizational level. (See *process performance baseline* for contrast.)

process database　See *organization's software process database*.

process description　The operational definition of the major components of a process. Documentation that specifies, in a complete, precise, verifiable manner, the requirements, design, behavior, or other characteristics of a process. It may also include the procedures for determining whether these provisions have been satisfied. Process descriptions may be found at the task, project, or organizational level.

process development　The act of defining and describing a process. It may include planning, architecture, design, implementation, and validation.

process measurement　The set of definitions, methods, and activities used to take measurements of a process and its resulting products for the purpose of characterizing and understanding the process.

process performance　A measure of the actual results achieved by following a process. (See *process capability* for contrast.)

process performance baseline　A documented characterization of the actual results achieved by following a process, which is used as a benchmark for comparing actual process performance against expected process performance. A process performance baseline is typically established at the project level, although the initial process performance baseline will usually be derived from the process capability baseline. (See *process capability baseline* for contrast.)

process tailoring　The activity of creating a process description by elaborating, adapting, and/or completing the details of process elements or other incomplete specifications of a process. Specific business needs for a project will usually be addressed during process tailoring.

product　See *software product* and *software work product*.

profile　A comparison, usually in graphical form, of plans or projections versus actuals, typically over time.

project　An undertaking requiring concerted effort that is focused on developing and/or maintaining a specific product. The product may include hardware, software, and other components. Typically a project has its own funding, cost accounting, and delivery schedule.

project's defined software process　The operational definition of the software process used by a project. The project's defined software process is well characterized and understood and is described in terms of software standards, procedures, tools, and methods. It is developed by tailoring the

The Capability Maturity Model   363

organization's standard software process to fit the specific characteristics of the project. (See also *organization's standard software process, effective process,* and *well-defined process.*)

project manager   The role with total business responsibility for an entire project. The individual who directs, controls, administers, and regulates a project building a software or hardware/software system. The project manager is the individual ultimately responsible to the customer.

project software manager   The role with total responsibility for all the software activities for a project. The project software manager controls all the software resources for a project and is the individual with whom the project manager deals in terms of software commitments.

quality   (1) The degree to which a system, component, or process meets specified requirements. (2) The degree to which a system, component, or process meets customer or user needs or expectations. [IEEE-STD-610]

quality assurance   See *software quality assurance.*

quantitative control   Any quantitative or statistically based technique appropriate to analyze a software process, identify special causes of variations in the performance of the software process, and bring the performance of the software process within well-defined limits.

repeatable level   See *maturity level.*

required training   Training designated by an organization to be required to perform a specific role.

risk   Possibility of suffering loss.

risk management   An approach to problem analysis that weighs risk in a situation by using risk probabilities to give a more accurate understanding of the risks involved. Risk management includes risk identification, analysis, prioritization, and control.

risk management plan   The collection of plans that describe the risk management activities to be performed on a project.

role   A unit of defined responsibilities that may be assumed by one or more individuals.

senior manager   A management role at a high enough level in an organization that the primary focus is the long-term vitality of the organization, rather than short-term project and contractual concerns and pressures. In general, a senior manager for engineering would have responsibility for multiple projects.

software architecture   The organizational structure of the software or module. [IEEE-STD-610]

software baseline audit   An examination of the structure, contents, and facilities of the software baseline library to verify that baselines conform to the documentation that describes them.

software baseline library   The contents of a repository for storing configuration items and the associated records.

software build   An operational version of a software system or component that incorporates a specified subset of the capabilities the final software system or component will provide. [IEEE-STD-610]

software capability evaluation   An appraisal by a trained team of professionals to identify contractors who are qualified to perform the software work or to monitor the state of the software process used on an existing software effort.

software configuration control board   A group responsible for evaluating and approving or disapproving proposed changes to configuration items and for ensuring implementation of approved changes.

software development plan   The collection of plans that describe the activities to be performed for the software project. It governs the management of the activities performed by the software engineering group for a software project. It is not limited to the scope of any particular planning standard, such as DoD-STD-2167A and IEEE-STD-1058, which may use similar terminology.

software engineering group   The collection of individuals (both managers and technical staff) who have responsibility for performing the software development and maintenance activities (i.e., requirements analysis, design, code, and test) for a project. Groups performing software-related work, such as the software quality assurance group, the software configuration management group, and the software engineering process group, are not included in the software engineering group.

software engineering process group   A group of specialists who facilitate the definition, maintenance, and improvement of the software process used by the organization. In the key practices, this group is generically referred to as "the group responsible for the organization's software process activities."

software engineering staff   The software technical people (e.g., analysts, programmers, and engineers), including software task leaders, who perform the software development and maintenance activities for the project, but who are not managers.

software integration   A process of putting together selected software components to provide the set or specified subset of the capabilities the final software system will provide.

software life cycle   The period of time that begins when a software product is conceived and ends when the software is no longer available for use. The software life cycle typically includes a concept phase, requirements phase, design phase, implementation phase, test phase, installation and checkout phase, operation and maintenance phase, and, sometimes, retirement phase. [IEEE-STD-610]

software manager   Any manager, at a project or organizational level, who has direct responsibility for software development and/or maintenance.

software plans   The collection of plans, both formal and informal, used to express how software development and/or maintenance activities will be performed. Examples of plans that could be included: software development plan, software quality assurance plan, software configuration management plan, software test plan, risk management plan, and process improvement plan.

software process   A set of activities, methods, practices, and transformations to develop and maintain software and the associated products (e.g., project plans, design documents, code, test cases, and user manuals).

software process assessment   An appraisal by a trained team of software professionals to determine the state of an organization's current software process, to determine the high-priority software process-related issues facing an organization, and to obtain the organizational support for software process improvement.

software process assets   See *organization's software process assets.*

software process capability   See *process capability.*

software process description   The operational definition of a major software process component identified in the project's defined software process or the organization's standard software process. It documents, in a complete, precise, verifiable manner, the requirements, design, behavior, or other characteristics of a software process. (See also *process description.*)

software process element   A constituent element of a software process description. Each process element covers a well-defined, bounded, closely related set of activities (e.g., software estimating element, software design element, coding element, and peer review element). The descriptions of the process elements may be templates to be filled in, fragments to be completed, abstractions to be refined, or complete descriptions to be modified or used unmodified.

software process improvement plan   A plan, derived from the recommendations of a software process assessment, that identifies the specific actions that will be taken to improve the software process and outlines the plans for implementing those actions. Sometimes referred to as an action plan.

software process improvement proposal   A documented suggestion for change to a process or process-related item that will improve software process capability and performance. (See also *action proposal.*)

software process maturity   The extent to which a specific process is explicitly defined, managed, measured, controlled, and effective. Maturity implies a potential for growth in capability and indicates both the richness of an organization's software process and the consistency with which it is applied in projects throughout the organization.

software process maturity questionnaire   A set of questions about the software process that sample the key practices in each key process area of the CMM. The maturity questionnaire is used as a springboard to appraise the capability of an organization or project to execute a software process reliably.

software process performance   See *process performance.*

software process-related documentation   Example documents and document fragments that are expected to be of use to future projects when they are tailoring the organization's standard software process. The examples may cover subjects such as a project's defined software process, standards, procedures, software development plans, measurement plans, and process training materials.

software product   The complete set, or any of the individual items of the set, of computer programs, procedures, and associated documentation and data designated for delivery to a customer or end user. [IEEE-STD-610] (See *software work product* for contrast.)

software project   An undertaking requiring concerted effort and focusing on analyzing, specifying, designing, developing, testing, and/or maintaining the software components and associated documentation of a system. A software project may be part of a project building a hardware/software system.

software quality assurance   (1) A planned and systematic pattern of all actions necessary to provide adequate confidence that a software work product conforms to established technical requirements. (2) A set of activities designed to evaluate the process by which software work products are developed and/or maintained. [Derived from IEEE-STD-610]

software quality goal   Quantitative quality objectives defined for a software work product.

software quality management   The process of defining quality goals for a software product, establishing plans to achieve these goals, and monitoring and adjusting the software plans, software work products, activities, and quality goals to satisfy the needs and desires of the customer and end users.

software-related group   A collection of individuals (both managers and technical staff) representing a software engineering discipline that supports, but is not directly responsible for, performing software development and/or maintenance. Examples of software engineering disciplines include software quality assurance and software configuration management.

software requirement   A condition or capability that must be met by software needed by a user to solve a problem or achieve an objective. [IEEE-STD-610]

software work product   Any artifact created as part of defining, maintaining, or using a software process. They can include process descriptions, plans, procedures, computer programs, and associated documentation, which may or may not be intended for delivery to a customer or end user. (See *software product* for contrast.)

special cause (of a defect)   A cause of a defect that is specific to some transient circumstance and not an inherent part of a process. Special causes provide random variation (noise) in process performance. (See *common cause* for contrast.)

staff   The individuals, including task leaders, who are responsible for accomplishing an assigned function, such as software development or software configuration management, but who are not managers.

stage   A partition of the software effort that is of a manageable size and that represents a meaningful and measurable set of related tasks performed by the project. A stage is usually considered a subdivision of a software life cycle and is often ended with a formal review (or other well-defined criteria) prior to the onset of the following stage.

standard   Mandatory requirements employed and enforced to prescribe a disciplined uniform approach to software development. [Derived from IEEE-STD-610]

standard software process   See *organization's standard software process*.

statement of work   A description of all the work required to complete a project, which is provided by the customer.

subcontract manager   A manager in the prime contractor's organization who has direct responsibility for administering and managing one or more subcontracts.

subcontractor   An individual, partnership, corporation, or association that contracts with an organization (i.e., the prime contractor) to design, develop, and/or manufacture one or more products.

system   A collection of components organized to accomplish a specific function or set of functions. [IEEE-STD-610]

system engineering group   The collection of individuals (both managers and technical staff) who have responsibility for specifying the system requirements; allocating the system requirements to the hardware, software, and other components; specifying the interfaces between the hardware, software, and other components; and monitoring the design and development of these components to ensure conformance with their specifications.

system requirement   A condition or capability that must be met or possessed by a system or system component to satisfy a condition or capability needed by a user to solve a problem. [IEEE-STD-610]

system requirements allocated to software   The subset of the system requirements that are to be implemented in the software components of the system. The allocated requirements are a primary input to the software development plan. Software requirements analysis elaborates and refines the allocated requirements and results in documented software requirements.

tailor   To modify a process, standard, or procedure to better match process or product requirements.

target computer   The computer on which delivered software is intended to operate. (See *host computer* for contrast.)

task   (1) A sequence of instructions treated as a basic unit of work. [IEEE-STD-610] (2) A well-defined unit of work in the software process that provides management with a visible checkpoint into the status of the project. Tasks have readiness criteria (preconditions) and completion criteria (postconditions). (See *activity* for contrast.)

task kick-off meeting   A meeting held at the beginning of a task of a project for the purpose of preparing the individuals involved to perform the activities of that task effectively.

task leader   The leader of a technical team for a specific task who has technical responsibility and provides technical direction to the staff working on the task.

team   A collection of people, often drawn from diverse but related groups, assigned to perform a well-defined function for an organization or a project. Team members may be part-time participants of the team and have other primary responsibilities.

testability   (1) The degree to which a system or component facilitates the establishment of test criteria and the performance of tests to determine whether those criteria have been met. (2) The degree to which a requirement is stated in terms that permit establishment of test criteria and performance of tests to determine whether those criteria have been met. [IEEE-STD-610]

technical requirements   Those requirements that describe what the software must do and its operational constraints. Examples of technical requirements include functional, performance, interface, and quality requirements.

technology   The application of science and/or engineering in accomplishing some particular result.

total quality management   The application of quantitative methods and human resources to improve the material and services supplied to an organization, all the processes within an organization, and the degree to which the needs of the customer are met, now and in the future.

traceability   The degree to which a relationship can be established between two or more products of the development process, especially products having a predecessor–successor or master–subordinate relationship to each other. [IEEE-STD-610]

train   To make proficient with specialized instruction and practice. (See also *orientation*.)

training group   The collection of individuals (both managers and staff) who are responsible for coordinating and arranging the training activities for an organization. This group typically prepares and conducts most of the training courses and coordinates use of other training vehicles.

training program   The set of related elements that focus on addressing an organization's training needs. It includes an organization's training plan, training materials, development of training, conduct of training, training facilities, evaluation of training, and maintenance of training records.

training waiver   A written approval exempting an individual from training that has been designated as required for a specific role. The exemption is granted because it has been objectively determined that the individual already possesses the needed skills to perform the role.

unit   (1) A separately testable element specified in the design of a computer software component. (2) A logically separable part of a computer program. (3) A software component that is not subdivided into other components. [IEEE-STD-610]

user   See *end user*.

validation   The process of evaluating software during or at the end of the development process to determine whether it satisfies specified requirements. [IEEE-STD-610]

verification   The process of evaluating software to determine whether the products of a given development phase satisfy the conditions imposed at the start of that phase. [IEEE-STD-610]

verifying implementation   See *common features*.

waiver   See *training waiver*.

well-defined process   A process that includes readiness criteria, inputs, standards and procedures for performing the work, verification mechanisms (such as peer reviews), outputs, and completion criteria. (See also *effective process*.)

Appendix D

Abridged Version of the Key Practices

This abridged version of the key practices provides a high-level overview of the CMM. It can be used to get a "quick look" at each key process area, but it does not provide the specific activities for, nor cover, all the key practices. It is intended for informational purposes, not for determining compliance to the key practices or planning process improvements.

This abridgment contains a short description of the key process area, its goals, and the key practice statements from the Activities Performed common feature of the key process area. These items are extracted verbatim from the detailed key practice tables.

A number of other practices specified under the other common features (i.e., Commitment to Perform, Ability to Perform, Measurement and Analysis, and Verifying Implementation) are not contained in this appendix. These other key practices must be in place to ensure the key practices are implemented appropriately and effectively, are solidly established, will be maintained and not erode over time, and can be effectively applied to new work. To establish a key process area appropriately, the full set of key practices should be used.

Commitment to Perform typically involves establishing organizational policies and senior management sponsorship. Ability to Perform typically involves resources, organizational structures, and training. Measurement and Analysis typically includes examples of the measurements that could be taken to determine the status and effectiveness of the Activities Performed. Verifying Implementation typically encompasses reviews and audits by management and software quality assurance.

Level 2: Abridged Practices for Requirements Management

The purpose of Requirements Management is to establish a common understanding between the customer and the software project of the customer's requirments that will be addressed by the software project.

Requirements Management involves establishing and maintaining an agreement with the customer on the requirements for the software project. This agreement is referred to as the "system requirements allocated to the software." The "customer" may be interpreted as the system engineering group, the marketing group, another internal organization, or an external customer. The agreement covers both the technical and nontechnical (e.g., delivery dates) requirements. The agreement forms the basis for estimating, planning, performing, and tracking the software project's activities throughout the software life cycle.

The allocation of the system requirements to software, hardware, and other system components (e.g., humans) may be performed by a group external to the software engineering group (e.g., the system engineering group), and the software engineering group may have no direct control of this allocation. Within the constraints of the project, the software engineering group takes appropriate steps to ensure that the system requirements allocated to software, which they are responsible for addressing, are documented and controlled.

To achieve this control, the software engineering group reviews the initial and revised system requirements allocated to software to resolve issues before they are incorporated into the software project. Whenever the system requirements allocated to software are changed, the affected software plans, work products, and activities are adjusted to remain consistent with the updated requirements.

The goals of Requirements Management are:

1. System requirements allocated to software are controlled to establish a baseline for software engineering and management use.

2. Software plans, products, and activities are kept consistent with the system requirements allocated to software.

The top-level activities performed for Requirements Management are:

1. The software engineering group reviews the allocated requirements before they are incorporated into the software project.

2. The software engineering group uses the allocated requirements as the basis for software plans, work products, and activities.

3. Changes to the allocated requirements are reviewed and incorporated into the software project.

Level 2: Abridged Practices for Software Project Planning

The purpose of Software Project Planning is to establish reasonable plans for performing the software engineering and for managing the software project.

Software Project Planning involves developing estimates for the work to be performed, establishing the necessary commitments, and defining the plan to perform the work.

The software planning begins with a statement of the work to be performed and other constraints and goals that define and bound the software project (those established by the practices of the Requirements Management key process area). The software planning process includes steps to estimate the size of the software work products and the resources needed, produce a schedule, identify and assess software risks, and negotiate commitments. Iterating through these steps may be necessary to establish the plan for the software project (i.e., the software development plan).

This plan provides the basis for performing and managing the software project's activities and addresses the commitments to the software project's customer according to the resources, constraints, and capabilities of the software project.

The goals of Software Project Planning are:

1. Software estimates are documented for use in planning and tracking the software project.
2. Software project activities and commitments are planned and documented.
3. Affected groups and individuals agree to their commitments related to the software project.

The top-level activities performed for Software Project Planning are:

1. The software engineering group participates on the project proposal team.
2. Software project planning is initiated in the early stages of, and in parallel with, the overall project planning.
3. The software engineering group participates with other affected groups in the overall project planning throughout the project's life.
4. Software project commitments made to individuals and groups external to the organization are reviewed with senior management according to a documented procedure.
5. A software life cycle with predefined stages of manageable size is identified or defined.
6. The project's software development plan is developed according to a documented procedure.
7. The plan for the software project is documented.
8. Software work products that are needed to establish and maintain control of the software project are identified.
9. Estimates for the size of the software work products (or changes to the size of software work products) are derived according to a documented procedure.
10. Estimates for the software project's effort and costs are derived according to a documented procedure.
11. Estimates for the project's critical computer resources are derived according to a documented procedure.
12. The project's software schedule is derived according to a documented procedure.
13. The software risks associated with the cost, resource, schedule, and technical aspects of the project are identified, assessed, and documented.

14. Plans for the project's software engineering facilities and support tools are prepared.

15. Software planning data are recorded.

Level 2: Abridged Practices for Software Project Tracking and Oversight

The purpose of Software Project Tracking and Oversight is to provide adequate visibility into actual progress so that management can take effective actions when the software project's performance deviates significantly from the software plans.

Software Project Tracking and Oversight involves tracking and reviewing the software accomplishments and results against documented estimates, commitments, and plans, and adjusting these plans based on the actual accomplishments and results.

A documented plan for the software project (i.e., the software development plan, as described in the Software Project Planning key process area) is used as the basis for tracking the software activities, communicating status, and revising plans. Software activities are monitored by the management. Progress is primarily determined by comparing the actual software size, effort, cost, and schedule to the plan when selected software work products are completed and at selected milestones. When it is determined that the software project's plans are not being met, corrective actions are taken. These actions may include revising the software development plan to reflect the actual accomplishments and replanning the remaining work or taking actions to improve the performance.

The goals of Software Project Tracking and Oversight are:

1. Actual results and performance are tracked against the software plans.

2. Corrective actions are taken and managed to closure when actual results and performance deviate significantly from the software plans.

3. Changes to software commitments are agreed to by the affected groups and individuals.

The top-level activities performed for Software Project Tracking and Oversight are:

1. A documented software development plan is used for tracking the software activities and communicating status.

2. The project's software development plan is revised according to a documented procedure.

3. Software project commitments and changes to commitments made to individuals and groups external to the organization are reviewed with senior management according to a documented procedure.

4. Approved changes to commitments that affect the software project are communicated to the members of the software engineering group and other software-related groups.

5. The size of the software work products (or size of the changes to the software work products) are tracked, and corrective actions are taken as necessary.

6. The project's software effort and costs are tracked, and corrective actions are taken as necessary.

7. The project's critical computer resources are tracked, and corrective actions are taken as necessary.

8. The project's software schedule is tracked, and corrective actions are taken as necessary.

9. Software engineering technical activities are tracked, and corrective actions are taken as necessary.

10. The software risks associated with cost, resource, schedule, and technical aspects of the project are tracked.

11. Actual measurement data and replanning data for the software project are recorded.

12. The software engineering group conducts periodic internal reviews to track technical progress, plans, performance, and issues against the software development plan.

13. Formal reviews to address the accomplishments and results of the software project are conducted at selected project milestones according to a documented procedure.

Level 2: Abridged Practices for Software Subcontract Management

The purpose of Software Subcontract Management is to select qualified software subcontractors and manage them effectively.

Software Subcontract Management involves selecting a software subcontractor, establishing commitments with the subcontractor, and tracking and reviewing the subcontractor's performance and results. These practices cover the management of a software (-only) subcontract, as well as the management of the software component of a subcontract that includes software, hardware, and possibly other system components.

The subcontractor is selected based on its ability to perform the work. Many factors contribute to the decision to subcontract a portion of the prime contractor's work. Subcontractors may be selected based on strategic business alliances as well as technical considerations. The practices of this key process area address the traditional acquisition process associated with subcontracting a defined portion of the work to another organization.

When subcontracting, a documented agreement covering the technical and nontechnical (e.g., delivery dates) requirements is established and is used as the basis for managing the subcontract. The work to be done by the subcontractor and the plans for the work are documented. The standards that are to be followed by the subcontractor are compatible with the prime contractor's standards.

The software planning, tracking, and oversight activities for the subcontracted work are performed by the subcontractor. The prime contractor ensures that these planning, tracking, and oversight activities are performed appropriately and that the software products delivered by the subcontractor satisfy their acceptance criteria. The prime contractor works with the subcontractor to manage their product and process interfaces.

The goals of Software Subcontract Management are:

1. The prime contractor selects qualified software subcontractors.

2. The prime contractor and the software subcontractor agree to their commitments to each other.

3. The prime contractor and the software subcontractor maintain ongoing communications.

4. The prime contractor tracks the software subcontractor's actual results and performance against its commitments.

The top-level activities performed for Software Subcontract Management are:

1. The work to be subcontracted is defined and planned according to a documented procedure.

2. The software subcontractor is selected, based on an evaluation of the subcontract bidders' ability to perform the work, according to a documented procedure.

3. The contractual agreement between the prime contractor and the software subcontractor is used as the basis for managing the subcontract.

4. A documented subcontractor's software development plan is reviewed and approved by the prime contractor.

5. A documented and approved subcontractor's software development plan is used for tracking the software activities and communicating status.

6. Changes to the software subcontractor's statement of work, subcontract terms and conditions, and other commitments are resolved according to a documented procedure.

7. The prime contractor's management conducts periodic status/coordination reviews with the software subcontractor's management.

8. Periodic technical reviews and interchanges are held with the software subcontractor.

9. Formal reviews to address the subcontractor's software engineering accomplishments and results are conducted at selected milestones according to a documented procedure.

10. The prime contractor's software quality assurance group monitors the subcontractor's software quality assurance activities according to a documented procedure.

11. The prime contractor's software configuration management group monitors the subcontractor's activities for software configuration management according to a documented procedure.

12. The prime contractor conducts acceptance testing as part of the delivery of the subcontractor's software products according to a documented procedure.

13. The software subcontractor's performance is evaluated on a periodic basis, and the evaluation is reviewed with the subcontractor.

Level 2: Abridged Practices for Software Quality Assurance

The purpose of Software Quality Assurance is to provide management with appropriate visibility into the process being used by the software project and of the products being built.

Software Quality Assurance involves reviewing and auditing the software products and activities to verify that they comply with the applicable procedures and standards and providing the software project and other appropriate managers with the results of these reviews and audits.

The software quality assurance group works with the software project during its early stages to establish plans, standards, and procedures that will add value to the software project and satisfy the constraints of the project and the organization's policies. By participating in establishing the plans, standards, and procedures, the software quality assurance group helps ensure they fit the project's needs and verifies that they will be usable for performing reviews and audits throughout the software life cycle. The software quality assurance group reviews project activities and audits software work products throughout the life cycle and provides management with visibility as to whether the software project is adhering to its established plans, standards, and procedures.

Compliance issues are first addressed within the software project and resolved there if possible. For issues not resolvable within the software project, the software quality assurance group escalates the issue to an appropriate level of management for resolution.

This key process area covers the practices for the group performing the software quality assurance function. The practices identifying the specific activities and work products that the software quality assurance group reviews and/or audits are generally contained in the Verifying Implementation common feature of the other key process areas.

The goals of Software Quality Assurance are:

1. Software quality assurance activities are planned.

2. Adherence of software products and activities to the applicable standards, procedures, and requirements is verified objectively.

3. Affected groups and individuals are informed of software quality assurance activities and results.

4. Noncompliance issues that cannot be resolved within the software project are addressed by senior management.

The top-level activities performed for Software Quality Assurance are:

1. A SQA plan is prepared for the software project according to a documented procedure.

2. The SQA group's activities are performed in accordance with the SQA plan.

3. The SQA group participates in the preparation and review of the project's software development plan, standards, and procedures.

4. The SQA group reviews the software engineering activities to verify compliance.

5. The SQA group audits designated software work products to verify compliance.

6. The SQA group periodically reports the results of its activities to the software engineering group.

7. Deviations identified in the software activities and software work products are documented and handled according to a documented procedure.

8. The SQA group conducts periodic reviews of its activities and findings with the customer's SQA personnel, as appropriate.

Level 2: Abridged Practices for Software Configuration Management

The purpose of Software Configuration Management is to establish and maintain the integrity of the products of the software project throughout the project's software life cycle.

Software Configuration Management involves identifying the configuration of the software (i.e., selected software work products and their descriptions) at given points in time, systematically controlling changes to the configuration, and maintaining the integrity and traceability of the configuration throughout the software life cycle. The work products placed under software configuration management include the software products that are delivered to the customer (e.g., the software requirements document and the code) and the items that are identified with or required to create these software products (e.g., the compiler).

A software baseline library is established containing the software baselines as they are developed. Changes to baselines and the release of software products built from the software baseline library are systematically controlled via the change control and configuration auditing functions of software configuration management.

This key process area covers the practices for performing the software configuration management function. The practices identifying specfic configuration items/units are contained in the key process areas that describe the development and maintenance of each configuration item/unit.

The goals of Software Configuration Management are:

1. Software configuration management activities are planned.
2. Selected software work products are identified, controlled, and available.
3. Changes to identified software work products are controlled.
4. Affected groups and individuals are informed of the status and content of software baselines.

The top-level activities performed for Software Configuration Management are:

1. An SCM plan is prepared for each software project according to a documented procedure.
2. A documented and approved SCM plan is used as the basis for performing the SCM activities.
3. A configuration management library system is established as a repository for the software baselines.
4. The software work products to be placed under configuration management are identified.
5. Change requests and problem reports for all configuration items/units are initiated, recorded, reviewed, approved, and tracked according to a documented procedure.
6. Changes to baselines are controlled according to a documented procedure.
7. Products from the software baseline library are created and their release is controlled according to a documented procedure.
8. The status of configuration items/units is recorded according to a documented procedure.
9. Standard reports documenting the SCM activities and the contents of the software baseline are developed and made available to affected groups and individuals.
10. Software baseline audits are conducted according to a documented procedure.

Level 3: Abridged Practices for Organization Process Focus

The purpose of Organization Process Focus is to establish the organizational responsibility for software process activities that improve the organization's overall software process capability.

Organization Process Focus involves developing and maintaining an understanding of the organization's and projects' software processes and coordinating the activities to assess, develop, maintain, and improve these processes.

The organization provides the long-term commitments and resources to coordinate the development and maintenance of the software processes across current and future software projects via a group such as a software engineering process group. This group is responsible for the organization's software process activities. It is specifically responsible for the development and maintenance of the organization's standard software process and related process assets (as described in the Organization Process Definition key process area), and it coordinates the process activities with the software projects.

The goals of Organization Process Focus are:

1. Software process development and improvement activities are coordinated across the organization.
2. The strengths and weaknesses of the software processes used are identified relative to a process standard.
3. Organization-level process development and improvement activities are planned.

The top-level activities performed for Organization Process Focus are:

1. The software process is assessed periodically, and action plans are developed to address the assessment findings.
2. The organization develops and maintains a plan for its software process development and improvement activities.
3. The organization's and projects' activities for developing and improving their software processes are coordinated at the organization level.
4. The use of the organization's software process database is coordinated at the organizational level.

5. New processes, methods, and tools in limited use in the organization are monitored, evaluated, and, where appropriate, transferred to other parts of the organization.

6. Training for the organization's and projects' software processes is coordinated across the organization.

7. The groups involved in implementing the software processes are informed of the organization's and projects' activities for software process development and improvement.

Level 3: Abridged Practices for Organization Process Definition

The purpose of Organization Process Definition is to develop and maintain a usable set of software process assets that improve process performance across the projects and provide a basis for cumulative, long-term benefits to the organization.

Organization Process Definition involves developing and maintaining the organization's standard software process, along with related process assets, such as descriptions of software life cycles, process tailoring guidelines and criteria, the organization's software process database, and a library of software process-related documentation.

These assets may be collected in many ways, depending on the organization's implementation of Organization Process Definition. For example, the descriptions of the software life cycles may be an integral part of the organization's standard software process or parts of the library of software process-related documentation may be stored in the organization's software process database.

The organization's software process assets are available for use in developing, implementing, and maintaining the projects' defined software processes. (The practices related to the development and maintenance of the project's defined software process are described in the Integrated Software Management key process area.)

The goals of Organization Process Definition are:

1. A standard software process for the organization is developed and maintained.

2. Information related to the use of the organization's standard software process by the software projects is collected, reviewed, and made available.

The top-level activities performed for Organization Process Definition are:

1. The organization's standard software process is developed and maintained according to a documented procedure.

2. The organization's standard software process is documented according to established organization standards.

3. Descriptions of software life cycles that are approved for use by the projects are documented and maintained.

4. Guidelines and criteria for the projects' tailoring of the organization's standard software process are developed and maintained.

5. The organization's software process database is established and maintained.

6. A library of software process-related documentation is established and maintained.

Level 3: Abridged Practices for Training Program

The purpose of the Training Program key process area is to develop the skills and knowledge of individuals so they can perform their roles effectively and efficiently.

Training Program involves first identifying the training needed by the organization, projects, and individuals, then developing or procuring training to address the identified needs.

Each software project evaluates its current and future skill needs and determines how these skills will be obtained. Some skills are effectively and efficiently imparted through informal vehicles (e.g., on-the-job training and informal mentoring), whereas other skills need more formal training vehicles (e.g., classroom training and guided self-study) to be effectively and efficiently imparted. The appropriate vehicles are selected and used.

This key process area covers the practices for the group performing the training function. The practices identifying the specific training topics (i.e., knowledge or skill needed) are contained in the Ability to Perform common feature of the individual key process areas.

The goals of Training Program are:

1. Training activities are planned.

2. Training for developing the skills and knowledge needed to perform software management and technical roles is provided.

3. Individuals in the software engineering group and software-related groups receive the training necessary to perform their roles.

The top-level activities performed for Training Program are:

1. Each software project develops and maintains a training plan that specifies its training needs.

2. The organization's training plan is developed and revised according to a documented procedure.

3. The training for the organization is performed in accordance with the organization's training plan.

4. Training courses prepared at the organization level are developed and maintained according to organization standards.

5. A waiver procedure for required training is established and used to determine whether individuals already possess the knowledge and skills required to perform in their designated roles.

6. Records of training are maintained.

Level 3: Abridged Practices for Integrated Software Management

The purpose of Integrated Software Management is to integrate the software engineering and management activities into a coherent, defined software process that is tailored from the organization's standard software process and related process assets, which are described in Organization Process Definition.

Integrated Software Management involves developing the project's defined software process and managing the software project using this defined software process. The project's defined software process is tailored from the organization's standard software process to address the specific characteristics of the project.

The software development plan is based on the project's defined software process and describes how the activities of the project's defined software process will be implemented and managed. The management of the software project's size, effort, cost, schedule, staffing, and other resources is tied to the tasks of the project's defined software process.

Since the project's defined software processes are all tailored from the organization's standard software process, the software projects can share process data and lessons learned.

The basic practices for estimating, planning, and tracking a software project are described in the Software Project Planning and Software Project Tracking and Oversight key process areas. They focus on recognizing problems when they occur and adjusting the plans and/or performance to address the problems. The practices of this key process area built on, and are in addition to, the practices of those two key process areas. The emphasis of Integrated Software Management shifts to anticipating problems and acting to prevent or minimize the effects of these problems.

The goals of Integrated Software Management are:

1. The project's defined software process is a tailored version of the organization's standard software process.

2. The project is planned and managed according to the project's defined software process.

The top-level activities performed for Integrated Software Management are:

1. The project's defined software process is developed by tailoring the organization's standard software process according to a documented procedure.

2. Each project's defined software process is revised according to a documented procedure.

3. The project's software development plan, which describes the use of the project's defined software process, is developed and revised according to a documented procedure.

4. The software project is managed in accordance with the project's defined software process.

5. The organization's software process database is used for software planning and estimating.

6. The size of the software work products (or size of changes to the software work products) is managed according to a documented procedure.

7. The project's software effort and costs are managed according to a documented procedure.

8. The project's critical computer resources are managed according to a documented procedure.

9. The critical dependencies and critical paths of the project's software schedule are managed according to a documented procedure.

10. The project's software risks are identified, assessed, documented, and managed according to a documented procedure.

11. Reviews of the software project are periodically performed to determine the actions needed to bring the software project's performance and results in line with the current and projected needs of the business, customer, and end users, as appropriate.

Level 3: Abridged Practices for Software Product Engineering

The purpose of Software Product Engineering is to perform consistently a well-defined engineering process that integrates all the software engineering activities to produce correct, consistent software products effectively and efficiently.

Software Product Engineering involves performing the engineering tasks to build and maintain the software using the project's defined software process (which is described in the Integrated Software Management key process area) and appropriate methods and tools.

The software engineering tasks include analyzing the system requirements allocated to software (these system requirements are described in the Requirements Management key process area), developing the software requirements, developing the software architecture, designing the software, implementing the software in the code, integrating the software components, and testing the software to verify that it satisfies the specified requirements (i.e., the system requirements allocated to software and the software requirements).

Documentation needed to perform the software engineering tasks (e.g., software requirements document, software design document, test plan, and test procedures) is developed and reviewed to ensure that each task addresses the results of predecessor tasks and the results produced are appropriate for the subsequent tasks (including the tasks of operating and maintaining the software). When changes are approved, affected software work products, plans, commitments, processes, and activities are revised to reflect the approved changes.

The goals of Software Product Engineering are:

1. The software engineering tasks are defined, integrated, and consistently performed to produce the software.

2. Software work products are kept consistent with one another.

The top-level activities performed for Software Product Engineering are:

1. Appropriate software engineering methods and tools are integrated into the project's defined software process.

2. The software requirements are developed, maintained, documented, and verified by systematically analyzing the allocated requirements according to the project's defined software process.

3. The software design is developed, maintained, documented, and verified, according to the project's defined software process, to accommodate the software requirements and to form the framework for coding.

4. The software code is developed, maintained, documented, and verified, according to the project's defined software process, to implement the software requirements and software design.

5. Software testing is performed according to the project's defined software process.

6. Integration testing of the software is planned and performed according to the project's defined software process.

7. System and acceptance testing of the software are planned and performed to demonstrate that the software satisfies its requirements.

8. The documentation that will be used to operate and maintain the software is developed and maintained according to the project's defined software process.

9. Data on defects identified in peer reviews and testing are collected and analyzed according to the project's defined software process.

10. Consistency is maintained across software work products, including the software plans, process descriptions, allocated requirements, software requirements, software design, code, test plans, and test procedures.

Level 3: Abridged Practices for Intergroup Coordination

The purpose of Intergroup Coordination is to establish a means for the software engineering group to participate actively with the other engineering groups so the project is better able to satisfy the customer's needs effectively and efficiently.

Intergroup Coordination involves the software engineering group's participation with other project engineering groups to address system-level requirements, objectives, and issues. Representatives of the project's engineering groups participate in establishing the system-level requirements, objectives, and plans by working with the customer and end users, as appropriate. These requirements, objectives, and plans become the basis for all engineering activities.

The technical working interfaces and interactions between groups are planned and managed to ensure the quality and integrity of the entire system. Technical reviews and interchanges are regularly conducted with representatives of the project's engineering groups to ensure that all engineering groups are aware of the status and plans of all the groups and that system and intergroup issues receive appropriate attention.

The software-specific practices related to these engineering tasks are described in the Requirements Management and Software Product Engineering key process areas.

The goals of Intergroup Coordination are:

1. The customer's requirements are agreed to by all affected groups.
2. The commitments between the engineering groups are agreed to by the affected groups.
3. The engineering groups identify, track, and resolve intergroup issues.

The top-level activities performed for Intergroup Coordination are:

1. The software engineering group and the other engineering groups participate with the customer and end users, as appropriate, to establish the system requirements.
2. Representatives of the project's software engineering group work with representatives of the other engineering groups to monitor and coordinate technical activities and resolve technical issues.
3. A documented plan is used to communicate intergroup commitments and to coordinate and track the work performed.
4. Critical dependencies between engineering groups are identified, negotiated, and tracked according to a documented procedure.
5. Work products produced as input to other engineering groups are reviewed by representatives of the receiving groups to ensure that the work products meet their needs.

6. Intergroup issues not resolvable by the individual representatives of the project engineering groups are handled according to a documented procedure.

7. Representatives of the project engineering groups conduct periodic technical reviews and interchanges.

Level 3: Abridged Practices for Peer Reviews

The purpose of Peer Reviews is to remove defects from the software work products early and efficiently. An important corollary effect is to develop a better understanding of the software work products and of defects that might be prevented.

Peer Reviews involve a methodical examination of software work products by the producers' peers to identify defects and areas where changes are needed. The specific products that will undergo a peer review are identified in the project's defined software process and scheduled as part of the software project planning activities, as described in Integrated Software Management.

This key process area covers the practices for performing peer reviews. The practices identifying the specific software work products that undergo peer review are contained in the key process areas that describe the development and maintenance of each software work product.

The goals of Peer Reviews are:

1. Peer review activities are planned.

2. Defects in the software work products are identified and removed.

The top-level activities performed for Peer Reviews are:

1. Peer reviews are planned, and the plans are documented.

2. Peer reviews are performed according to a documented procedure.

3. Data on the conduct and results of the peer reviews are recorded.

Level 4: Abridged Practices for Quantitative Process Management

The purpose of Quantitative Process Management is to control the process performance of the software project quantitatively. Software process performance represents the actual results achieved from following a software process.

Quantitative Process Management involves establishing goals for the performance of the project's defined software process, which is described in the Integrated Software Management key process area, taking measurements of the process performance, analyzing these measurements, and making adjustments to maintain process performance within acceptable limits. When the process performance is stabilized within acceptable limits, the project's defined software process, the associated measurements, and the acceptable limits for the measurements are established as a baseline and used to control process performance quantitatively.

The organization collects process performance data from the software projects and uses these data to characterize the process capability (i.e., the process performance a new project can expect to attain) of the organization's standard software process, which is described in the Organization Process Definition key process area. Process capability describes the range of expected results from following a software process (i.e., the most likely outcomes that are expected from the next software project the organization undertakes). These process capability data are, in turn, used by the software projects to establish and revise their process performance goals and to analyze the performance of the projects' defined software processes.

The goals of Quantitative Process Management are:

1. The quantitative process management activities are planned.
2. The process performance of the project's defined software process is controlled quantitatively.
3. The process capability of the organization's standard software process is known in quantitative terms.

The top-level activities performed for Quantitative Process Management are:

1. The software project's plan for quantitative process management is developed according to a documented procedure.

2. The software project's quantitative process management activities are performed in accordance with the project's quantitative process management plan.

3. The strategy for the data collection and the quantitative analyses to be performed are determined based on the project's defined software process.

4. The measurement data used to control the project's defined software process quantitatively are collected according to a documented procedure.

5. The project's defined software process is analyzed and brought under quantitative control according to a documented procedure.

6. Reports documenting the results of the software project's quantitative process management activities are prepared and distributed.

7. The process capability baseline for the organization's standard software process is established and maintained according to a documented procedure.

Level 4: Abridged Practices for Software Quality Management

The purpose of Software Quality Management is to develop a quantitative understanding of the quality of the project's software products and achieve specific quality goals.

Software Quality Management involves defining quality goals for the software products, establishing plans to achieve these goals, and monitoring and adjusting the software plans, software work products, activities, and quality goals to satisfy the needs and desires of the customer and end user for high-quality products.

The practices of Software Quality Management build on the practices of the Integrated Software Management and Software Product Engineering key process areas, which establish and implement the project's defined software process, and the Quantitative Process Management key process area, which establishes a quantitative understanding of the ability of the project's defined software process to achieve the desired results.

Quantitative goals are established for the software products based on the needs of the organization, the customer, and the end users. So that these goals may be achieved, the organization establishes strategies and plans, and the project specifically adjusts its defined software process, to accomplish the quality goals.

The goals of Software Quality Management are:

1. The project's software quality management activities are planned.
2. Measurable goals for software product quality and their priorities are defined.
3. Actual progress toward achieving the quality goals for the software products is quantified and managed.

The top-level activities performed for Software Quality Management are:

1. The project's software quality plan is developed and maintained according to a documented procedure.
2. The project's software quality plan is the basis for the project's activities for software quality management.
3. The project's quantitative quality goals for the software products are defined, monitored, and revised throughout the software life cycle.
4. The quality of the project's software products is measured, analyzed, and compared to the products' quantitative quality goals on an event-driven basis.
5. The software project's quantitative quality goals for the products are allocated appropriately to the subcontractors delivering software products to the project.

Level 5: Abridged Practices for Defect Prevention

The purpose of Defect Prevention is to identify the cause of defects and prevent them from recurring.

Defect Prevention involves analyzing defects that were encountered in the past and taking specific actions to prevent the occurrence of those types of defects in the future. The defects may have been identified on other projects as well as in earlier stages or tasks of the current project. Defect prevention activities are also one mechanism for spreading lessons learned between projects.

Trends are analyzed to track the types of defects that have been encountered and to identify defects that are likely to recur. Based on an understanding of the project's defined software process and how it is implemented (as described in the Integrated Software Management and Software Product Engineering key process areas), the root causes of the defects and the implications of the defects for future activities are determined.

Both the project and the organization take specific actions to prevent recurrence of the defects. Some of the organizational actions may be handled as described in the Process Change Management key process area.

The goals of Defect Prevention are:

1. Defect prevention activities are planned.

2. Common causes of defects are sought out and identified.

3. Common causes of defects are prioritized and systematically eliminated.

The top-level activities performed for Defect Prevention are:

1. The software project develops and maintains a plan for its defect prevention activities.

2. At the beginning of a software task, the members of the team performing the task meet to prepare for the activities of that task and the related defect prevention activities.

3. Causal analysis meetings are conducted according to a documented procedure.

4. Each of the teams assigned to coordinate defect prevention activities meets on a periodic basis to review and coordinate implementation of action proposals from the causal analysis meetings.

5. Defect prevention data are documented and tracked across the teams coordinating defect prevention activities.

6. Revisions to the organization's standard software process resulting from defect prevention actions are incorporated according to a documented procedure.

7. Revisions to the project's defined software process resulting from defect prevention actions are incorporated according to a documented procedure.

8. Members of the software engineering group and software-related groups receive feedback on the status and results of the organization's and project's defect prevention activities on a periodic basis.

Level 5: Abridged Practices for Technology Change Management

The purpose of Technology Change Management is to identify new technologies (i.e., tools, methods, and processes) and incorporate them into the organization in an orderly manner.

Technology Change Management involves identifying, selecting, and evaluating new technologies and incorporating effective technologies into the organization. The objective is to improve software quality, increase productivity, and decrease the cycle time for product development.

The organization establishes a group (such as a software engineering process group or a technology support group) to work with the software projects, introduce and evaluate new technologies, and manage changes to existing technologies. Particular emphasis is placed on technology changes that are likely to improve the capability of the organization's standard software process (as described in the Organization Process Definition key process area).

By maintaining an awareness of software-related technology innovations and systematically evaluating and experimenting with them, the organization selects appropriate technologies to improve the quality of its software and the productivity of its software activities. Pilot efforts are performed to assess new and unproven technologies before they are incorporated into normal practice. With appropriate sponsorship of the organization's management, the selected technologies are incorporated into the organization's standard software process and current projects, as appropriate.

Changes to the organization's standard software process (as described in the Organization Process Definition key process area) and the projects' defined software processes (as described in the Integrated Software Management key process area) resulting from these technology changes are handled as described in the Process Change Management key process area.

The goals of Technology Change Management are:

1. Incorporation of technology changes is planned.

2. New technologies are evaluated to determine their effect on quality and productivity.

3. Appropriate new technologies are transferred into normal practice across the organization.

The top-level activities for Technology Change Management are:

1. The organization develops and maintains a plan for technology change management.

2. The group responsible for the organization's technology change management activities works with the software projects in identifying areas of technology change.

3. Software managers and technical staff are kept informed of new technologies.

4. The group responsible for the organization's technology change management systematically analyzes the organization's standard software process to identify areas that need or could benefit from new technology.

5. Technologies are selected and acquired for the organization and software projects according to a documented procedure.

6. Pilot efforts for improving technology are conducted, where appropriate, before a new technology is introduced into normal practice.

7. Appropriate new technologies are incorporated into the organization's standard software process according to a documented procedure.

8. Appropriate new technologies are incorporated into the projects' defined software processes according to a documented procedure.

Level 5: Abridged Practices for Process Change Management

The purpose of Process Change Management is to continually improve the software processes used in the organization with the intent of improving software quality, increasing productivity, and decreasing the cycle time for product development.

Process Change Management involves defining process improvement goals and, with senior management sponsorship, proactively and systematically identifying, evaluating, and implementing improvements to the organization's standard software process and the projects' defined software processes on a continuous basis.

Training and incentive programs are established to enable and encourage everyone in the organization to participate in process improvement activities. Improvement opportunities are identified and evaluated for potential payback to the organization. Pilot efforts are performed to assess process changes before they are incorporated into normal practice.

When software process improvements are approved for normal practice, the organization's standard software process and the projects' defined software processes are revised as appropriate. The practices for revising the organization's standard software process are found in the Organization Process Definition key process area, and the practices for revising the projects' defined software processes are found in the Integrated Software Management key process area.

The goals of Process Change Management are:

1. Continuous process improvement is planned.
2. Participation in the organization's software process improvement activities is organization wide.
3. The organization's standard software process and the projects' defined software processes are improved continuously.

The top-level activities performed for Process Change Management are:

1. A software process improvement program is established to empower the members of the organization to improve the processes of the organization.
2. The group responsible for the organization's software process activities (e.g., software engineering process group) coordinates the software process improvement activities.
3. The organization develops and maintains a plan for software process improvement according to a documented procedure.
4. The software process improvement activities are performed in accordance with the software process improvement plan.
5. Software process improvement proposals are handled according to a documented procedure.
6. Members of the organization actively participate in teams to develop software process improvements for assigned process areas.
7. Where appropriate, the software process improvements are installed on a pilot basis to determine their benefits and effectiveness before they are introduced into normal practice.

8. When the decision is made to transfer a software process improvement into normal practice, the improvement is implemented according to a documented procedure.

9. Records of software process improvement activities are maintained.

10. Software managers and technical staff receive feedback on the status and results of the software process improvement activities on an event-driven basis.

Appendix **E**

Mapping the Key Practices
to Goals

Since satisfying a key process area implies addressing each of the goals for that key process area, it may be helpful to understand the relationships between the key practices and the goals. The following tables map each of the key practices to its associated goal(s).

Practices, like key process areas, are not independent of one another. Many key practices map to more than one goal. For example, there is usually only one policy statement per key process area, and it covers all of the goals for that key process area.

Even when a practice is mapped to a single goal, there may be subpractices that contribute to achieving another goal. For example, the subpractices on configuration management in Software Product Engineering (Activities 1.4, 2.11, 3.10, 4.5, 5.7, 7.8, and 8.6) contribute to Goal 2 on maintaining consistent software work products, even though the associated key practices contribute directly to Goal 1, as is indicated in this appendix.

REQUIREMENTS MANAGEMENT

Goal	Commitment	Ability	Activity	Measurement	Verification
1	1	1, 2, 3, 4	1	1	1, 2, 3
2	1	3, 4	2, 3	1	1, 2, 3

SOFTWARE PROJECT PLANNING

Goal	Commitment	Ability	Activity	Measurement	Verification
1	1, 2	1, 3, 4	9, 10, 11, 12, 15	1	1, 2, 3
2	1, 2	1, 2, 3, 4	2, 5, 6, 7, 8, 13, 14	1	1, 2, 3
3	1, 2	1, 3, 4	1, 3, 4	1	1, 2, 3

SOFTWARE PROJECT TRACKING AND OVERSIGHT

Goal	Commitment	Ability	Activity	Measurement	Verification
1	1, 2	1, 2, 3, 4, 5	1, 5, 6, 7, 8, 9, 10, 11, 12, 13	1	1, 2, 3
2	1, 2	1, 2, 3, 4, 5	2, 5, 6, 7, 8, 9, 11	1	1, 2, 3
3	1, 2	1, 2, 3, 4, 5	3, 4	1	1, 2, 3

SOFTWARE SUBCONTRACT MANAGEMENT

Goal	Commitment	Ability	Activity	Measurement	Verification
1	1, 2	1, 2	1, 2	1	2, 3
2	1, 2	1, 2, 3	3, 4, 6	1	1, 2, 3
3	1, 2	1, 2, 3	7, 8, 9, 13	1	2, 3
4	1, 2	1, 2, 3	3, 5, 7, 9, 10, 11, 12, 13	1	1, 2, 3

SOFTWARE QUALITY ASSURANCE

Goal	Commitment	Ability	Activity	Measurement	Verification
1	1	1, 2, 3	1, 2	1	2, 3
2	1	1, 2, 3, 4	2, 3, 4, 5	1	2, 3
3	1	1, 2, 3, 4	6, 7, 8	1	1, 2, 3
4	1	1, 2, 3, 4	7	1	1, 2, 3

SOFTWARE CONFIGURATION MANAGEMENT

Goal	Commitment	Ability	Activity	Measurement	Verification
1	1	2, 3, 4	1, 2	1	2, 4
2	1	1, 2, 3, 4, 5	2, 3, 4, 7	1	4
3	1	1, 2, 3, 4, 5	5, 6	1	4
4	1	2, 3, 4, 5	8, 9, 10	1	1, 2, 3, 4

ORGANIZATION PROCESS FOCUS

Goal	Commitment	Ability	Activity	Measurement	Verification
1	1, 2, 3	1, 2, 3, 4	3, 4, 5, 6, 7	1	1
2	1, 2, 3	1, 2, 3, 4	1	1	1
3	1, 2, 3	1, 2, 3, 4	2	1	1

ORGANIZATION PROCESS DEFINITION

Goal	Commitment	Ability	Activity	Measurement	Verification
1	1	1, 2	1, 2, 3, 4	1	1
2	1	1, 2	5, 6	1	1

TRAINING PROGRAM

Goal	Commitment	Ability	Activity	Measurement	Verification
1	1	1, 2, 3, 4	1, 2, 3	1	1, 3
2	1	1, 2, 3, 4	3, 4	1, 2	1, 2, 3
3	1	1, 2, 3, 4	5, 6	1, 2	2, 3

INTEGRATED SOFTWARE MANAGEMENT

Goal	Commitment	Ability	Activity	Measurement	Verification
1	1	1, 2	1, 2, 3	1	2, 3
2	1	1, 3	3, 4, 5, 6, 7, 8, 9, 10, 11	1	1, 2, 3

SOFTWARE PRODUCT ENGINEERING

Goal	Commitment	Ability	Activity	Measurement	Verification
1	1	1, 2, 3, 4	1, 2, 3, 4, 5, 6, 7, 8, 9	1, 2	1, 2, 3
2	1	1, 2, 3, 4	10	1, 2	1, 2, 3

INTERGROUP COORDINATION

Goal	Commitment	Ability	Activity	Measurement	Verification
1	1	1, 2, 3, 4, 5	1	1	2, 3
2	1	1, 2, 3, 4, 5	3, 4, 5	1	2, 3
3	1	1, 2, 3, 4, 5	2, 6, 7	1	1, 2, 3

PEER REVIEWS

Goal	Commitment	Ability	Activity	Measurement	Verification
1	1	1, 2	1	1	1
2	1	1, 2, 3	2, 3	1	1

QUANTITATIVE PROCESS MANAGEMENT

Goal	Commitment	Ability	Activity	Measurement	Verification
1	1, 2	1, 2, 4, 5	1, 2, 3	1	2, 3
2	1	1, 2, 3, 4, 5	2, 4, 5, 6	1	1, 2, 3
3	2	1, 2, 3, 4, 5	7	1	1, 3

SOFTWARE QUALITY MANAGEMENT

Goal	Commitment	Ability	Activity	Measurement	Verification
1	1	1, 2, 3	1, 2	1	2, 3
2	1	1, 2, 3	3, 5	1	2, 3
3	1	1, 2, 3	2, 4	1	1, 2, 3

DEFECT PREVENTION

Goal	Commitment	Ability	Activity	Measurement	Verification
1	1, 2	1, 2, 3, 4	1, 2	1	2, 3
2	1, 2	3, 4	3, 5	1	3
3	1, 2	1, 2, 3, 4	4, 6, 7, 8	1	1, 2, 3

TECHNOLOGY CHANGE MANAGEMENT

Goal	Commitment	Ability	Activity	Measurement	Verification
1	1, 2, 3	1, 2, 5	1	1	2
2	1, 2, 3	1, 2, 3, 4, 5	2, 4, 5, 6	1	1, 2
3	1, 2, 3	1, 2, 5	3, 7, 8	1	1, 2

PROCESS CHANGE MANAGEMENT

Goal	Commitment	Ability	Activity	Measurement	Verification
1	1, 2	1, 2, 3	2, 3, 4	1	2
2	1, 2	1, 2, 3, 4	1, 6, 10	1	1, 2
3	1, 2	1, 2, 3, 4	4, 5, 7, 8, 9	1	1, 2

Appendix F

Comparing ISO 9001 and the CMM

The CMM and the ISO 9000 series of standards developed by the International Standards Organization share a common concern about quality and process management. The two are driven by similar concerns and are intuitively correlated.

The specific standard in the ISO 9000 series of concern to software organizations is ISO 9001. Three questions are frequently asked:

- At what level in the CMM would an ISO 9001–compliant organization be?
- Can a Level 2 (or 3) organization be considered compliant with ISO 9001?
- Should my software quality management and process improvement efforts be based on ISO 9001 or on the CMM?

The purpose of this appendix is to compare the CMM and ISO 9001, identify their differences and similarities, and answer these questions. This appendix is based on papers [Paulk93d, Paulk94b], which discuss the relationship in both lesser and greater detail.

F.1 The ISO 9000 Series

The ISO 9000 series of standards is a set of documents dealing with quality systems that can be used for external quality assurance purposes. They specify quality system requirements for use where a contract between two parties requires the demonstration of a supplier's capability to design and supply product. The two parties could be an external client and the supplier, or both could be internal, for example, marketing and engineering groups in a company.

ISO 9000 proper is a guideline that clarifies the distinctions and interrelationships between quality concepts and provides guidelines for the selection and use of a series of international standards on quality systems that can be used for internal quality management purposes (ISO 9004) and for external quality assurance purposes (ISO 9001, 9002, and 9003). The quality concepts addressed by these standards are:

- An organization should achieve and sustain the quality of the product or service produced so as to meet continually the purchaser's stated or implied needs.

- An organization should provide confidence to its own management that the intended quality is being achieved and sustained.

- An organization should provide confidence to the purchaser that the intended quality is being, or will be, achieved in the delivered product or service provided. When contractually required, this provision of confidence may involve agreed demonstration requirements.

ISO 9001, "Quality systems—Model for quality assurance in design/development, production, installation, and servicing," is intended for use when conformance to specified requirements is to be assured by the supplier during several stages, which may include design, development, production, installation, and servicing. Of the ISO 9000 series, it is the standard that is pertinent to software development and maintenance. There is a guideline, ISO 9000-3, for applying ISO 9001 to the development, supply, and maintenance of software. A British guide [TickIT] for applying ISO 9001 to software provides additional information on using ISO 9000-3 and 9001 in the software arena.

F.2 Mapping ISO 9001 to the CMM

This section summarizes and compares 20 clauses in Chapter 4 of ISO 9001 to the practices in the CMM. The comparison, based on an analysis of ISO 9001, ISO 9000-3, TickIT, and the TickIT training materials [Lloyd's94], involves judgment, and so there are differences of interpretation for both ISO 9001 and the CMM. A common challenge for CMM-based appraisals and ISO 9001 certification is reliability and consistency of assessments, which is partially addressed by strict training prerequisites for TickIT auditors and CMM appraisers. ISO 9000-3 elaborates significantly on ISO 9001, and TickIT training provides significant guidance on how to interpret both ISO 9000-3 and ISO 9001.

Each clause in ISO 9001 will be discussed, but not on a sentence-for-sentence basis. A detailed mapping, at the sentence-to-subpractice level, was performed as part of this analysis and published as an SEI technical report [Paulk94b].

Clause 4.1 Management Responsibility

ISO 9001 requires that the quality policy be defined, documented, understood, implemented, and maintained; that responsibilities and authorities for all personnel specifying, achieving, and monitoring quality be defined; and that in-house verification resources be defined, trained, and funded. A designated manager ensures that the quality program is implemented and maintained.

Management responsibility for quality policy and verification activities is primarily addressed in Software Quality Assurance, although Software Project Planning and Software Project Tracking & Oversight assist by assigning responsibility for performing all project roles.

Management's responsibility at both the senior management and project management levels to oversee the software project are addressed in the Verifying Implementation common feature. More generically, leadership issues are addressed in the Commitment to Perform common feature, and organizational structure and resource issues are addressed in the Ability to Perform common feature.

One could argue that the quality policy described in Software Quality Management at Level 4 is also addressed by this clause, but the Level 4 quality policy is quantitative. ISO 9001 is somewhat ambiguous about the role of measurement in the quality management system, as is discussed for Clause 4.20, but it only requires that quality objectives be defined and documented, not that they be quantitative.

Clause 4.2 Quality System

ISO 9001 requires that a documented quality system, including procedures and instructions, be established. ISO 9000-3 characterizes this quality system as an integrated process throughout the entire life cycle.

Quality system activities are primarily addressed in the CMM in Software Quality Assurance. The procedures that would be used are distributed throughout the key process areas in the various Activities Performed practices.

The specific procedures and standards that a software project would use are specified in the software development plan described in Software Project Planning. Compliance with these standards and procedures is assured in Software Quality Assurance and by the auditing practices in the Verifying Implementation common feature.

Software Product Engineering requires that the software engineering tasks be defined, integrated, and consistently performed, which corresponds directly to the ISO 9000-3 guidance for interpreting this clause.

One arguable correspondence is to Organization Process Definition, which describes a set of software process assets, including standards, procedures, and process descriptions, at the organization level. Addressing Organization Process Definition would certainly contribute to achieving this clause. ISO 9001 specifies the supplier's quality system, but it does not discuss the relationship between organizational support and project implementation as the CMM does. ISO 9000-3, on the other hand, has two sections on quality planning: Clause 4.2.3 discusses quality planning across projects; Clause 5.5 discusses quality planning within a particular development effort.

Clause 4.3 Contract Review

ISO 9001 requires that contracts be reviewed to see whether the requirements are adequately defined, agree with the bid, and can be implemented.

Review of the customer requirements, as allocated to software, is described in the CMM in Requirements Management. The software organization (supplier) ensures that the system requirements allocated to software are documented and reviewed and that missing or ambiguous requirements are clarified. Since the CMM is constrained to the software perspective, the customer requirements as a whole are beyond the scope of this key process area.

Software Project Planning describes the development of a proposal, a statement of work, and a software development plan, which are reviewed by the software engineering group and by senior management, in establishing external (contractual) commitments.

The CMM also explicitly addresses the acquisition of software through subcontracting by the software organization, as described in Software Subcontract Management. Contracts may be with an external customer or with a subcontractor, although that distinction is not explicitly made in this clause of ISO 9001.

Clause 4.4 Design Control

ISO 9001 requires that procedures to control and verify the design be established. This includes planning design and development activities, defining organizational and technical interfaces, identifying inputs and outputs, reviewing, the design, verifying the design, validating the design and controlling design changes. ISO 9000-3 elaborates this clause with clauses on the purchaser's requirements specification (5.3), development planning (5.4), quality planning (5.5), design and implementation (5.6), testing and validation (5.7), and configuration management (6.1).

In the CMM, the life cycle activities of requirements analysis, design, code, and test are described in Software Product Engineering. Planning these activities is described in Software Project Planning. Control of these life cycle activities is described in Software Project Tracking & Oversight. Configuration management is described in Software Configuration Management.

ISO 9001 requires holding design reviews. ISO 9000-3 states that the supplier should carry out reviews to ensure the requirements are met and design methods are correctly carried out. There is a wide range of flexibility in what kind of design review is implemented. In contrast, the CMM calls out a specific design control mechanism: peer reviews. The Peer Reviews key process area supports processes throughout the life cycle, from requirements analysis through testing.

TickIT training clarifies this issue by listing three examples of design reviews: Fagan inspections, structured walkthroughs, and peer reviews (in the sense of a desk check). The training also states that "an auditor will need to be satisfied from the procedures and records available that the reviews within an organization are satisfactory considering the type and criticality of the project under review" [Lloyd's94, p. 17.10–11]

More formal, quantitative aspects of the design process are described in Software Quality Management, but this degree of formality is not necessarily required by ISO 9001.

Clause 4.5 Document and Data Control

ISO 9001 requires that the distribution and modification of documents and data be controlled.

The configuration management practices characterizing document control are described in Software Configuration Management. The specific procedures, standards, and other documents that may be placed under configuration management in the CMM are distributed throughout the key process areas in the various Activities Performed practices. The documentation required to operate and maintain the system is specifically called out in Activity 8 of Software Product Engineering.

Clause 4.6 Purchasing

ISO 9001 requires that purchased products conform to their specified requirements. This includes the evaluation of potential subcontractors and verification of purchased products.

The CMM addresses this issue in Software Subcontract Management. Evaluation of subcontractors is described in Activity 2. Acceptance testing of subcontracted software is addressed in Activity 12.

Clause 4.7 Control of Customer-Supplied Product

ISO 9001 requires that any customer-supplied material be verified, controlled, and maintained. ISO 9000-3 discusses this clause in the context of included software product (6.8), including commercial-off-the-shelf software.

Activity 6.3 in Integrated Software Management is the only practice in the CMM describing the use of purchased software. It does so in the context of identifying off-the-shelf or reusable software as part of planning. Integration of off-the-shelf and reusable software is one of the areas where the CMM is weak. This clause, especially as expanded in ISO 9000-3, cannot be considered adequately covered by the CMM. It would be reasonable, though not sufficient, to apply the acceptance testing practice for subcontracted software in Activity 12 of Software Subcontract Management to any included software product.

A change request has been written for CMM v1.1 to incorporate practices in Software Product Engineering that address product evaluation and the inclusion of off-the-shelf and nondevelopmental software.

Clause 4.8 Product Identification and Traceability

ISO 9001 requires that the product be identified and traceable during all stages of production, delivery, and installation.

The CMM covers this clause primarily in Software Configuration Management, but Activity 10 of Software Product Engineering states the specific need for consistency and traceability between software work products.

Clause 4.9 Process Control

ISO 9001 requires that production processes be defined and planned. This includes carrying out production under controlled conditions, according to documented instructions. When the results of processes cannot be fully verified after the fact the processes are continuously monitored and controlled. ISO 9000-3 includes design and implementation (5.6); rules, practices, and conventions (6.5); and tools and techniques (6.6).

The procedures defining the software production process in the CMM are distributed throughout the key process areas in the various Activities Performed practices. The specific procedures and standards that would be used are specified in the software development plan, as described in Activity 7 of Software Project Planning. The definition and integration of software "production" processes are described in Software Product Engineering. The tools to support these processes are called out in Ability 1.2 of Software Product Engineering. Process assurance is specified in Activity 4 of Software Quality Assurance (product assurance is in Activity 5).

Quantitative Process Management addresses the quantitative aspect of control exemplified by statistical process control, but would typically not be required to satisfy this clause.

It is also worth noting that Clause 6.6 in ISO 9000-3 states that "the supplier should improve these tools and techniques as required," which corresponds to transitioning new technology into the organization as discussed in Technology Change Management.

Clause 4.10 Inspection and Testing

ISO 9001 requires that incoming materials be inspected or verified before use and that in-process inspection and testing be performed. Final inspection and testing are performed prior to release of finished product. Records of inspection and test are kept.

The issues surrounding the inspection of incoming material have already been discussed for Clause 4.7. The CMM describes testing in Activities 5, 6, and 7 in Software Product Engineering. In-process inspections in the software sense are addressed in Peer Reviews.

Clause 4.11 Control of Inspection, Measuring, and Test Equipment

ISO 9001 requires that equipment used to demonstrate conformance be controlled, calibrated, and maintained. Test hardware or software are checked to prove they are capable of verifying the acceptability of product and rechecked at prescribed intervals. ISO 9000-3 clarifies this clause with clauses on testing and validation (5.7); rules, practices, and conventions (6.5); and tools and techniques (6.6).

This clause is generically addressed in the CMM under the testing practices in Software Product Engineering. Test software is specifically called out in Ability 1.2, which describes the tools that support testing.

Clause 4.12 Inspection and Test Status

ISO 9001 requires that the status of inspections and tests be maintained for items as they progress through various processing steps.

This clause is addressed in the CMM by the testing practices in Software Product Engineering and by Activities 5 and 8 on problem reporting and configuration status, respectively, in Software Configuration Management.

Clause 4.13 Control of Nonconforming Product

ISO 9001 requires that nonconforming product be controlled to prevent inadvertent use or installation. ISO 9000-3 maps this concept to design and implementation (5.6); testing and validation (5.7); replication, delivery, and installation (5.9); and configuration management (6.1).

Design, implementation, testing, and validation are addressed in Software Product Engineering. In Software Configuration Management, Activity 8 addresses the status of configuration items, which would include the status of items that contain known defects not yet fixed. Installation is not addressed in the CMM, as is discussed for Clause 4.15.

In the manufacturing world, this clause is important because it is sometimes necessary to build products using components that do not conform to all of the requirements. When such decisions are made, the resulting nonconforming products must be carefully controlled.

Nonconforming product is not specifically addressed in the CMM. In ISO 9000-3, it essentially disappears among a number of related processes spanning the software life cycle.

Clause 4.14 Corrective and Preventive Action

ISO 9001 requires that the causes of nonconforming product be identified. Corrective action is directed toward eliminating the causes of actual nonconformities, and preventive action is directed toward eliminating the causes of potential nonconformities [Durand93, p. 27]. Potential causes of nonconforming product are eliminated; procedures are changed resulting from corrective action. ISO 9000-3 quotes this clause verbatim, with no elaboration, from the 1987 release of ISO 9001.

A literal reading of this clause would imply many of the practices in Defect Prevention. Based upon the TickIT Auditors' Guide [TickIT, pp. 139–140] and discussions with ISO 9000 auditors, one interpretation is that the corrective action is driven by customer complaints. The software engineering group should look at field defects, analyze why they occurred, and take corrective action. This would typically occur through software updates and patches distributed to the fielded software. Under this interpretation, an appropriate mapping of this clause would be problem reporting, followed with controlled maintenance of baselined work products, as described in Software Configuration Management.

A complementary interpretation described in TickIT training [Lloyd's94, Section 23] is that the corrective action is to address noncompliances identified in an audit, whether external or internal. This would be addressed in Software Quality Assurance in the CMM.

This is a controversial issue in applying ISO 9001 to software. Some auditors seem to expect a defect prevention process similar to that found in the manufacturing environment. Others only require addressing user problem reports. It is arguable how much, if any, of the in-process causal analysis and defect prevention described in Defect Prevention is necessary to satisfy this clause.

Clause 4.15 Handling, Storage, Packaging, and Preservation Delivery

ISO 9001 requires that procedures for handling, storage, packaging, and delivery be established and maintained. ISO 9000-3 maps this to acceptance (5.8) and replication, delivery, and installation (5.9).

Replication, delivery, and installation are not covered in the CMM. Acceptance testing is addressed in Activity 7 of Software Product Engineering, and Activity 7 of Software Configuration Management describes the creation and release of software products, but the actual delivery and installation of the product is not described in the CMM.

A change request has been written for CMM v1.1 to incorporate a practice in Software Product Engineering on delivery and installation of the software product.

Clause 4.16 Control of Quality Records

ISO 9001 requires that quality records be collected, maintained, and dispositioned.

The practices defining the quality records to be maintained in the CMM are distributed throughout the key process areas in the various Activities Performed practices. Specifically pertinent to this clause are the testing and peer review practices in Software Product Engineering, especially the collection and analysis of defect data in Activity 9. Problem reporting is addressed by Activity 5 in Software Configuration Management, and the collection of peer review data is described in Activity 3 of Peer Reviews.

Clause 4.17 Internal Quality Audits

ISO 9001 requires that audits be planned and performed. The results of audits are communicated to management, and any deficiencies found are corrected.

The auditing process is described in Software Quality Assurance. Specific audits in the CMM are called out in the auditing practices of the Verifying Implementation common feature.

Clause 4.18 Training

ISO 9001 requires that training needs be identified and that training be provided, since selected tasks may require qualified personnel. Records of training are maintained.

Specific training needs in the CMM are identified in the training and orientation practices in the Ability to Perform common feature. The general training infrastructure is described in Training Program, including maintaining training records in Activity 6.

Clause 4.19 Servicing

ISO 9001 requires that servicing activities are performed as specified. ISO 9000-3 addresses this clause as maintenance.

Although the CMM is intended to be applied in both the software development and maintenance environments, the practices in the CMM do not directly address the unique aspects that characterize the maintenance environment. Maintenance is embedded throughout the practices of the CMM, and they must be appropriately interpreted in the development or maintenance contexts.

Maintenance therefore is not a separate process in the CMM. Change requests for CMM v1.0 expressed a concern about using the CMM for maintenance projects, and some wording was changed for CMM v1.1 to better address the maintenance environment. We anticipate that this will remain a topic of discussion as we provide guidance for tailoring the CMM to different environments, such as maintenance, and begin the next revision cycle for the CMM.

Clause 4.20 Statistical Techniques

ISO 9001 states that statistical techniques shall be identified and used to verify the acceptability of process capability and product characteristics. ISO 9000-3 simply characterizes this clause as measurement (6.4).

The practices describing measurement in the CMM are distributed throughout the key process areas. Product measurement is typically incorporated into the various Activities Performed practices. Process measurement is described in the Measurement and Analysis common feature.

Activity 5 of Organization Process Definition describes the establishment of an organization process database for collecting process and product data. This database is maintained at the organization level, and it seems likely that most auditors would accept project-level data (as described in the project management key process areas at Level 2) to satisfy this clause. At least a few auditors do, however, require an organization-level historical database and the use of simple statistical control charts.

If statistical process control is inferred from this clause, it would be satisfied by Quantitative Process Management and Software Quality Management. Some auditors look for use of any statistical tools, such as Pareto analysis. Other auditors are satisfied by any consistently collected and used measurement data. There is a significant degree of interpretation of this clause by auditors.

F.3 Contrasting ISO 9001 and the CMM

Clearly, there is a strong correlation between ISO 9001 and the CMM, although some issues in ISO 9001 are not covered in the CMM and vice versa. The levels of detail differ significantly: Chapter 4 in ISO 9001 is about 5 pages long, sections 5, 6, and 7 in ISO 9000-3 comprise about 11 pages, and the CMM is over 500 pages long. Some judgment is involved in deciding the exact correspondence, given the different levels of abstraction.

The clauses in ISO 9001 with no strong relationships to the CMM key process areas, and which are not well-addressed in the CMM, are control of customer-supplied product (4.7) and handling, storage, packaging, preservation and delivery (4.15). The clause in ISO 9001 that is addressed in the CMM in a completely distributed fashion is servicing (4.19). The clauses in ISO 9001 for which the exact relationship to the CMM is subject to significant debate are corrective and preventive action (4.14) and statistical techniques (4.20).

The biggest difference between these two documents, however, is the emphasis of the CMM on continuous process improvement. ISO 9001 addresses the minimum criteria for an acceptable quality system.[1] It should also be noted that the CMM focuses strictly on software, while ISO 9001 has a much broader scope: hardware, software, processed materials, and services [Marquardt91].

The biggest similarity is that for both the CMM and ISO 9001, the bottom line is "Say what you do; do what you say." The fundamental premise of ISO 9001 is that every important process should be documented and every deliverable should have its quality checked through a quality control activity. ISO 9001 requires documentation that contains instructions or guidance on what should be done or how it should be done. The CMM shares this emphasis on processes that are documented and practiced as documented. Phrases such as conducted "according to a documented procedure" and following "a written organizational policy" characterize the key process areas in the CMM.

The CMM also emphasizes the need to record information for later use in the process and for improvement of the process, which is equivalent to the quality records of ISO 9001 that record the achievement (or otherwise) of the required quality and the effective operation (or otherwise) of the quality system [TickIT, p. 120].

F.3.1 The Need for Judgment

When making a more detailed comparison, some clauses in ISO 9001 are easily mapped to their equivalent CMM practices. Other relationships map in a many-to-many fashion, since the two documents are structured differently. For example, the training clause (4.18) in ISO 9001 maps to both the Training Program key process area and the training and orientation practices in all of the key process areas.

Satisfying a key process area depends on both implementing and institutionalizing the process. Implementation is described in Activities Performed; institutionalization is described by the other common features.

In general, practices in Commitment to Perform (policies, leadership) can be considered addressed under ISO 9001's clause on management responsibility (4.1). Practices in Ability to Perform (training, resource allocation, tools, and organizational structures) can be considered addressed under ISO 9001's

---

[1]This statement is controversial in itself. Some members of the international standards community maintain that if you read ISO 9001 with insight (between the lines so to speak), it does address continuous process improvement. There is faith that weaknesses will improve over time, especially given regular surveillance audits. This will undoubtedly be one of the major topics for the next revision cycle for ISO 9001.

clauses on management responsibility (4.1) and training (4.18) and ISO 9000-3's clauses on rules, practices, and conventions (6.5) and tools and techniques (6.6). Practices in Measurement and Analysis can be considered addressed under ISO 9001's clauses on quality records (4.16) and statistical techniques (4.20) and ISO 9000-3's clause on measurement (6.4). Practices in Verifying Implementation (senior management oversight, project management review, and audits) can be considered addressed under ISO 9001's clauses on management responsibility (4.1) and quality system (4.2).

As this illustrates, the element of judgment in making this comparison is significant. A preliminary comparison of the concepts in ISO 9001 and the CMM would suggest that an organization with an ISO 9001 certificate should be at Level 3 or 4. In reality, there are Level 1 organizations with certificates. One reason is variability of interpretation; it is clear that the design reviews in ISO 9001 correspond directly to the CMM's peer reviews if one has gone through the TickIT training. Another reason, however, is that achieving Level 2 implies mastering the Level 2 key process areas. Due to the high level of abstraction in ISO 9001, it is unclear what degree of sophistication is required to satisfy an auditor.

F.3.2 The CMM Profile of an ISO 9001–Compliant Organization

What would be the maturity level of an ISO 9001–compliant organization if it implemented no management or engineering practices beyond those called out by ISO 9001? This is an extreme case, but it gives a lower bound for the maturity of an ISO 9001–compliant organization.

Figure F.1 illustrates the key process area profile of an ISO 9001–compliant organization that has no quality practices beyond those directly called out in ISO 9001. Where a matter of judgment may be involved, that interpretation is also illustrated in the profile. The dark shading indicates practices that are directly addressed by ISO 9001 or ISO 9000-3; the light shading indicates practices that may be addressed depending on an interpretation of ISO 9001; and the unshaded areas indicate practices not addressed by ISO 9001. Key process areas may therefore be partially or fully satisfied, satisfied under some interpretations, or not satisfied.

Note the following about Fig. F.1:

▫ Every key process area at Level 2 is strongly related to ISO 9001.

▫ Every key process area is at least weakly related to ISO 9001.

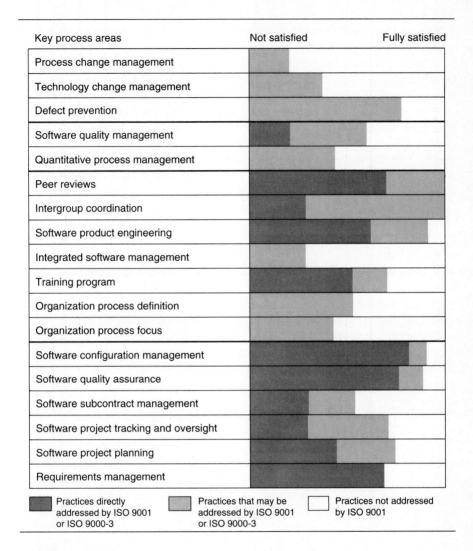

Key process areas	Not satisfied	Fully satisfied

FIGURE F.1
Key process area profile for an ISO 9001–complaint organization.

Based on this profile, a Level 1 organization according to the CMM could be certified as compliant with ISO 9001. That organization would, however, have significant process strengths at Level 2 and noticeable strengths at Level 3.

Private discussions indicate that many Level 1 organizations have received ISO 9001 certificates. Surveillance audits may identify deficiencies later that result in loss of certification. Other organizations have identified significant problems during a CMM-based assessment that had not surfaced during a previous ISO 9001 audit [Coallier94].

Given a reasonable implementation of the software process, however, an organization that obtains and retains ISO 9001 certification should at least be close to Level 2.

Can a Level 3 organization be considered compliant with ISO 9001? Even a Level 3 organization would need to ensure that the delivery and installation process described in Clause 4.15 of ISO 9001 is adequately addressed and should consider the use of included software product, as described in Clause 6.8 of ISO 9000-3, but even a Level 2 organization would have comparatively little difficulty in obtaining ISO 9001 certification.

F.4 Concluding Remarks on ISO 9001 and the CMM

Although there are specific issues that are not adequately addressed in the CMM, in general the concerns of ISO 9001 are encompassed by the CMM. The converse is less true. ISO 9001 describes the minimum criteria for an adequate quality management system rather than process improvement, although future revisions of ISO 9001 may address this concern. The differences are sufficient to make a rote mapping impractical, but the similarities provide a high degree of overlap.

Should software process improvement be based on the CMM, with perhaps some extensions for ISO 9001 specific concerns, or should the improvement effort focus on certification concerns? A market may require ISO 9001 certification, and Level 1 organizations would certainly profit from addressing the concerns of ISO 9001. It is also true that addressing the concerns of the CMM would help organizations prepare for an ISO 9001 audit. Although either document could be used to structure a process improvement program, the more detailed guidance and greater breadth provided to software organizations by the CMM suggest that it is the better choice (a perhaps biased answer).

In any case, building competitive advantage should be focused on improvement, not on achieving a score, whether the score is a maturity level or a certificate. We would advocate addressing the larger context encompassed by the CMM, but even then there is a need to address the still larger business context, as exemplified by Total Quality Management.

Appendix G

An Overview of ISO's SPICE Project

The International Organization for Standardization (ISO) is developing a suite of standards on software process under the rubric of SPICE— Software Process Improvement and Capability dEtermination. SPICE was inspired by the numerous efforts on software process around the world, including the SEI's work with the Capability Maturity Model (CMM) [Paulk93a, Paulk93b], Bell Canada's Trillium [Trillium], ESPRIT's Bootstrap [Koch93], and many others.

The SPICE standards focus on software process issues but will also be concerned with people, technology, management practices, customer support and quality, as well as software development and maintenance practices. Organizations will be able to use this standard in many ways:

- In capability determination mode, to help a purchasing organization determine the capability of a potential software supplier against a recognized international standard.

- In process improvement mode, to help a software organization improve its own software development and maintenance processes.
- In self-assessment mode, to help an organization determine its ability to implement a new software project.

The benefits of an international standard on software process assessment are as follows:

- It will help purchasers determine the capability of software suppliers and assess the risks involved in selecting one supplier over another.
- Software suppliers will only submit to one process assessment scheme, not go through numerous schemes as is the case today.
- Software organizations will have an internationally recognized tool to support their continuous process improvement programs.
- It will help managers ensure that the process is aligned with the business needs of the organization.

G.1 Background of SPICE

The effort to create an ISO standard for software process assessment officially began at the June 1991 ISO plenary meeting for JTC1/SC7.[1] Alec Dorling of the U.K. proposed a study group on process management, preparatory to proposing an international standard in this area. Part of the proposal submission included the "ImproveIT" report [Dorling91], which compared a number of different process management schemes, including the CMM. The study group was established under ISO/IEC JTC1/SC7/WG7.[2]

At the June 1992 plenary meeting of ISO/IEC JTC1/SC7 in London, a new working group, JTC1/SC7/WG10, was established,[3] based on the recommendations in the study group's report [ISO-N944R]. The SPICE project was created to coordinate the different development activities for the set of software process

---

[1]JTC1 is the joint technical committee between ISO and the International Electrotechnical Commission (IEC) responsible for information technology standards; SC7 is the subcommittee of JTC1 responsible for software engineering standards. (Note that the ISO 9000 series of standards are under a different technical committee, ISO TC176.)

[2]WG7 is responsible for standards on software life cycle processes.

[3]Completion of the formal balloting process was completed in January 1993. The vote was unanimously in favor of forming WG10.

standards. The international convenor for WG10, and the head of the SPICE project, is Alec Dorling of the U.K. Mark Paulk leads the U.S. activities for WG10, and Mike Konrad coordinates U.S. participation in SPICE.

Four Technical Centers were established to administer SPICE activities:

- Europe: Defence Research Agency Malvern
- United States: Software Engineering Institute
- Canada: Bell Canada
- Pacific Rim: Griffith University

Additional Technical Centers may be established as needed.

The suite of proposed SPICE standards will be published as technical reports during early 1995. A pilot testing period will follow, and the revised suite of SPICE products will be submitted for consideration as ISO standards in the 1996 time frame.

For further information on SPICE, and how to participate, contact:

Mike Konrad
U.S. SPICE Technical Center Manager
Software Engineering Institute
Carnegie Mellon University
Pittsburgh, PA 15213-3890
Internet: mdk@sei.cmu.edu
Tel: (412) 268-5813
Fax: (412) 268-5758

G.2 The SPICE Products

The SPICE project began with a set of requirements, initially drafted in the process management study report and refined in subsequent meetings. Based on those requirements, a number of products have been identified for the international standard.

G.2.1 The Requirements for SPICE

The requirements for the SPICE suite of products are listed below. The process assessment standard shall:

A. encourage predictable quality products.

B. encourage optimum productivity.

C. promote a repeatable software process.

D. provide guidance for improving software processes aligned to business goals, including starting point and target.

E. support process capability determination for risk identification and analysis within an organization.

F. support process capability determination for risk identification and analysis within a two-party contractual situation.

G. be capable of being employed reliably and consistently.

H. be simple to use and understand.

I. be culturally independent.

J. not presume specific organizational structures, management philosophies, software life cycle models, software technologies, or software development methods.

K. recognize different application domains, business needs, and sizes of organizations.

L. for each process, define baseline practices that are appropriate across all application domains, business needs, and sizes of organization. The baseline practices should be extensible to allow for industry or business variants.

M. define standard requirements for the development of industry or business variants of the baseline practices.

N. be applicable at the project and organizational levels with connectivity between the two.

O. focus on process, but also address people and application of technology.

P. be objective.

Q. be quantitative wherever possible.

R. support output as process profiles that allow views at different levels of detail. The profiling method should support comparisons against other similar entities or industry "norms."

S. require that agreement be reached over ownership and confidentiality of assessment results prior to assessment.

T. define the initial and ongoing qualification of assessors.

U. be supportive of and consistent with other ISO JTC1/SC7 standards and projects.

V. be supportive of, and consistent with, the ISO 9000 series of standards.

W. be subject to continuous improvement through periodic reviews to maintain consistency with current good practice.

A more detailed analysis of the SPICE requirements can be found in the "Requirements Specification for a Software Process Assessment Standard" [ISO-N017R]. This analysis breaks these requirements into goals, functional requirements, and nonfunctional requirements and derives additional requirements.

G.2.2 The SPICE Product Suite

The core set of SPICE products comprising the software process assessment standard are:

- Introductory Guide
- Baseline Practices Guide
- Assessment Instrument
- Process Assessment Guide
- Process Improvement Guide
- Process Capability Determination Guide
- Assessor Training and Qualification Guide

Introductory Guide

The Introductory Guide (IG) is the top-level architecture document that describes how the various parts of the standard fit together and provides guidance for their selection, use, and the creation of conformant variants. The product manager for the IG is Terry Rout (Australia). The SPICE Architect is Peter Simms (U.K.).

Baseline Practices Guide

The Baseline Practices Guide (BPG) will define, at a high level, the goals and fundamental activities that are essential to good software engineering. The guide will describe what activities are required, not how they are to be implemented. The baseline practices may be extended through the generation of application/sector specific Practice Guides to take account of specific industry, sector, or other requirements. The BPG is the SPICE equivalent of the SEI's CMM; the CMM is an example of a sector-specific Practice Guide. The product managers for the BPG are Al Graydon (Canada) and Mark Paulk (U.S.).

Assessment Instrument

The Assessment Instrument (AI) is a guide for designing instruments that extract data related to the process(es) undergoing assessment. It provides guidance on how to achieve adequate coverage of the BPG, confirming the presence of the set of baseline practices. Any conformant assessment instrument must provide complete coverage of the Baseline Practices Guide. This document will specify how this is to be demonstrated. As an example, the AI describes criteria that the SEI's maturity questionnaire must satisfy to be conformant to the SPICE standard. The product managers for the AI are Mary Campbell (U.S.) and Peter Hitchcock (Canada).

Process Assessment Guide

The Process Assessment Guide (PAG) specifies the assessment method, which defines how to conduct an assessment using the Assessment Instrument and the Baseline Practices Guide and sets out the basis for profiling, rating, and scoring. The PAG is the SPICE equivalent of the SEI's CMM Appraisal Framework. The product manager for the PAG is Harry Barker (U.K.).

Process Improvement Guide

The Process Improvement Guide (PIG) will provide guidance on how to use the results of an assessment for the purposes of process improvement. Embedded within, or companion to, the Process Improvement Guide will be a number of guidance models applicable to particular situations. The PIG is the SPICE equivalent of the SEI's IDEAL[4] approach to software process improvement. The product managers for the PIG are Adriana Bicego (Italy) and Pasi Kuvaja (Finland).

Process Capability Determination Guide

The Process Capability Determination Guide (PCDG) will provide generic guidance on how to use the results of an assessment for the purposes of capability evaluation. Embedded within the Guide, or companion to it, will be a number of guidance models applicable to particular situations. The PCDG is the SPICE equivalent of the SEI's Software Capability Evaluation method. The product manager for the PCDG is John Hamilton (U.K.).

Assessor Training and Qualification Guide

The Assessor Training and Qualification Guide (ATQG) will provide generic guidance for the development of programs for the training of people to act as

---

[4]IDEAL is an acronym standing for initiate, diagnose, evaluate, act, and leverage.

assessors using this standard. The guide will also define procedures for the qualification of assessors who intend to act in a third-party situation. The product manager for the ATQG is Ron Meegoda (Australia).

G.3 Relationship to ISO 9000

The assumption is frequently made that the SPICE project is a part of ISO 9000. The ISO 9000 standards were developed by ISO TC176, which is responsible for standards for quality management systems. The ISO 9000 series deals with quality systems that can be used for external quality assurance purposes. They specify quality system requirements for use where a contract between two parties requires the demonstration of a supplier's capability to design and supply product, as is discussed in Appendix F.

In contrast, the SPICE standards are being developed under ISO/IEC JTC1/SC7, which is responsible for standards in software engineering. SC7 and TC176 are separate bodies within ISO and have different charters. There is overlap between the scopes of SC7 and TC176 when looking at quality management for software. One of the SPICE requirements (Requirement V) is to be supportive of, and consistent with, the ISO 9000 series of standards. Nonetheless, SPICE and ISO 9000-3 are separate efforts by different bodies within ISO. One of the challenges for both WG10 and TC176 is to harmonize these efforts when the ISO 9000 series is being revised in parallel with the development of the SPICE series. Both the SPICE series and a revised set of ISO 9000 standards are planned to enter the standardization process in the 1996 time frame.

Refer to Appendix F for a discussion of the relationship between ISO 9001 and the CMM.

Appendix H

Change History of the CMM

Date	Version	Change Description
1 Mar 90	0.0	Rough draft of the key practice tables; distributed to the CMM User Working Group. Version for review at the March 1990 CMM Workshop.
1 May 90	0.1	Rough draft of the key practice tables appendix to incorporate recommendations made at the March 1990 CMM Workshop against Version 0.0. Version for internal SEI peer review.
6 Jun 90	0.2	Draft, revision to the key practice tables to incorporate comments from the SEI peer review of Version 0.1. Version distributed to the CMM User Working Group for its review and comments. (Baselined version of the key practice tables)

Date	Version	Change Description
26 Feb 91	0.3	Draft, revision to the key practice tables (Level 2 key process areas only) to incorporate comments from the CMM User Working Group and the Questionnaire Advisory Board made against Version 0.2. Version for internal SEI peer review. Rough draft (first version) of overview and definitions to assist in the SEI peer review of the key practice tables, Level 2 key process areas.
18 Mar 91	0.4	Draft, revision to the key practice tables, Level 2 key process areas to incorporate comments from the SEI peer review of Version 0.3. Version distributed to the CMM User Working Group and Questionnaire Advisory Board for their review and comments. Rough draft, revision of overview and definitions to assist the CMM User Working Group and the Questionnaire Advisory Board in their review of the key practice tables, Level 2 key process areas.
10 Apr 91	0.41	Draft, revision to the key practice tables (Level 3 key process areas only, except Software Product Engineering key process area is not included) to incorporate comments from the CMM User Working Group and the Questionnaire Advisory Board made against Version 0.2. Version for internal SEI peer review.
22 Apr 91	0.5	Draft, revision to the key practice tables, Level 3 key process areas (except the Software Product Engineering key process area is not included) to incorporate comments from the SEI peer review of Version 0.41. Version distributed to the CMM User Working Group and Questionnaire Advisory Board for their review and comments. Rough draft, revision of overview and definitions to assist the CMM User Working Group and the Questionnaire Advisory Board in their review of the key practice tables, Level 3 key process areas.
17 May 91	0.51	Draft, revision to the Level 2 key practice areas to incorporate comments from the CMM User Working Group made against Version 0.4 and make practices of each key process area at a single maturity level. Version for internal SEI peer review.
23 May 91	0.52	Draft, revision to the key practice tables (initial version of Software Requirements Management key process area, and consolidation of Software Requirements Analysis, Software Design, and Software Testing key process areas and addition of coding practices into the single key process area, Software Product Engineering) to incorporate comments from the CMM User Working Group and the Questionnaire Advisory Board. Version for internal SEI peer review.
5 Jun 91	0.53	Preliminary baseline, revision to the Level 2 key practice areas to incorporate comments from the internal SEI peer review of Version 0.51. Version submitted to SEI's Information Management.

Date	Version	Change Description
7 Jun 91	0.54	Draft, revision to the key practice tables (initial version of Software Project Management key process area only). Version for internal SEI peer review.
14 Jun 91	0.6	Draft, revision to the key practice tables to incorporate comments from the SEI peer review of Software Requirements Management (Version 0.52), Software Project Management (Version 0.54), and Software Product Engineering (Version 0.52) key process areas; incorporated Version 0.53 of other Level 2 key process areas. Version distributed to the CMM User Working Group and Questionnaire Advisory Board for their review and comments. Rough draft, revision of overview and definitions to assist the CMM User Working Group and the Questionnaire Advisory Board in their review of the key practice tables (Software Requirements Management, Software Project Management, and Software Product Engineering key process areas). Significant changes include (1) restructuring key process area practice tables by changing the common key features, (2) modifying the set of key process areas, and (3) rearranging the practice statements so that each key process area contains practices for a single maturity level.
21 Jun 91	0.61	Draft, revision to the key practice tables (Level 4 and 5 key process areas only) to incorporate comments from the CMM User Working Group and the Questionnaire Advisory Board made against Version 0.2. Version for internal SEI peer review.
28 Jun 91	0.7	Draft, revision to the key practice tables appendix, (Level 4 and 5 key process areas only) to incorporate comments from the SEI peer review of Version 0.61. Version distributed to the CMM User Working Group and Questionnaire Advisory Board for their review and comments.
10 Jul 91	0.71	Draft, revision to the Level 3 key process areas and Software Requirements Management key process area to incorporate comments from the CMM User Working Group made against Versions 0.5 and 0.6; make practices of each key process area at a single maturity level; and renamed three key process areas (Software Requirements Management to Requirements Management, Software Project Management to Integrated Software Management, and Technical Team Coordination to Intergroup Coordination). Version for internal SEI peer review.
14 Jul 91	0.72	Draft, revision to the Level 3 key process areas and Software Requirements Management key process area to incorporate comments from the internal SEI peer review against Version 0.71. Version for internal SEI peer review.
15 Jul 91	0.73	Draft, revision to the Level 3 key process areas and Software Requirements Management key process area to incorporate comments from the internal SEI peer review.

Date	Version	Change Description
15 Jul 91	0.74	Preliminary baseline, revision to the Level 3 key process areas and Software Requirements Management key process area (reformatting and fixing editorial defects). Version submitted to SEI's Information Management.
22 Jul 91	0.75	Draft, revision to the Level 4 and 5 key process areas to incorporate comments from the CMM User Working Group made against Version 0.7. Version for internal SEI peer review.
30 Jul 91	0.76	Preliminary baseline, revision to Level 4 and 5 key process areas to incorporate comments from internal SEI peer review. Version submitted to SEI's Information Management.
30 Jul 91	0.77	Draft, revision to the preliminary baseline of the Requirements Management key process area to incorporate comments from the 30 July 1991 Questionnaire Advisory Board meeting. Version for internal SEI peer review.
5 Aug 91	0.78	Draft, revision to Version 0.77 of the Requirements Management key process area to incorporate comments from the 31 July 1991 Questionnaire Advisory Board meeting. Version for internal SEI peer review.
7 Aug 91	0.79	Revised preliminary baseline of the Requirements Management key process area to incorporate comments from the Questionnaire Advisory Board and the internal SEI peer review against Version 0.78.
7 Aug 91	0.80	Draft, revision of overview and definitions to incorporate comments received from the CMM User Working Group and the Questionnaire Advisory Board in their review of Versions 0.4, 0.5, and 0.6 and restructure the document. Version for internal SEI peer review.
15 Aug 91	1.0	Baseline version for public release.
1 Sep 92	1.01	Draft, revision to Version 1.0 based on change requests received by 17 January 92 and recommendations from the CMM Workshop held 6-7 April 92. Training Program key process area replaced with Skills Building. Title of Technology Innovation changed to Technology Change Management.
8 Dec 92	1.02	Draft, revision to Version 1.01 to incorporate recommendations of CMM Advisory Board and comments from the internal SEI peer review. Training Program key process area restored, with minor upgrades to address skills-building concerns. Title of Process Measurement and Analysis key process area changed to Quantitative Process Management. Version for internal SEI peer review.
14 Dec 92	1.03	Draft, revision to Version 1.02 to incorporate comments from the internal SEI peer review. Title of Quality Management key process area changed to Software Quality Management. Version for internal SEI peer review.

Date	Version	Change Description
18 Dec 92	1.04	Draft, revision to Version 1.03 to incorporate comments from the internal SEI peer review. Distributed to reviewers of version 1.01 and the CMM Advisory Board for comment and feedback.
15 Jan 93	1.05	Draft, revision to Version 1.04 to incorporate recommendations of CMM Advisory Board and comments from the internal SEI peer review. Version for internal SEI peer review.
10 Feb 93	1.1	Baseline version for public release.
19 Nov 93	1.11	Correction of minor grammatical errors for book in SEI series from Addison-Wesley. The changes are:

  □ In PTO.GO.1, "performances" was changed to "performance."

  □ In IC.VE.2, "even-driven" was changed to "event-driven."

  □ In the intro to TCM, first paragraph, "track [new technologies]" was changed to "transition [new technologies]."

  □ In TCM.GO.1, "are" was changed to "is."

Appendix **I**

Change Request Form

The CMM is a living document. We encourage feedback on how the CMM can be improved, and we plan to continue evolving the CMM in response to the needs of the software community. To facilitate that feedback, the following change request form is included. Make copies of this form, or create your own using this template, and mail your comments to:

CMM Change Requests
Software Process Program
Software Engineering Institute
Carnegie-Mellon University
Pittsburgh, PA 15213-3890

Send packages to:

CMM Change Requests
Software Process Program
Software Engineering Institute

431

4500 Fifth Avenue
Carnegie-Mellon University
Pittsburgh, PA 15213-2691

Fax comments to: (412) 268-5758.

E-mail comments to: cmmchange@sei.cmu.edu.

For the SEI to take appropriate action on a change request, we must have a clear description of the recommended change, along with a supporting rationale.

Change Request—Capability Maturity Model for Software, Version 1.1

Product: CMM v1.1   SEI Assigned Tracking Number: _____

Name of Submitting Organization: _____

Organization Contact: _____ **Telephone:** _____

Mailing Address:

Date: _____ **Short Title:** _____

Change Location Tag: _____
(use section #, figure #, key process area ID, practice ID, etc.)

Proposed Change:

Rationale for Change:

Index

Ability to perform, 43–44,
  48–51
  configuration management
    and, 182–184
  defect prevention and,
    307–309
  explanation of, 48–51
  integrated software
    management and,
    224–226
  intergroup coordination
    and, 263–264
  organization process focus
    and, 196–198
  peer reviews and, 271–273
  process change
    management and,
    332–334
  product engineering and,
    242–246
  project planning and,
    136–138
  project tracking and
    oversight and,
    149–151
  quality assurance and,
    173–175
  quality management and,
    294–295

  quantitative process
    management and,
    280–282
  requirements management
    and, 128–129
  subcontract management
    and, 161–162
  technology change
    management and,
    321–324
  training programs and,
    215–217
Activities performed
  according to documented
    procedure, 52–53
  configuration management
    and, 184–189
  defect prevention and,
    309–317
  integrated software
    management and,
    226–239
  intergroup coordination
    and, 264–268
  key practices in, 51–52
  organization process focus
    and, 198–201
  peer reviews and,
    273–275

  process change
    management and,
    334–342
  product engineering and,
    246–259
  project planning and,
    138–146
  project tracking and
    oversight and,
    151–156
  quality assurance and,
    175–178
  quality management and,
    295–302
  quantitative process
    management and,
    282–290
  requirements management
    and, 129–132
  subcontract management
    and, 162–169
  technology change
    management and,
    324–329
  training programs and,
    217–221
Appraisal method
  CMM-based, 83–85
  explanation of, 82–83

435